Oral Tradition in Ancient Israel

Biblical Performance Criticism Series
David Rhoads, Series Editor

The ancient societies of the Bible were overwhelmingly oral. People originally experienced the traditions now in the Bible as oral performances. Focusing on the ancient performance of biblical traditions enables us to shift academic work on the Bible from the mentality of a modern print culture to that of an oral/scribal culture. Conceived broadly, biblical performance criticism embraces many methods as means to reframe the biblical materials in the context of traditional oral cultures, construct scenarios of ancient performances, learn from contemporary performances of these materials, and reinterpret biblical writings accordingly. The result is a foundational paradigm shift that reconfigures traditional disciplines and employs fresh biblical methodologies such as theater studies, speech-act theory, and performance studies. The emerging research of many scholars in this field of study, the development of working groups in scholarly societies, and the appearance of conferences on orality and literacy make it timely to inaugurate this series. For further information on biblical performance criticism, go to www.biblicalperformancecriticism.org.

Books in the Series

Holly Hearon and Philip Ruge-Jones, editors
The Bible in Ancient and Modern Media: Story and Performance

James Maxey
From Orality to Orality:
A New Paradigm for Contextual Translation of the Bible

Antoinette Clark Wire
The Case for Mark Composed in Performance

Robert D. Miller II, SFO
Oral Tradition in Ancient Israel

Forthcoming

David Rhoads
Biblical Performance Criticism:
An Emerging Discipline in New Testament Studies

Joanna Dewey
Orality, Scribality, and the Gospel of Mark

Pieter J. J. Botha
Orality and Literacy in Early Christianity

Oral Tradition in Ancient Israel

ROBERT D. MILLER II, SFO

CASCADE *Books* • Eugene, Oregon

ORAL TRADITION IN ANCIENT ISRAEL

Biblical Performance Criticism 4

Cascade Books
An Imprint of Wipf and Stock Publishers
199 W. 8th Ave., Suite 3
Eugene, OR 97401
www.wipfandstock.com

ISBN 13: 978-1-61097-271-0

Cataloging-in-Publication data:

Miller, Robert D., II.

Oral tradition in ancient Israel / Robert D. Miller II.

Biblical Performance Criticism 4

xvi + 154 pp.; 23 cm—Includes bibliographical references and index.

ISBN 13: 978-1-61097-271-0

1. Bible—O.T.—Criticism, interpretation, etc. 2. Oral tradition. 3. Folklore in the Bible. 4. Sagas—Criticism and interpretation. I. Title. II. Series.

BS535. M55. 2011

Manufactured in the USA.

Nihil Obstat:
Rev. Christopher Begg
Censor Deputatus

Imprimatur:
Most Rev. Barry C. Knestout
Auxiliary Bishop of Washington
Archdiocese of Washington
June 14, 2010

The nihil obstat and imprimatur are official declarations that a book or pamphlet is free of doctrinal or moral error. There is no implication that those who have granted the nihil obstat and the imprimatur agree with the content, opinions, or statements expressed therein.

Contents

Acknowledgments

This book grew out of a desire to understand the process of authorship in ancient Israel, and it was originally intended as an essay for inclusion in a Festschrift for my teacher, Charles Krahmalkov. It quickly became apparent that the scope of the work was far larger than would suit such a chapter. Yet it should still be noted that many of the avenues explored herein owe their rudiments to discussions in Charles' classes at Michigan over a decade ago.

I thank the School of Graduate Studies of the Catholic University of America for a Grant-in-Aid to further the research for this book. Great assistance was given by Professor Terry Gunnell of the University of Iceland, my e-mail dialogue partner for nine months, although all conclusions—including those about Icelandic literature—are my own. It was during a three-month period when my family was between houses and living in borrowed homes of generous, hospitable friends that the majority of the actual writing took place, and I must thank them all for the kitchen tables and other work space. My graduate students, Nathan LaMontagne and Thaddeus Winker, were of great help in the initial editing of this book. And, finally, I express to my wife and constant support, Anne-Marie, my unceasing gratitude.

Abbreviations

AB	Anchor Bible
ABD	*The Anchor Bible Dictionary.* 6 vols. Edited by David Noel Freedman. New York: Doubleday, 1992
ABL	*Assyrian and Babylonian Letters.* 14 vols. Edited by R. F. Harper. Chicago: University of Chicago Press, 1892–1914
ABRL	Anchor Bible Reference Library
ACh Supp.	*L'Astrologie chaldéenne Supplément.* Edited by C. Virolleaud. Paris: Geuthner, 1905
AcOr	*Acta Orientalia*
AJA	*American Journal of Archaeology*
Akk.	Akkadian
AnBib	Analecta biblica
ANET	*Ancient Near Eastern Texts Relating to the Old Testament.* Edited by James B. Pritchard. 3rd ed. Princeton: Princeton University Press, 1969
ANVAO	Avhandlinger utgitt av det Norske Videnskaps-Akademi i Oslo
AnOr	Analecta orientalia
AOAT	Alter Orient und Altes Testament
AoF	*Altorientalische Forschungen*
AOS	American Oriental Series
ArbT	Arbeiten zur Theologie
ASTI	*Annual of the Swedish Theological Institute*
ATD	Das Alte Testament Deutsch
ATR	*Anglican Theological Review*
BA	*Biblical Archaeologist*
BASOR	*Bulletin of the American Schools of Oriental Research*
BEATAJ	Beiträge zur Erforschung des Alten Testaments und des antiken Judentums

Abbreviations

BETL	Bibliotheca ephemeridum theologicarum lovaniensium
Bib	*Biblica*
BibInt	*Biblical Interpretation*
BiOr	*Biblica et Orientalia*
BN	*Biblische Notizen*
BSOAS	*Bulletin of the School of Oriental and African Studies*
CBQ	*Catholic Biblical Quarterly*
CIS	Corpus Inscriptionem Semiticarum
COS	*The Context of Scripture.* Edited by William Hallo. 3 vols. Leiden: Brill, 2003
CTA	*Corpus des tablettes en cunéiformes alphabétiques découvertes à Ras Shamra-Ugarit.* Edited by A. Herdner. Paris: Imprimerie Nationale, 1963
CTH	*Catalogue des textes hittites.* Edited by L. Laroche. Paris, 1956; repr. 1971
DDD	*Dictionary of Deities and Demons in the Bible.* Edited by Karel van der Toorn et al. Leiden: Brill, 1995
EA	Tell el-Amarna Tablets
ErIsr	*Eretz-Israel*
FAT	Forschungen zum Alten Testament
HKAT	Handkommentar zum Alten Testament
HR	*History of Religions*
HSCP	*Harvard Studies in Classical Philology*
HSM	Harvard Semitic Monographs
HTR	*Harvard Theological Review*
IEJ	*Israel Exploration Journal*
Int	*Interpretation*
JANES	*Journal of the Ancient Near Eastern Society of Columbia University*
JAOS	*Journal of the American Oriental Society*
JBL	*Journal of Biblical Literature*
JCS	*Journal of Cuneiform Studies*
JETS	*Journal of the Evangelical Theological Society*
JQR	*Jewish Quarterly Review*
JSNTSup	Journal for the Study of the New Testament Supplement Series
JSOT	*Journal for the Study of the Old Testament*
JSOTSup	Journal for the Study of the Old Testament. Supplement Series

Abbreviations

JSS	*Journal of Semitic Studies*
JTS	*Journal of Theological Studies*
KAI	*Kanaanäische und aramäische Inschriften.* Edited by H. Donner and W. Röllig. 3 vols. Wiesbaden: Harrassowitz, 1962
KBo	*Keilschrifttexte aus Boghazköi.* Wissenschaftliche Veröffentlichungen der Deutchen Orient-Gesellschaft 30/36/68-70/72-. Leipzig, 1916–23; Berlin, 1954–
KTU	*Die keilalphabetischen Texte aus Ugarit*
LAS	*Letters from Assyrian Scholars.* Compiled by Simo Parpola. 2 vols. Winona Lake: Eisenbrauns, 2007
OTE	*Old Testament Essays*
OTL	Old Testament Library
OtSt	Oudtestamentische Studiën
PÄ	Probleme der Ägyptologie
Proof	*Prooftexts*
RelSRev	*Religious Studies Review*
RHR	*Revue d'histoire des religions*
Rm	Museum signlum of the British Museum
SBL	Society of Biblical Literature
SBLABib	Society of Biblical Literature Academia Biblica
SBLABS	Society of Biblical Literature: Archaeology and Biblical Studies
SBLDS	Society of Biblical Literature Dissertation Series
SBLStBl	Society of Biblical Literature Studies in Biblical Literature
SBLSymS	Society of Biblical Literature Symposium Series
SBT	Studies in Biblical Theology
SEÅ	*Svensk Exegetisk Årsbok*
Sem	*Semitica*
SemeiaSt	Semeia Studies
SJOT	*Scandinavian Journal of the Old Testament*
ST	*Studia Theologica*
TAPA	*Transactions of the American Philological Association*
TynBul	*Tyndale Bulletin*
UT	*Ugaritic Textbook.* C. H. Gordon. AnOr 38. Rome, 1965
UUÅ	Uppsala universitets Årsskrift
WUNT	Wissenschaftliche Untersuchungen zum Neuen Testament

Abbreviations

VT	*Vetus Testamentum*
ZÄS	*Zeitschrift für Ägyptische Sprache und Altertumskunde*
ZDPV	*Zeitschrift des deutschen Palästina-Vereins*
ZRGG	*Zeitschrift für Religions- und Geistesgeschichte*

Introduction

A decade ago, John Van Seters wrote, "A comprehensive study on 'literacy and orality in ancient Israel' remains to be written."[1] To claim that this short book fulfills that desideratum would be the height of cheek. What is entailed can better be described as a volume to replace Eduard Nielsen's 1954 *Oral Tradition*,[2] a comprehensive study of "oral tradition" in the narrative books of the Old Testament. The notion of oral tradition plays an important role in nearly all areas of biblical scholarship, although all too often scholars themselves admit the tentative nature of anything they hope to say about it. We write, "It began, as far as I can determine, with oral creation."[3]

Actual study of the nature of oral tradition has greatly waned in recent decades, though not entirely to be sure. Patricia Kirkpatrick, the author twenty years ago of a then-seminal study of oral tradition in the Bible,[4] now writes, "Whereas the beginning of the twentieth century augured well for the recovery of original ancient oral composition forms preserved in the biblical text, the twenty-first century seems to have all but abandoned such quests."[5] To abandon such a quest simply because it is difficult or unpopular would be a shame. I will argue, not merely for the sake of novelty, that oral tradition ought not be dismissed as antiquated, outmoded, nineteenth-century, Romantic, or some other fashion-conscious, wand-waving term of rejection. This volume tries to understand the nature of oral tradition and the forms it would have taken in ancient Israel, along with brief discussion of the "remains" of oral tradition in the

1. Van Seters, Review of *Oral World and Written Word*, 437.

2. Nielsen, *Oral Tradition*.

3. Rofé, *Introduction to the Composition of the Pentateuch*, 130.

4. Kirkpatrick, *The Old Testament and Folklore Study*. As Kirkpatrick herself realizes, this study is now quite outdated and need not be refuted or reexamined now.

5. Kirkpatrick, "The Jacob-Esau Narratives," 1.

narrative books of the Hebrew Bible. But to be clear, in spite of the exploration of such "remnants," this study is not a quest of markers in texts that might indicate some relationship to oral composition.

The first chapter briefly surveys the history of the study of oral tradition in ancient Israel. It then presents the Oral Formulaic school of thought on oral tradition, associated with the work of Milman Parry and Albert Lord. It also explains the related theories on orality of Walter Ong and Jack Goody. Finally, the chapter illustrates the extent to which this theory has been adapted in biblical studies, noting the indebtedness to Oral Formulaicism in Old Testament research. Chapter 2 explains what has happened to Oral Formulaicism in the past decades, how the theory has been seriously undercut and bypassed. The particular areas of challenge to Parry-Lord and to the theories of Good and Ong will be discussed. In particular, the chapter presents areas of the world—especially the ancient Near East—where orality and literacy co-existed. Chapter 3 presents three specific cases of oral/written interaction that provide the best ethnographic analogies for ancient Israel. Homer, Icelandic sagas, and Arabic epic poetry will be shown to be of key interest. Insights from their study suggest a model of transmission in oral-written societies valid for ancient Israel.[6] Chapter 4 draws on the insights of pre-Formulaic Scandinavian traditions historians and on the most recent studies of Israelite literacy. Drawing on current archaeology, the extent of literacy in ancient Israel and the nature of early Israelite literature are discussed in dialogue with William Schniedewind, Susan Niditch, and John Van Seters. The conclusion of this chapter is that Israel was "always oral" and "always literate."

Chapter 5 forays into reconstructing what ancient Israelite oral literature would have been. Its focus is on the reconstruction of the oral literature of preexilic Israel, not on the Hebrew Bible. The chapter demonstrates the validity of using ethnographic analogies of Icelandic and Arabic poetry, rather than working back from written biblical texts to oral precursors. Chapter 6 considers various criteria for identifying orally derived material in the narrative books of the Old Testament. Drawing on the previous chapters, these criteria tentatively mark several passages from the biblical text as possible oral derivations. Using ethnographic data and ancient Near Eastern examples, the chapter also proposes per-

6. The term "oral-written" is David Carr's (Carr, "Torah on the Heart," 19).

formance settings for both this material and the hypothetical material of chapter 5.

An epilogue treats the contentious topic of historicity and whether orally derived texts are somehow more historically reliable than other texts in the Bible. A conclusion brings together the main ideas of this monograph.

1

Oral Formulaicism in Old Testament Study

Oral Tradition in the Hebrew Bible

For over a century, since Hermann Gunkel first suggested that behind the written Pentateuchal sources of Julius Wellhausen and the Documentary Hypothesis lay oral traditions, biblical scholars have spoken of oral tradition. From 1910, Gunkel had become acquainted with Wilhelm Wundt's "Folk Psychology."[1] Wundt maintained that the movement of human societies follows historical stages, and the description of these stages was very similar to the forms and complexity of language and its development.[2] Gunkel adopted this thesis, and from it concluded that oral folklore was at the origin of Israel's sagas.[3] From this point on, the form-critical and traditions-history methods operated under the presumption that the written literature was dependent on oral tradition.[4] Form critics and traditions historians detected oral "substrata" by various means beneath many parts of the Old Testament. The history of this movement was thoroughly reviewed by Douglas Knight decades ago.[5] Biblical scholars, like many other historians, "given the slightest hint of orality, however distant and unfounded, will allow their Romantic presuppositions (and ultimately their positivism!) of an elemental orality to hold forth: in the beginning there was the Oral."[6]

1. Wundt, *Völkerpsychologie*
2. Wundt, *Logik der Gfeisteswissenschaften*, 225–26.
3. Mitchell, "War, Folklore, and the Mystery of a Disappearing Book," 116.
4. Knierim, "Old Testament Form Criticism," 457.
5. Knight, *Rediscovering the Traditions of Israel*.
6. Zumthor, *Oral Poetry*, 44.

Accompanying the early traditions-historical quest for oral tradition was often an agenda that promoted traditions criticism as an alternative to source and redaction criticism, proving that what appeared to be doublets and variants indicative of multiple sources in, say, the Pentateuch were actually merely signs of oral composition.[7] There was no need for late J, E, D, and P, and biblical veracity might be salvaged. In the twentieth century, oral sources were considered by all varieties of historians to be "somehow impervious to many of the factors which historians usually take account of in critical assessment of sources."[8] And so a Romantic perception of illiterate peoples' powers of cultural memory assured some that what was contained in the Bible's oral tradition was historically reliable.[9]

In the past several decades, the term "oral tradition" has become increasingly controversial and suspect. In part, this is because it had been defined rather loosely and often only on the basis of common sense. Modern academic traditions burgeoned as one biblical scholar merely cited another in identifying "literary and linguistic characteristics" or "typical syntactical characteristics" of oral tradition.[10] Moreover, "'Orality' itself is a loaded, or at least ambiguous term, and when it is treated as a functional dimension of a written text, it can be especially problematic."[11]

So in a search for theoretical grounding, biblical scholars used studies in folklore and the theory of oral tradition. In 1950, Adolphe Lods used the work of the folklorist Andrew Lang.[12] Eduard Nielsen's 1954 *Oral Tradition* drew on Nordic studies of folklore from 1900 to 1915.[13] Yet biblical scholars were as dilatory at reading theoretical literature on oral tradition as they were in most subjects of anthropology. Frank Moore Cross's 1998 *From Epic to Canon* used the work of many folklorists, but nothing more recent than 1981, and most sources were considerably

7. Lods, "Le rôle de la tradition orale," 54–55.

8. Finnegan, "A Note on Oral Tradition,"195.

9. Finnegan, *Oral Traditions and the Verbal Arts*, 116. But cf. Gandz, "Oral Tradition in the Bible," 256, who had no such illusions.

10. Gómez Aranda, "Transmisión Oral y Transmisión Escrita," 247, 249; Hahn, "Zur Verschriftlichung mündlicher Tradition in der Bibel," 310; Gunn, "'Threading the Labyrinth,'" 78.

11. Graham, *Beyond the Written Word*, 7; Schier, "Einige methodische Überlegungen," 101.

12. Lods, *Histoire de la littérature hébraïque et juive*, 130.

13. Nielsen, *Oral Tradition*.

earlier.[14] In 1988, Klaus Seybold referred to the 1909 work of Axel Olrik and the 1960s work of Claude Lévi-Strauss as "newer methods."[15] John Van Seters' seminal *Abraham in History and Tradition* likewise relied on Olrik's "laws."[16]

Biblical scholars did not hesitate to "make reference to some general principles from the sociology of tradition"[17] and then authoritatively tell their readers that, for example, "sociologists of tradition reject the notion that any distinction should be made between the so-called primitive or traditional society and modern society in the study of tradition."[18] I cannot imagine any theorist of such an opinion; the references given were from the 1970s.[19]

The Oral Formulaic Theory

Most of the time biblical scholars cite or work with scholarship on oral tradition and folklore, they draw on the "Oral Formulaic Theory" or "Parry-Lord" school of thought. This movement is associated with the work of Milman Parry and his student Albert Lord,[20] as well as with the scholars Walter J. Ong and Jack Goody.[21]

In the 1930s, the Harvard scholar Milman Parry sought to understand Homeric Greek epic poetry by studying modern South Slavic oral

---

14. Cross, *From Epic to Canon*, 23–27. In Assyriology and Egyptology, the situation is generally better, as will be seen herein; but note Edzard's reliance on Vladimir Propp and the "Aarne-Thompson" index of folklore motifs; "Sumerian Epic," 7–14.

15. Seybold, "Zur mündlichen Überlieferung," 145. Olrik himself applied his "laws" to some of the legends of Genesis; Olrik, *Principles for Oral Narrative Research*, 116–33.

16. Van Seters, *Abraham in History and Tradition*, 156–57, 160–61, 164–65, 168–70. He also briefly draws on the 1960s work of Einar Sveinsson, *Abraham*, 162–63.

17. Van Seters, "Myth, Legend, and History," 2.

18. Ibid.

19. The folklorist foray into the biblical world by Alan Dundes (*Holy Writ as Oral Lit*) is highly problematic, in that every source-critical and text-critical variant is considered a sign of folklore; e.g., pp. 20, 24, etc. Cf. William Schniedewind, Review of *Holy Writ as Oral Lit* by Alan Dundes; and Susan Niditch, *Underdogs and Tricksters: A Prelude to Biblical Folklore*, 334–35.

20. E.g.,. Lord, *The Singer of Tales* (1960) and other works of Lord and Parry in the bibliography herein.

21. See the works of Ong and Goody in the bibliography.

tradition.[22] He and his student Albert Lord undertook extensive ethnographic research on Serbo-Croatian oral epic and, in particular, on Muslim oral poets of Herzegovina. They explicitly intended to test the hypothesis that Homer was a traditional oral poet and that the *Iliad* and *Odyssey* bore unmistakable signs of an oral heritage.[23] Together with their native assistant Nikola Vujnović, they recorded hundreds of epic narratives from local oral poets or *guslari*, and conducted interviews with the singers and others. The epics they recorded ran from six hundred to thirteen thousand lines apiece.

Parry had previously authored the basic work on Homeric *noun + epithet* diction (e.g, "swift-footed Achilles," "wine-dark sea"), beginning with his 1928 Paris dissertation "*L'Epithète traditionelle dans Homère.*" He had been alerted by his own teachers, Antoine Meillet and the Slavic philologist Matija Murko, to the possible relevance of South Slavic oral epic for Homeric studies.[24] After his fieldwork, Parry's key conclusion about this poetry, a conclusion that he then applied to the Homeric epics, was that its authors were illiterate poets who composed in a special "formulaic" language, a language that could not deviate significantly from what the audience expected verbally and thematically.[25]

Parry's work was cut short by his death in 1935, almost immediately after returning from Yugoslavia with "a 'half-ton of epic' on large aluminum disks and in notebooks."[26] Lord elaborated the theory in his now classical work of 1960, *The Singer of Tales*, originally his 1949 Harvard dissertation begun under Parry. "No book in the last fifty years," wrote Albert Friedman in 1983, "has so fluttered the dovecots of philology as *The Singer of Tales.*"[27] Lord returned to Yugoslavia in the 1950s and 1960s for more fieldwork.

22. Such issues as Parry explored had already been important to Prague school thinkers like Roman Jacobson and Peter Bogatyrev (e.g., Bogatyrev, "Folklore as a Special Form of Creativity," 32–46. The fact that Parry (and Lord) were at Harvard is an important factor in the oral formulaic theory's amazing growth and in its influence on Frank Moore Cross and his students; Russo, "Oral Theory," 7.

23. Foley, "Editing and Translating the Traditional Oral Epic," 3.

24. Foley, Review of *The Singer of Tales*, by Albert Lord (2000), *Cultural Analysis* 1 (2000) 85.

25. Lord, *The Singer of Tales* (2000), 17.

26. Foley, Review of *The Singer of Tales* (2000), 85. Much of this material is available in Bartok and Lord, *Serbo-Croatian Folksongs*.

27. Friedman, "The Oral-Formulaic Theory of Balladry," 215.

Parry and Lord defined the "formula" as "a group of words which is regularly employed under the same metrical condition to express a given essential idea."[28] Lord then established a methodology wherein a percentage of formula could be calculated for a given *written* text and then used as an unmistakable indicator of oral composition.[29] Lord set up his South Slavic model as the sole form of orality and felt free to define any nonliterate composition that did not fit the mold as "written composition without writing."[30]

Lord also isolated "theme" as a component of oral composition distinct from formulaic language.[31] Lord defined a "theme" as "a recurrent element of narration or description . . . not restricted, as is the formula, by metrical considerations; hence, it should not be limited to exact word-for-word repetition,"[32] or, elsewhere as, "groups of ideas regularly used in telling a tale in the formulaic style," although "not any fixed set of words."[33] It was clear that "themes" included such things as type-scenes, but Lord's definitions remained elusively vague. In general, and perhaps for this reason, the presence or absence of themes never gained popularity as a test for oral or written composition the way formula did,[34] although Lord suggested (without explanation) that in the Old Testament it could be more pertinent than formulas.[35]

A major conclusion of Parry and Lord was that the oral "tradent" really composes his "text" in its performance.[36] Each iteration of an oral text was original in detail, in spite of its formulaic and thematic consistency.[37] The same tale is different each time it is performed.[38] As will be seen in

---

28. Parry, *The Making of Homeric Verse*, 172; Lord, *The Singer of Tales* (1960), 30.

29. Lord, "Homer as Oral Poet," 1–46.

30. Lord, "The Traditional Song," 175–76.

31. In 1936, Parry had written a review of Walter Arend's *Die typischen Scenen bei Homer* (1933) that first compared "theme" in Homer and the Slavic oral poetry.

32. Lord, "Composition by Theme in Homer and Southslavic Epos," 73.

33. Lord, *The Singer of Tales* (1960), 68–69.

34. Russo, "Oral Theory," 17.

35. Lord, "Formula and Non-Narrative Theme," 102.

36. Lord, *The Singer of Tales* (1960), 100.

37. Ibid., 13, 141.

38. Ibid., 101.

what follows, "composition-in-performance" may be the most enduring contribution of the Parry-Lord enterprise.[39]

Most scholars were convinced of Parry and Lord's applicability to Homeric poetry. "A consensus exists among classicists that the work of Milman Parry and Albert Lord has provided satisfactory answers to some parts of the Homeric question."[40] Homer was oral composition because of its formulaic nature, and this was based on "the *rules* derived from research done in Yugoslavia" that must be applicable to "all oral poets,"[41] including tradents of oral *prose*. This latter point is of great importance.

The impact of Parry and Lord was therefore widespread beyond Classics. So pivotal was *The Singer of Tales* for the field, that even in 1997, a national survey of university offerings on oral tradition showed it still central to undergraduate coursework.[42] Lord himself stated that their work was applicable "to all oral poetries."[43] But the followers of Parry and Lord went well beyond poetry, extending the analysis to "every conceivable genre"[44]—prose included. "The spread of the Parry and Lord theory after 1960 led to refinements, of the idea, albeit of a grossly overgeneralized version. Many researchers, mostly from English-speaking countries, in fact, wasted no time in setting forth the equation: oral style = formulaic style."[45] The work of Parry and Lord, which "seemed to sweep all before it,"[46] had, in fact, more impact on the study of *written* texts than on the study of oral tradition. "The more a text has formulas, the more likely is its oral origin."[47]

For Parry and Lord, oral poets are always illiterate. This means that there is a clear dichotomy between orality and literacy. The literate do not compose oral poetry,[48] and written text is either orally derived or liter-

---

39. Vet, "Context and the Emerging Story," 161.

40. Vet, "The Joint Role of Orality and Literacy," 43.

41. Ibid.; italics added.

42. Foley, Review of *The Singer of Tales* (2000), 86.

43. In Parry and Lord, *Serbo-Croatian Heroic Songs*, 1:4.

44. Finnegan, *Oral Traditions and the Verbal Arts*, 119.

45. Zumthor, *Oral Poetry*, 97.

46. Finnegan, *The Oral and Beyond*, 96; Finnegan, *Oral Traditions and the Verbal Arts*, 42.

47. Honko, "Oral and Semiliterary Epics," 3. Honko does not agree with this view.

48. Lord, *The Singer of Tales* (1960), 129; Parry, "Have We Homer's *Iliad*?," 212–15.

ary.[49] The implications of this were developed by Walter J. Ong and Jack Goody[50] in what became known as the "Literacy Hypothesis."[51] According to this school's "interminable number of studies that keep coming out on orality *vs.* literacy in various disciplines in the humanities as well as in the social sciences,"[52] there is both a qualitative difference between oral and written language, and a particular oral mindset.[53] For example, in an oral culture, spoken words have power, and naming an object gives one power over it.[54] Not only do particular features reveal oral composition, but those features also reveal thought patterns. Oral composition, therefore, along with its telltale features, is tied to social organization.[55] Oral societies were said to be "highly traditionalist or conservative."[56] Literacy brought "quicker and more radical innovation."[57]

Admittedly, it was not the ability to write itself that constituted this vast cultural change. So long as "literature" continued to be predominately oral, the radical change was only incipient.[58] It was when the poet moved beyond the aims and methods of oral poetry to principles aimed

49. The emphasis on this point was due to the Homeric focus, not the Slavic evidence.

50. Goody, *The Domestication of the Savage Mind*; Goody, *The Logic of Writing and the Organization of Society*.

51. Lord, in fact, backtracked from this view in later years; Lord, *Epic Singers and Oral Tradition*, 25–27. But it was too late to stop the Ong-Goody juggernaut.

52. Michałowski, "Orality and Literacy and Early Mesopotamian Literature," 231.

53. Goody, *Domestication*, chapter 7.

54. Ong, *Orality and Literacy*, 32–33.

55. Griffiths, *Religious Readings*, 29.

56. Ong, *Orality and Literacy*, 41.

57. W. J. Henderson, "Tradition and Originality in Early Greek Lyric," 249. Jan Assmann has independently proposed a different "Great Divide" that writing introduces. "With writing this history divides into two phases: the phase of rite-based repetition and the phases of text-based repetition" (Assmann, *Religion and Cultural Memory*, 39. Assmann argues for the exact opposite of the view of Goody and Ong when he writes, "In the world of nonwritten memory transmission the heir to tradition is measured by" fidelity to the tradition, while writing values innovation (ibid., 83, 114). Writing supports novelty; orality inhibits it (ibid., 84, 109). Assmann marshals no evidence in support of this anti-Lordian view, but it allows him to conclude that the precise knowledge of oral texts required in oral societies limits cultural literacy to an elite few "in a sharper form than in written cultures" (ibid.,106). Assmann does have the valid point that variants between oral versions of the same tale will only become manifest to anyone with their written recording (ibid., 114).

58. Zwettler, *The Oral Tradition*, 26.

at a reading audience[59] that one reached a reading and writing society—this was "literacy."

"The acquisition of literacy, . . . the most profound of all revolutions in technology, it marks a 'Great Divide' in human history, and the changes it brings are qualitative, placing oral societies on the one side and literate ones on the other."[60] Even those who held that, "This shift is certainly not to be described as an event, a drastic change, but instead as a slow process," agreed that "the shift from an oral society to a writing society . . . has decisive implications for a culture, to such an extent that it becomes the fundamental basis for an intellectual revolution."[61] Since literacy "provides a substitute for memory, . . . [it] restructures consciousness, enabling the development of analytical skill and logical, sequential reasoning."[62] In other words, man emerges from the primitive mires of savagery into the light of Civilization![63]

The Impact of the Parry-Lord School
in Old Testament Scholarship

When most Old Testament scholars talk about theory in oral tradition, they are talking about the Oral Formulaic school.[64] At one time, this made perfect sense. W. F. Albright was conversant with the work of Parry and Lord the moment it first appeared.[65] As conversant with scholarship on

59. Ibid., 22.

60. Jolles, "Interfaces between Oral and Literate Societies," 396. Goody, *Domestication*, chap. 1.

61. Brink, "*Verba Volant, Scripta Manent?*," 78.

62. Draper, "'Less Literate Are Safer,'" 304.

63. Ong did not ascribe to all that his purported followers espoused, and would not have agreed with the statements of this last paragraph. For Ong's resistance to such moves, see Ong, "A Comment on 'Arguing about Literacy,'" 700.

64. "A few Assyriologists have given lip service through passing reference to the work of Parry and Lord and a handful of brave souls have attempted [Oral Formulaic analysis] . . . [But it] has had a remarkably small effect on the larger scholarly community of Assyriologists who, for the most part, have little interest in such nontraditional approaches" (Michałowski, "Orality," 228). One such "brave soul" was Alster, *Dumuzi's Dream*. Alster concluded that Oral Formulaicism was not applicable to Mesopotamia Alster, "Interaction of Oral and Written Poetry," 27–28. In Egyptology, Parkinson relies on Goody and Ong's literacy divide and formulaic tests for orality; Parkinson, *Poetry and Culture in Middle Kingdom Egypt*, 55–58.

65. Albright, "Some Oriental Glosses," 162.

oral folklore as he was in all cross-disciplinary fields,[66] Albright attempted a small-scale application of Oral Formulaic insights to Ugaritic epics.[67]

In the 1960s and 70s, several biblical scholars used the work of Lord for their understanding of oral tradition, in spite of warnings from Lord himself that "application of the formulaic test for orality requires special adaption if it is to work at all . . . in biblical poetry."[68] As will be seen in the following chapter, cracks were only beginning to appear in the Oral Formulaic edifice, and scholars of most of the world's literatures remained unaware of these. Foremost among oral-formulaic biblical studies was the work of Robert Culley.[69] Culley's 1963 dissertation on oral language in the psalms, published in 1967,[70] was the first work to extensively apply the Oral Formulaic insights to the Old Testament. Culley's 1976 study of Old Testament narrative referenced a number of more recent field studies, including those of Ruth Finnegan, that pose the greatest challenges to Parry and Lord, discussed in the following chapter.[71] Yet Culley concluded that nothing significantly detracted from the findings of Parry and Lord.[72]

Ronald Hendel's Harvard dissertation, published in 1987 as *The Epic of the Patriarch*, is entirely dependent on Lord, whose *Singer of Tales* is cited on nearly every page.[73] Hendel's dissertation was under Frank Moore Cross at Harvard, where Parry began the oral formulaic school and where it greatly influenced biblical studies. It is not too much to say that Cross's students reenvisioned traditions history with Oral Formulaicism substi-

66. See Miller, "How Post-Modernism (and W. F. Albright) Can Save Us from Malarkey."

67. Albright, "Some Oriental Glosses," 162–76.

68. Lord, "Formula and Non-Narrative Theme," 96. Nevertheless, Lord dismissed those who hesitated in making the attempt (e.g., Robert Coote) as "a bit too pessimistic" (Lord, "Formula and Non-Narrative Theme," 99).

69. David Gunn's works are also noteworthy for this period, although Gunn tried to apply Lord's concept of theme to prose narratives. Gunn writes, "I read it [*The Singer of Tales*], and it changed my life" (Gunn, "'Threading the Labyrinth,'" 19). Gunn concluded that the precise relationship of particular biblical texts to oral tradition could not be proven (Gunn, *The Story of King David*, 62). See the works of both Culley and Gunn in the bibliography. Dorothy Irvin's 1970 dissertation on ancient Near Eastern folkloric themes, published in 1978, relied extensively on Parry's work (but not Lord's); Irvin, *Mytharion*, 9–10.

70. Culley, *Oral Formulaic Language in the Biblical Psalms*.

71. Culley, *Studies in the Structure of Hebrew Narrative*, 3, 7–10.

72. Ibid., 17, 20.

73. Hendel, *The Epic of the Patriarch*, esp. 35, 37, 137.

tuted for form criticism.[74] Cross himself liberally identified formulas in early Israelite poetry and prose.[75] Lordian "themes," too, were identified, as type-scenes became markers of the "oral literature which preceded written biblical literature."[76] Likewise, the notion of an epic poet who neither memorizes scripts nor composes whole cloth has been widely adopted.[77]

Parry-Lord was used to dismantle the very form criticism that first introduced oral tradition into biblical scholarship. Based on what "A. B. Lord has demonstrated," one could no longer hold with Gunkel that short narratives evolved into longer cycles, since such distinctions of length were merely matters of storytellers' and audiences' preferences.[78]

Frank Polak has an idiosyncratic method for distinguishing biblical Hebrew of oral origin that is quite unlike Lord's formula test.[79] Yet his linguistic criteria for tracing the development of Hebrew syntax depend on Goody's pronouncements about the stylistic differences of oral and scribal texts.[80] While the accuracy of Polak's conclusions about the history of the Hebrew language may be debated,[81] it is only on the authority of Goody that he can say, "the specific features by which the three main classes [phases of the language of narrative] differ from one another are connected to the characterization of written language as against oral discourse."[82]

Susan Niditch's magisterial *Oral World and Written Word* (1997) depends on Parry, Lord, Goody, and Ong.[83] Yet she is keenly aware of the misunderstandings and shortcomings of this school.[84] "No longer are

74. Kawashima, *Biblical Narrative and the Death of the Rhapsode*, 7.

75. Cross, *From Epic to Canon*, 24. So too Jason, "The Story of David and Goliath," 36–70.

76. Zakovitch, "Humor and Theology," 78.

77. Cross, *From Epic to Canon*, 26; Kofoed, "Remember the Days of Old (Deut 32, 7)," 9–10; Silver, *The Story of Scripture*, 53.

78. Hendel, *The Epic of the Patriarch*, 137.

79. Polak, "The Oral and the Written," 59–105. See further discussion in chapter 6, below.

80. Ibid., 59–61, 101.

81. Susan Niditch, *Judges*, 16–17; Niditch, "Epic and History in the Hebrew Bible," 91.

82. Polak, "The Oral and the Written," 101.

83. Niditch, *Oral World and Written Word*, 8–10, 117.

84. Niditch, "The Hebrew Bible and Oral Literature," 3, 5.

many scholars convinced . . . that the most seemingly oral-traditional or formulaic pieces are earliest in date," she writes. "The most formulaic may be the latest in date."[85] Nevertheless, the presence of oral formulas in the eighth-century BCE Siloam tunnel inscription and graffiti from Kuntillet Ajrud (ca. 800 BCE) is "writing in the oral mode."[86] Though acknowledging, "Written works may have been performed orally, while oral works may have been written down . . . Oral works can become quite fixed, a virtual 'text,' while written works can display the qualities of performance,"[87] there exists nevertheless a "style indicative of oral-style aesthetics."[88]

A cursory poll of contemporary biblical scholarship finds the oral-formulaic school still firmly entrenched. Raymond Person still relies on the Parry-Lord school and the Goody-Ong notion of an "oral mindset" for his understanding of ancient authorship,[89] although he rejects the notion of a "great divide" between oral and literate cultures.[90] Robert Kawashima writes, "Compositions exhibiting signs of oral-formulaic composition provide us with our best glimpse into Israel's prebiblical narrative traditions."[91] He considers written literature and oral tradition "autonomous categories."[92] Jean-Louis Ska uses Lord to define biblical redaction processes.[93] Jens Kofoed refers to Lord and Ong as "Current research on mnemonic techniques of modern oral societies."[94] William

85. Niditch, "Oral Tradition and Biblical Scholarship," 43.

86. Niditch, *Oral World and Written Word*, 54–55.

87. Niditch, *Judges*, 17. The quotation is essentially reproduced in Niditch, "Epic and History," 92. See also Niditch, "The Hebrew Bible," 6.

88. Niditch, *Judges*, 17, with a nod to "Lord and Parry."

89. Person, "A Rolling Corpus and Oral Tradition," 263–71; Person, *The Deuteronomic School*, 88–91; Person, *The Deuteronomic History and the Book of Chronicles*, ix, 20, 44, 70.

90. Person, *Deuteronomic History*, 46–47, 67

91. Kawashima, "From Song to Story," 152; Kawashima, "Comparative Literature and Biblical Studies," 331. He applies the Parry-Lord formulaic test to the Song of Deborah ("From Song to Story," 155).

92. Kawashima, "Comparative Literature and Biblical Studies," 324. Kawashima emphasizes "the landmark comparative studies of Milman Parry and Albert Lord" ("Comparative Literature," 334), but also uses the 1960s theoretical work of Walter Benjamin and Victor Shklovsky; Kawashima, "Comparative Literature and Biblical Studies," 332.

93. Ska, "A Plea on Behalf of the Biblical Redactors," 11; Ska, "Le Pentateuque à l'heure de ses usagers," 100.

94. Kofoed, "Remember the Days of Old (Deut 32, 7)," 8.

Schniedewind bases his work on the "new approaches"[95] of Goody and Ong: "Writing is a technology that transforms culture," he writes.[96] So "determining the degree of literacy in Judah is critical for placing the Hebrew Bible on the orality-literacy continuum."[97] Since Goody and Ong propose that literacy devalues the art of memory, Schniedewind is able to imagine conflict in ancient Israel between "literary elites whose authority was threatened by the oral tradition" and "a critique of the written word by those with a vested interest in the authority of . . . the oral tradition."[98] Ong is key to the work of Joachim Schaper on writing.[99] His recent work on Deuteronomy and Joshua is still constantly dependent on Parry, Lord, Goody, and Ong.[100] In short, biblical scholars, though not all of them to be sure, seem bound to the Oral Formulaic gibbet.

95. Schneidewind, "How the Bible Became a Book."

96. Schniedewind, *How the Bible Became a Book*, 35, 91, 108, 219 n. 1. Schniedewind is explicit in his rejection of Goody and Ong's detractors, John Miles Foley and Rosalind Thomas, on which see the following chapter; Schniedewind, "Orality and Literacy in Ancient Israel," 328.

97. Schniedewind, "Orality and Literacy in Ancient Israel," 331. This notion builds on existing ideas that the rise of writing in Israel spelled the end of oral tradition; Rendtorff, *The Problem of the Process*, 120. On the necessity of determining the degree of literacy in ancient Israel, see chapter 6, below.

98. Schniedewind, "How the Bible Became a Book."

99. Schaper, "A Theology of Writing," 97–99.

100. Schaper, "The Living Word Engraved in Stone," 9–10, 15, 20.

2

The Bathos of the Oral Formulaic School

Empirical and analytical research in this field is governed by a number of controlling factors: the very questions that one wants to have answered in the end; the attitudes that one holds about the standards that answers are expected to satisfy (e.g., standards of verity, certainty, coherence, heuristic value, vividness, intuitive soundness, faithfulness to experience, aesthetic value); the form in which one prefers to put together answers (e.g., a historical narrative—and if so, what narrative models are chosen); ideas about what constitutes an explanation; the concepts with which one works and the ways that one conceives them (concepts, in this subject, like "formula," "tradition,"... "orality," "literacy").[1]

Although rare contemporary folklore scholars continue to work in the Parry-Lord school of thought,[2] by the late 1980s its "unnuanced deterministic view"[3] had been called into question by folklorists, classicists, anthropologists, and ethnomusicologists alike.[4] "Today there are few, if any, oralists who would classify themselves as Oral Formulaicists, and one

---

1. Treitler, "Sinners and Singers," 140.
2. E.g., Sale, "The Oral-Formulaic Theory Today," 54; Jensen, "The Oral-Formulaic Theory Revisited," 50; Gísli Sigurðsson, "On the Classification of Eddic Heroic Poetry," 245–55; Sigurðsson, *The Medieval Icelandic Saga*, 38–41—although Gísli's more recent work has withdrawn from this somewhat; see below. N.B., because most modern Icelanders have no surnames, it is conventional to refer to them in bibliographies by first name rather than patronymic.
3. Griffiths, *Religious Reading*, 34.
4. Finnegan, *Literacy and Orality*, 13.

would be hard pressed to find many who subscribe to the hard Parryist position that dominated the field for so long."[5]

While the South Slavic epic poet "provided an excellent analogue for Homeric epic in many ways, . . . the model that was generalized outward to hundreds of other traditions and forms was too narrow to be widely applicable."[6] For example, Old Norse-Icelandic Skaldic poetry, to be discussed in chapter 3, "does not use formulas."[7] In India, "the tendency towards greater frequency of formulaic *pādas* in the later parts of the *Ramayana*, as of the *Mahabharata*, seems in fact to be a symptom of the breakdown of the true oral tradition."[8] "Recurring elements are of different kinds and functions."[9] On the other hand, formulaic language can often be found in literature composed in writing,[10] and in written literature *never intended* to be recited, such as fourteenth-century BCE Amarna letters to Pharaoh, written in a hybrid Canaanite-Akkadian certainly incomprehensible to the Egyptian king.[11]

By the late 1970s, scholars were admitting that it was difficult "to find oral material which is formulaic."[12] "Gradually people began to lose confidence in the notion that formula research provided an infallible guide to whether a particular text was of oral origin or not."[13] Formulaic language, rather, seemed to be more concurrent with long tales about heroes.[14] "No one these days believes that there is any one touchstone for the oral style."[15]

5. Amodio, "Contemporary Critical Approaches and Studies in Oral Tradition," 96.

6. Foley, "The Challenge of Translating Traditional Oral Epic," 260; Dagmar Burkhart, "Märchen nach dem Märchen," 49; Finnegan, "Problems in the Processing of 'Oral Texts,'" 2.

7. Würth, "Skaldic Poetry and Performance," in *Learning and Understanding in the Old Norse World*, 264; Jesse L. Byock, "Saga Form, Oral Prehistory, and the Icelandic Social Context," 156.

8. Brockington, "The Textualization of the Sanskrit Epics," 201.

9. Clark, *Theme in Oral Epic and in Beowulf*, 221. "Complexity of meanings beyond the surface of a text does not distinguish oral from literary narrative," either (ibid., 214).

10. Finnegan, *Oral Traditions*, 119–20; Green, *Medieval Listening and Reading*, 7.

11. Shlomo Izre'el, "The Study of Oral Poetry," 193.

12. O'Nolan, "Formula in Oral Tradition," 25; Friedman, "The Oral-Formulaic Theory," 229.

13. Sigurðsson, "Orality Harnessed," 19.

14. O'Nolan, "Formula in Oral Tradition," 32.

15. Niles, "The Myth of the Anglo-Saxon Oral Poet," 10; Finnegan, *The Oral and Beyond*, 111.

Field studies of Rosalind Thomas and others also challenged the compositional theories of Parry and Lord.[16] Parry, Lord, Goody, and Ong had denied poetic intention in composition and had underrated the role of memorization.[17] Lord had insisted not only on "composition-in-performance," but that "oral narrative is not, *cannot*, be memorized."[18] But oral poems are regularly composed in advance of performance in Tonga, the Gilbert Islands, and among the Netsilik Eskimo.[19] Ethnographers note that word-for-word accuracy was important for the Eastern Cherokee.[20] Lord considers these singers no longer oral poets because he believes they cease innovating in performance.[21] Yet literacy in Bali "does not seem to inhibit a performer's improvisational skills, nor does it affect his ability to compose written poetry in an oral style."[22] "It is not so much the advent or existence of literacy that seem to cut short the improvisational nature of performance as . . . that once the context or social environment changes sufficiently and the influence and power of performances is lost."[23] Old Norse-Icelandic Skaldic performers "had only very limited opportunities for improvisation" on poems composed generations before,[24] and the same is true of English balladry.[25] "In a West and North European context the role of verbatim memorization has undoubtedly been underestimated," as well.[26] The Maori and Somali emphasize word-for-word memorization.[27]

On the other hand, there are clearly cases where oral narratives are "changing every time they are performed," as in performances of the Hindu Epic of *Ramayana*.[28] And Finnegan found many cases in Africa

16. Rosalind Thomas, *Literacy and Orality in Ancient Greece*, 17–19, 33.

17. Ibid., 34–36; Finnegan, "How Oral Is Oral Literature?" 60.

18. Lord, "Oral Poetry," 592.

19. Finnegan, "How Oral Is Oral Literature?," 61; Finnegan, *The Oral and Beyond*, 107.

20. Stahl, "Accuracy, Fidelity, and Stability?," n.p.

21. Lord, "What Is Oral Literature Anyway?," 175.

22. De Vet, "Context," 165. The same was true for Old English poetry; see Caie, "*Ealdgesegena worn*: What the Old English *Beowulf* Tells Us about Oral Forms," 116,

23. De Vet, "Context," 165.

24. Würth, "Skaldic Poetry and Performance," 264; cf. Poole, "Skaldic Verse and Anglo-Saxon History," 265.

25. Friedman, "Oral-Formulaic Theory," 217.

26. Chesnutt, "Orality in a Norse-Icelandic Perspective," 197.

27. Finnegan, *Oral Traditions and the Verbal Arts*, 115.

28. Bandhu, "Common Languages and Common Narratives," 24–25.

where extemporisation was more important than memorization.[29] In Nigeria, the expectation of word-for-word accuracy varies by the kind of story being told.[30] The potential for improvisation thus varies both cross-culturally and generically.[31]

The sharp dichotomy of oral and written composition also proved false. For Parry and Lord, oral poets were always illiterate, and the literate do not compose oral poetry. According to Finnegan, Lord had never presented solid evidence for incompatibility of oral and written composition strategies.[32] Both writing and oral composition share similar methods. Writers could be as influenced by audiences as bards could, both before and after a text was first written.[33] In fact, many societies produced oral and written literature simultaneously, as will be shown in the following section of this chapter.[34]

The Goody-Ong conclusion that oral societies were inherently, structurally different from literate did not hold up to field studies such as those of Ruth Finnegan in Africa.[35] "The cultural role of memory seems independent of orality and literacy . . . Writing and literary culture did not replace memory, it supported it." That writing was used to augment people's oral memory is proven by the widespread use in the Hellenistic world of treatises on memory such as *Ad herennium* (86–82 BCE).[36] Nor were analytical thinking and transformed cognitive structures the result of literacy. The rise of literacy among the Liberian Vai or the Zulu or

---

29. Finnegan, *The Oral and Beyond*, 84.

30. Stahl, "Accuracy, Fidelity, and Stability."

31. Clark, *Theme in Oral Epic*, 200; Mundal, "Introduction," 1. The range of variation in epic, for example, appears to be quite limited (Oesterreicher, "Types of Orality," 211). At Hattusa, epic texts that must have been performed were stored at the temple, while rituals and other practical texts likely to have been consulted in writing were stored at the palace; Archi, "Orality, Direct Speech and the Kumarbi Cycle," 224. For modern examples of improvisational potential dependent on genre, see Abrahams, "Creativity, Individuality, and the Traditional Singer," 8.

32. Finnegan, *The Oral and Beyond*, 105.

33. Thomas, *Literacy and Orality in Ancient Greece*, 33.

34. Thomas, "Performance Literature and the Written Word," 2; Thomas, *Literacy and Orality in Ancient Greece*, 89; Finnegan, *Literacy and Orality*, 111–13, 159–61, 168; O'Keeffe, "The Performing Body on the Oral-Literate Continuum," 46.

35. Finnegan, *Literacy and Orality*, 13; de Vet, "Context," 161. Ong himself considered the historical edge between orality and literacy to be ragged (Ong, "Comment," 700).

36. Ásdís Egilsdóttir, "From Orality to Literacy," 212.

Xhosa of South Africa produces no such philosophical changes.[37] Writing itself does not change a people's thought patterns.[38]

Given the overlap and interpenetration of the oral and written and the lack of any clear line between orality and literacy, Finnegan has gone to the extent of rejecting the term "oral tradition" and the "ethnocentric models implied in the binarism of oral/literate."[39] Nevertheless, she recognizes, "There are also a number of differences between literature in literate and in non-literate contexts."[40] Preferring the term "oral literature," she opens this classification to works composed orally, transmitted orally (even if of written origin), or orally performed.[41] "There are instances of oral literature where all three criteria unambiguously apply, and here there is no problem. But in the cases where the criteria conflict—and these are common enough not to count as the odd or untypical type—then there is no right answer: one has to make a choice."[42] Do we, then, call these oral tradition?

Writing, too, is not nearly as uniform a phenomenon as Ong and Goody present it. It has different functions in different socioeconomic settings. For example, in Mesopotamia, "the uses to which writing was put underwent rather dramatic and violent fluctuations."[43] In the Old

37. Draper, "'Less Literate are Safer,'" 305.

38. Assmann, *Religion*, 41, 64, 117–20.

39. Finnegan, "'Oral Tradition': Weasel Words," 84–85; *The Oral and Beyond*, 102. Ignored in most studies of orality and literacy is the frequent presence of written but nonlinguistic pictorial or symbolic communication; Louis-Jean Calvet, *La Tradition orale*, 59, 63, 69. Henkelman, "The Birth of Gilgameš (Ael. *NA* XII.21," sec. 1.3.3, considers the role of vase art in the transmission of Gilgamesh stories to Greece.

40. Ruth Finnegan, "Literacy versus Non-literacy: The Great Divide?" 135.

41. Finnegan, "How Oral Is Oral Literature?" 60; Finnegan, *Oral Traditions and the Verbal Arts*, 7. Izre'el ("Study," 197) and Michałowski ("Orality," 242) probably go too far in declaring these unrelated phenomena. Dundes rejects "oral literature" as a "term used by elitist literary scholars who are uncomfortable with the term 'folklore' and who are trying to upgrade the material by calling it 'literature'" (Dundes, *Holy Writ as Oral Lit*, 11). For Finnegan's explanation of the benefits of the appellation, see Finnegan, *Oral Traditions and the Verbal Arts*, 9–10. Niditch, *Oral World*, 130, has a different classification: 1) oral performance dictated to a writer—I find this to be quite unlikely; 2) slow movement of literature from oral to written media; 3) writing in an oral style; and 4) writing excerpting other writing. These sorts of classification schemes are treated on a more philosophical level by Wulf Oesterreicher ("Types of Orality," 190–95), with reference to the work of Giovanni Nencioni and Niyi Akinnaso.

42. Finnegan, "How Oral Is Oral Literature?," 63.

43. Larsen, "The Mesopotamian Lukewarm Mind," 218–19.

Babylonian period, in part thanks to the simplified script and syllabary of few signs, "many people could read and write," while around the middle of the second millennium BCE, complication of the script and use of logograms over syllabic signs "led to literacy becoming the prerogative of a restricted class of highly trained professionals."[44]

The most prolific contemporary representative of the Parry-Lord school is John Miles Foley.[45] Foley, however, has been able to move Oral Formulaic thought beyond Lord while incorporating most of the criticisms of Finnegan, Thomas, and others. He writes, "We may, and we should, continue to evolve newer and better methods for such studies, and inevitably such progress will lead to revision or perhaps outright dismissal of earlier theories and practices. That is the nature of a healthy field of intellectual inquiry . . . But *Singer* will always remain a cornerstone of whatever edifice we seek to erect."[46]

Foley recognizes, "The formulaic test *as it has generally been carried out* cannot prove oral provenance."[47] But the italics are Foley's; he hectors those who imported the model without taking into consideration differences in prosody, phraseology, and poetics between cultures, leaving Lord's method "a useless index."[48] Foley also recognizes the fuzziness of the oral/written, orality/literacy divide, advocating the term "oral-derived" for written texts with what Finnegan called oral aesthetics.[49] Foley provides a useful nuance on the issues of formulas, themes, memorization, and composition-in-performance:

> A traditional work depends primarily on elements and strategies that were in place long before the execution of the present version or text, long before the present nominal author learned the inherited craft. Because the idiom is metonymic, summoning conventional connotations to conventional structures, we may say

44. Ibid., 219–20.

45. See the list of works in the bibliography.

46. Foley, Review of *The Singer of Tales*, 87. So too Green, *Medieval Listening and Reading*, 5.

47. Foley, *Traditional Oral Epic*, 4.

48. Ibid.

49. Foley, *Immanent Art*, 15; Foley, "Plenitude and Diversity," 106; Finnegan, "Literacy versus Non-literacy: The Great Divide?," 135. Dundes makes the same point: oral folklore is still folklore when written down (Dundes, *Holy Writ as Oral Lit*, 9). "Oral-derived" is now a commonplace term (e.g., Edmunds, "Epic and Myth," 32), although Kawashima rejects it (Kawashima, *Biblical Narrative*, 162).

that the meaning it conveys is principally inherent. The "author" uses this idiom most felicitously when he or she orchestrates inherent meaning coherently, so that the performance or text makes sense not only at the superficial (that is, decontextualized) level but, more importantly, with reference to the tradition.[50]

While, "All this is not to say that there remains no difference between oral and written literatures . . . But during that period while the oral tradition lives and dominates a society's—and an individual's—aesthetic values, there may be as little difference as possible between them."[51]

Still, Finnegan's warning is essential:

> Precisely because the general insights of *The Singer of Tales* are, as I have suggested, so useful in the study of some forms of oral literature in Africa (and elsewhere), it is tempting to swallow the theory whole, and to go overboard for all the detailed analysis and implicit assumptions in the Parry-Lord thesis and its adherents. This would be a mistake, the more important to recognize because of the unquestionable attraction and applicability of many aspects of the theory.[52]

Unfortunately, as was shown in the previous chapter, few biblical scholars were aware of the problems with Oral Formulaic theory.[53] Some scholars who did criticize the application of the theory did so without referring to the broader attacks on it in related fields. So Ferdinand Hahn, Jean-Louis Ska, and Ernst Wendland all speak of the interdependence of oral and written literature.[54] John Van Seters pointed out that recurrent supposed "formulas" might merely be evidence of literary dependence, unless attention is given to multiple sources and the relationship between texts.[55] He also rejects the dichotomy of orality and literacy.[56] The work of

50. Foley, "The Implications of Oral Tradition," 35.

51. Clark, *Theme in Oral Epic*, 223.

52. Finnegan, *The Oral and Beyond*, 100.

53. An example of using ethnographic analogy directly, with no conversation with theoretical linguistics or sociology, is that of Macdonald, "Literacy in an Oral Environment," 49–118.

54. Hahn, "Verschriftlichung," 315; Ska, "From History Writing to Library Building,"145, 152, 166; Wendland, "Performance Criticism," 5.

55. Van Seters, "Oral Patterns or Literary Conventions in Biblical Narrative," 149.

56. Van Seters, "The Origins of the Hebrew Bible," 89–90. In this, he is well aware of the work of Thomas (ibid., 91).

Van Seters will be discussed in a later chapter, but the rejection of oral formulaicism by Van Seters and by Patricia Kirkpatrick is accompanied by a rejection of the search for oral literature in the Old Testament altogether.[57]

As described in the previous chapter, Susan Niditch is aware of some of the shortcomings of the Parry-Lord-Goody-Ong school.[58] Citing Finnegan, she emphatically rejects the Goody-Ong "Great Dichotomy,"[59] although she fails to reckon with Thomas's demolition of the formulaic orality index.[60] Katherine Hayes, in her study of prophetic language, works in the Oral Formulaic school, but is explicitly a "Foleyist," rather than a Parry-Lordist.[61] As such, most of the shortcomings of the Parry-Lord school are not applicable to her work. Nevertheless, her focus on identifying formulaic language in the prophets, albeit of a Foley variety,[62] still seems unnecessarily focused on matching a preexisting checklist for oral features.[63]

David Carr and Karel van der Toorn have explicitly rejected the Parry-Lord model, as have Roger Syren and Seth Sanders on smaller scales.[64] Their discussion of the oral-written relationship is quite close to that which I will articulate here.[65]

The Simultaneity of Orality and Literacy

"The simplistic binary of orality versus literacy has receded into the background and more nuanced theories have arisen."[66] Recent field studies in oral tradition and folklore have shown that many societies produced oral and written literature simultaneously.[67] Not only should oral tradi-

57. Van Seters, *The Edited Bible*, 181; Kirkpatrick, "The Jacob-Esau Narrative," 9.

58. E.g., Niditch, "Oral Tradition and Biblical Scholarship," 43.

59. Niditch, *Judges*, 18; Niditch, "The Challenge of Israelite Epic," 284; Niditch, "Epic and History," 93.

60. Van Seters, Review of *Oral World and Written Word*, 437.

61. Hayes, *The Earth Mourns*, 207.

62. Ibid., 208, 211; and also for "themes," 225.

63. Ibid., 216, 222.

64. Carr, *Writing on the Tablet*, 6–7; van der Toorn, *Scribal Culture*, 228; Syren, "Before the Text and After," 236; Sanders, "What Was the Alphabet For?" 38–40.

65. Carr, "The Rise of Torah," 45.

66. Foley, "Analogues: Modern Oral Epics," 206.

67. Thomas, *Literacy and Orality*, 89; Finnegan, *Literacy and Orality*, 111–13, 159–61,

tion and written literature not be considered unrelated phenomena,[68] but writing often supports oral tradition and vice versa.[69] "The role of literacy in the preservation of oral poetry and also in the creation of new (and old) oral poetry is now generally accepted, and now, at the beginning of the twenty-first century, has liberated research."[70]

Ancient Egypt, it may be argued, displays various interdependent modes of written and oral literature.[71] Works composed in writing were intended for performance, especially in the Middle Kingdom (2100–1650 BCE).[72] "For example, in several of the royal burial suites where Pyramid Texts are inscribed, each column begins with *ḏd mdw* 'to be spoken,' marking the whole as being for recitation; what is written is an ideal oral form."[73] Practice copies of some texts include red markings to aid in recitation.[74] Yet at the same time, there were written works of literature that drew on other written works of literature.[75] The advent of writing seems to have had little role in instituting change of a Goody-Ong sort.[76] Even in later Egyptian wisdom texts, the fictional audiences described in the "texts are very often groups of people, suggesting that the poems were intended for audiences rather than single readers."[77] Egypt was never a literate society in a modern sense. There was no audience for written literature. The only book for which there was a "market," the *Book of the Dead*, was not intended to be read. It served merely as an amulet to be worn by corpses.[78]

168; Finnegan, "How Oral Is Oral Literature?" 58. Carr notes this (Carr, *Writing on the Tablet*, 159–62).

68. Schier, "Einige methodische Überlegungen," 101.

69. Thorvaldsen, "The Eddic Form and Its Contexts," 160.

70. De Vet, "Context," 161.

71. Redford, "Scribe and Speaker," 151.

72. E.g., *Ipuwer* 4.11–13; Parkinson, *Poetry and Culture,* 55–56; Baines, "Myth and Literature," 373.

73. Baines, *Visual and Written Culture*, 150–51.

74. Carr, "Torah on the Heart," 21.

75. Spalinger, *The Transformation of an Ancient Egyptian Narrative*, 357–58.

76. Baines, *Visual and Written Culture*, 170. The first writing of "literature" should probably be assigned to the XII Dynasty (2000–1800 B.C.); ibid., 149.

77. Parkinson, "Individual and Society in Middle Kingdom Literature, 143.

78. Van der Toorn, *Scribal Culture*, 26. The Mesopotamian *Song of Erra* may have served similarly.

In earliest Mesopotamia, the logographic system of Sumerian, where signs stood for words,

> has the effect that Sumerian writing was really a mnemotechnic device, and that the texts were not meant to represent fully any spoken message. A text gave cues, so that for instance a literary text must be understood as an aid to oral performance . . . Without a previous knowledge of the composition a reader would hardly be able to understand a complete text. It was only when Sumerian was no longer a living language that Akkadian-speaking scribes wrote down the literary tradition in Sumerian.[79]

Thus, an oral tradition existed alongside the texts, as in the case of the Sumerian *Lugalbanda Epic*.[80] The Old Assyrian Sargon legend (nineteenth century BCE) has Sargon say, "Why should I elaborate on a tablet?" (lines 63–64), when the stories are well known orally.[81] Even long after literature was committed to writing, it was written *ana zamāri*, for singing.[82] *Atraḫasis* (seventeenth century BCE) is not a tale, but a *zamāru*, a song (8.16–19). A thousand years later, the *Song of Erra* (eighth century BCE) still refers to its bards (5.49.53–54). The written texts may have developed as improvisations based on oral registers of storylines, plot elements, and narrative excerpts.[83] And at the same time, purely oral texts were memorized ahead of performance.[84] In *Nin-me-šár-ra* (*Exaltation of Inana*), 138–40, En ḫeduanna memorizes a song the night before reciting it. "For centuries the written tradition runs alongside the oral one, the one fructifying and supporting the other and vice-versa."[85] Sometimes it is possible to tell if a tale was handed down orally or in writing, but sometimes it is not. For example, the third-millennium BCE Sumerian tale of *The Fox and Ur*[86] reappears in the Late Assyrian (post-900 BCE) tale of

---

79. Larsen, "The Mesopotamian Lukewarm Mind," 219.

80. Laessö, "Literacy and Oral Tradition in Ancient Mesopotamia," 209–11; Moor, *Mondelinge Overlevering in Mesopotamië*, 17.

81. Westenholz, "Historical Events," 30.

82. Kilmer, "Fugal Features of Atrahasis," 133.

83. Westenholz, "Historical Events," 30.

84. Alster, "Interaction," 29; Sasson, "Comparative Observations on the Near Eastern Epic Traditions," 224.

85. Van der Toorn, *Scribal Culture*, 218; Westenholz, "Historical Events," 30.

86. Gordon, *Sumerian Proverbs*, sec. 2, proverb 69.

The Fox and the City[87]—but with no attestations in between, the means of transmission is unclear.[88]

"Yet at some point," holds Karel van der Toorn, "the oral does not die, but its authority is subordinate to that of the written text."[89] The impulses for such fixation are usually sociopolitical.[90] For Mesopotamia, van der Toorn argues that this occurs after 1200 BCE, from which point lexigraphical texts occur in a stabilized form that ossifies for centuries. This stabilization of form is secured by attributing the texts to an antediluvian revelation from Ea to the *apkallu* sages.[91] Nevertheless, orality persisted long after. The second-millennium BCE "Poor Man of Nippur," preserved in eighth-century-BCE fragments found both in the library of Ashurbanipal and in Sultantepe in Anatolia, served as a forerunner for Herodotus's story (2.121) of "Pharaoh Rhampsinit's Thief" (fifth century BCE) and in twentieth-century oral tradition of Turks and Yeminite and Kurdish Jews.[92] A proverb found in a letter of Shashi-Adad I—"The bitch in her haste gives birth to blind pups"—reappears verbatim in modern Jewish and Arab Iraqi folk traditions.[93]

Hittite literature appears soon after the establishment of the Old Kingdom (ca. 1600 BCE) in a style so fully developed that some sort of oral transmission must have taken place in the time following the disappearance of Old Assyrian script from Anatolia around 1750 BCE But Hittite literature appears soon after the establishment of the Old Kingdom (1600 BCE) in a style so fully developed that some sort of oral transmission must have taken place in the time following the disappearance.[94] The Hurrian myth of *Ullikummi*, best preserved in Hittite texts (*ANET*, 121–25; *CTH*, 345; Table I A III 7–36), was found in "new script"

---

87. Lambert, *Babylonian Wisdom Literature*, 21–25.

88. Jason and Kempinski, "How Old Are Folktales?," 18.

89. Van der Toorn, *Scribal Culture*, 218.

90. Foley, "Analogues: Modern Oral Epics," 209.

91. Van der Toorn, *Scribal Culture*, 218–19. Another indication of this ossification is the use of *niṣirtu* and *piristu* secrecy colophons to preserve texts for the scribes (ibid., 219–20).

92. Sparks, *Ancient Texts for the Study of the Hebrew Bible*, 262; Gurney, "The Tale of the Poor Man of Nippur," 149–58; Jason, "The Poor Man of Nippur," 189, 194–95, 205–15.

93. Avishur, "Additional Parallels of an Akkadian Proverb," 37–38.

94. Ünal, "The Power of Narrative," 131–34.

in the storerooms on the east side of Temple 1 at Hattusa. It was also found there in some Hurrian fragments (*KBo* 27.217; 33.61; 45.61). But, "The Hittite version of the *Song of Ullikummi* is not the translation of the Hurrian text kept in the archives of Hattusa . . . It is a clear indicator of the role played by oral tradition."[95] The Hittite version reflects an oral variant of the Ullikummi tale. So too the Hittite edition of the *Romance of the Hunter Kašši* is not a translation of the Hurrian copy.[96] The same thing happened with the *Epic of Gilgamesh*. Hittite, Hurrian, and Akkadian versions were all found, but none is exactly a translation of the other.[97] "When a scriptorium felt the need to acquire a written Hurrian version, they turned to a 'singer:' a bard who dictated his version."[98] That such oral performers existed in ancient Anatolia is confirmed by the incipit "I will sing" that occurs in both Hittite and Hurrian epics, such as the Hurrian *Song of Kumarbi* and *Song of Silver* (frag. 1, 7–8).[99]

For the Neo-Assyrian period (900–600 BCE), Yaakov Elman made a convincing case that the phrase *ša pî ummâni* (literally, "from the mouth of the teacher/secretary") in certain texts (e.g., a letter to Assurbanipal)[100] refers to authoritative oral scholarly tradition.[101] The colophon with one such *ša pî ummâni* is a list of astrological omens,[102] illustrating what material in *ša pî ummâni* is: "a small unit of traditional lore."[103] "This, in turn, permits us to suppose, with due reserve, that an 'oral tradition' of such 'oral communications' (*mašālātu ša pî ummâni*) existed, and were considered authoritative,"[104] and which had (by virtue of the colophons) entered into written text.[105]

---

95. Archi, "Transmission of Recitative Literature," 191, 197.

96. Archi, "Orality," 209–10.

97. Gilan, "Epic and History in Hittite Anatolia," 57.

98. Archi, "Transmission of Recitative Literature," 197, based on comparison of the Akkadian (*KBo* 32.128), Hurrian (*KBo* 33.10), and Hittite (Manuscript E, *KBo* 10.47[+]46) versions found at Hattusa. The same thing happened when a Hittite version was needed; Archi, "Transmission," 198.

99. Archi, "Orality," 222.

100. *ABL* 519 (=*LAS* 13) rev. 2.

101. Elman, "Authoritative Oral Tradition," 23–26.

102. Rm 2, 126:26 = *ACh Supp.*, 52; Elman, "Authoritative Oral Tradition," 27.

103. Elman, "Authoritative Oral Tradition," 30.

104. Ibid., 31. On the *mašālātu*, see chapter 6, below.

105. Van der Toorn, *Scribal Culture*, 128.

It is, moreover, probable that the codes of customary law throughout ancient Western Asia were oral in nature.[106] We should also consider the possibilities that literary transfer of stories between parts of the ancient Near East was in part oral. Certainly written texts circulated between Egypt and Mesopotamia and to all places between, but some oral transmission is also possible. Some scholars, in fact, believe that "a direct relationship between *texts* is a rarity."[107] How, for example, does the Old Babylonian story of the *Eagle and the Serpent* (*ANET*, 114–17; 1800–1500 BCE) resurface as the twentieth dynasty (1200–1100 BCE) Egyptian tale of the *Vulture and the Cat*?[108]

In Mycenaean Greece (1600–1200 BCE), oral and written literature coexisted, with writing disappearing during the "Dark Age" (1200–800 BCE)[109] Following this period, "'Homer' continued to be a living oral tradition, unaffected by the event [of literacy]."[110] As will be discussed in more detail in the following chapter, Homeric poetry was written down slowly, moving in and out of the written medium while much was retained in oral memory.[111] And, "Although late fifth-century Athenians mostly *could* read, they still preferred and even expected to experience their literature *orally*."[112] Even in the Hellenistic period, "leading families often had orally preserved ancestral traditions."[113] In Pausanias 8.9.9–10, a Roman second-century CE citizen of Mantinea named Podarcs recounts an oral tradition of his descent from a war hero of the fourth century BCE. In all these periods of Greek literature, "the choice of the medium of transmission depends on the context."[114]

106. Miller, "Foreword: The Development of Ancient Near Eastern Law," 1627.

107. Henkelman, "The Birth of Gilgameš," sec. 1.3.1.

108. Jason and Kempinski, "How Old Are Folktales?," 12–13.

109. Shear, *Kingship in the Mycenaean World*, 86–87.

110. Jensen, "The Writing of the *Iliad* and the *Odyssey*," 66. "Homer" was likely a legend and not a historical figure; I use the term to refer to the epic tradition as an ongoing whole (Foley, "'Reading' Homer through Oral Tradition," 7.

111. De Vet, "Joint Rule," 68.

112. Barber and Barber, *When They Severed Earth from Sky*, 151 (italics original); Green, *Medieval Listening*, 30; Scodel, "Social Memory in Aeschylus' *Oresteia*," 118. As evidence, see Plato, *Phaedrus*, 275C, D; 276D.

113. Thomas, *Oral Tradition and Written Record*, 95–131; Pretzler, "Pausanias and Oral Tradition 239. E.g., *IVO* 449–50 (mid-second century), 486–87 (mid-third century)—two men called T. Flavius Polybius.

114. Pretzler, "Pausanias," 240.

Various classical Latin texts refer to their own "listeners *and* readers" (Fronto, *Epistulae ad M. Caes.* 4.3; Martial, *Epigrams,* 11.83.1—both second century AD). This phrase, *lector et auditor* or some variation, recurs in many medieval texts, as well.[115]

In early Judaism, singing of the laws was the norm (*t. Ohol.* 16.8; *t. Para* 4.7; Rabbi Jonathan, *Megilla* 32a).[116] The scrolls were more a storage system for texts kept in memory, akin to a computer backup directory.[117] In the Middle Ages, musical accents were added to the Mishnah to ensure oral preservation (e.g., the Parma [B] manuscript of the Order *Toharot*; the Sabbionetta edition of *m. Qidd.*). To Rabbi Yohanan ben Zakkai is attributed the saying, "He who reads without melody and repeats without song, concerning him the scripture says: 'Therefore I gave them statutes which were not to their advantage'" (*b. Meg.* 32a).[118]

The beginning of the transmission of Gregorian chant in Carolingian Europe was an essentially oral process.[119] The chants soon appear in books, but books too small for even a single cantor to sing from; they serve only as control against deviation.[120] England immediately prior to and after the Norman Conquest shows a dynamic relationship between orality and literacy.[121] Folk literature in sixteenth to eighteenth-century Finland shows a constant interplay of the written and the oral.[122] Japanese epics that appear in a civilization that had been literate for many centuries are not read, but recited.[123] In present-day Bali, texts "migrate from oral to written and back again."[124] The written versions of the text have

115. Listed in Green, *Medieval Listening and Reading*, 179.

116. Dov Zlotnick, "Memory and the Integrity of the Oral Tradition," 231–35.

117. Jaffee, *Torah in the Mouth*, 17, 100. This is also true for early writing in Iceland; Pernille Hermann, "Concepts of 304.

118. Jerome Rothenberg, "2 July 1975"; Stahl, "Accuracy," argues that this cantellation is a distinct phenomenon from oral performance since it is merely for memory and does not intend to convey meaning.

119. Treitler, "Sinners and Singers," 147. For the continuity of orality in Europe after the advent of printing, see Green, *Medieval Listening and Reading*, 15, 35. Green also challenges the reception-end distinction of a reader and a listener (ibid., 18).

120. Treitler, "Sinners and Singers," 148.

121. Amodio, *Writing the Oral Tradition*, 13.

122. Apo, "The Relationship between Oral and Literary Tradition," 19–24.

123. Goyet, "Narrative Structure and Political Construction," 27.

124. De Vet, "Context," 165.

secured the survival of the oral literature.[125] In Nepal, the *Ramayana* epic is found in written form in multiple languages alongside oral versions handed down with variations from generation to generation in the same languages;[126] and the Swahili *utenzi* epic poems function the same way.[127]

In fact, predominantly oral societies are *not* the most common settings for oral literature, nor literate societies the normal home of written texts.[128] "The largest majority of the examples of oral literature which we possess and analyze have *not* been collected from pure [oral] cultures."[129] Some of this literature has been collected from societies that have recently become literate but preserve much orality, but there are also many societies that have been literate from antiquity and yet oral literature has continued to flourish.[130] The oral and the written—"the two have interacted and overlapped for centuries in vast areas of our planet."[131]

In the following chapter, three specific cases of this oral-written interaction and overlapping will be introduced. These three will provide the best ethnographic analogies to the biblical material.

125. De Vet, "Joint Role," 73.

126. Bandhu, "Common Languages," 21.

127. Khamis, "From Written through Oral to Mediated Oral," 206.

128. Petrović, "Oral and Written Art Form in Serbian Medieval Literature," 103.

129. Finnegan, "How Oral Is Oral Literature?" 53 (italics original).

130. Calvet, *Tradition orale*, 6–7.

131. Finnegan, *The Oral and Beyond*, 103; Scodel, "Social Memory," 118.

3

Models for Biblical Literature

This chapter focuses on three specific cases of oral-written interaction and overlapping that provide the best ethnographic analogies to the biblical material, for reasons to be discussed below. Two are cases, like Israel, preserved only in written form, while the third remains in oral tradition to this day. This, of course, raises the question of the appropriateness of the comparative method. Study of oral tradition in societies around the world must be relevant to anything we wish to say about it for ancient Israel. "The comparative approach does not entail, a priori, any identification, full or partial, of the phenomena or developments which are being compared."[1] But, "reconstructions cannot be achieved without the help of the comparative method."[2] In fact, reconstruction by speculation alone is extremely tendentious: "If five percent of the intellectual power devoted to pure speculation around fragmentary text corpuses had been directed at empirical studies on oral composition and the textualization of oral epics," writes Lauri Honko, "we would certainly have more and better models than the South Slavic."[3] And because the nature of orality and writing varies by the socioeconomic and political makeup of societies (and not by geographic proximity), as Ivan Engnell was well aware, "Comparing Israelite material with relatively far-distant lands and cultures . . . actually can be more fruitful than comparing it with closer regions . . . As a matter of fact, the latter can even be characterized as distinctly dangerous."[4]

1. Gelb, "Comparative Method," 32. On the comparative method in philology in general, see Todorov, *The Poetics of Prose*, 236.
2. Gelb, "Comparative Method," 35.
3. Honko, "Oral and Semiliterary Epics," 2.
4. Engnell, *A Rigid Scrutiny*, 8.

George Widengren's bumptious barney with this conclusion—"From where, then, are we supposed to 'jump'?"[5]—was based on an underlying Romantic distinction between Indo-European and the Semitic.[6] Moreover, the classicist Rosalind Thomas notes that as the topic we are comparing is oral performance, "For historians who cannot experience any live performances at all in the societies they study, such diverse comparisons are extremely helpful."[7] "The knowledge attained from fieldwork in the present can serve as a key to opening the doors contained in the material of the past."[8]

Homer

There is broad consensus today that the texts of Homer are grounded in oral tradition.[9] The traces of Mycenaean material culture and the Mycenaean landscape[10] and the numerous linguistic evidences of composition-in-performance (Parry and Lord's included),[11] all support this conclusion, whether the texts were the result of dictation, memorization of an ossified performance, or the work of literate poets.[12] "To what extent Homer may have known of the art of writing remains uncertain; but it is beyond doubt that he was familiar with—in fact expert in—compositional techniques which were developed by singers who were ignorant of it."[13]

But we must think beyond a mere binary option of "Homer inventing things" and a long oral tradition—a binary opposition only too familiar in Old Testament research, where scholars frequently consider the text either a hoary tradition or whole-cloth fiction. As Ruth Scodel writes, "Homer may very well have invented a given detail in a subordi-

5. Widengren, "Oral Tradition and Written Literature," 223.

6. Ibid., 226.

7. Thomas, "Performance Literature," 4.

8. Gunnell, "Narratives, Space and Drama," 19.

9. Foley, "The Implications of Oral Tradition," 32. Five proofs are adduced in Richard P. Martin, "Homer's *Iliad* and *Odyssey*," 339. The *Odyssey* is somewhat less clearly orally derived (Hainsworth, *The Idea of Epic*, 37).

10. Hainsworth, *The Idea of Epic*, 15.

11. Hainsworth, "The Fallibility of an Oral Heroic Tradition," 115.

12. Scodel, *Listening to Homer*, 2; Jensen, "The Writing of the *Iliad* and the *Odyssey*," 61.

13. Edwards, "Homer's *Iliad*," 307.

nate narrative that serves the rhetorical purpose of its immediate context, but so may his teacher, his teacher's teacher, or another bard from whom he adapts this section."[14] Like the Icelandic sagas to be treated below, "our *Iliad* is a patchwork quilt of layers, joins, interpolations, and conflations of different versions, while still emphasizing that it is first and foremost a literary creation."[15] Since we do not have access to all previous performances, we cannot know which part is which.[16]

The *Iliad* epic was certainly preceded by poems that resemble the so-called Homeric Hymns (see Thucydides 3.104).[17] Poems of the Greek "Epic Cycle" (e.g., the *Little Iliad* and *Iliou Persis*) tell a variant tale of adventures of Odysseus after his return home—a variant unknown in the *Odyssey* but acknowledged in the prophecy of Teiresias in *Od.* 11.119–37.[18] The *Odyssey* is also aware of variant traditions about Helen in Egypt (*Od.* 3.299–312; 4.81–89), known from Herodotus (2.113).[19] Moreover, the Epic of Gilgamesh, perhaps via its Hurrian or Hittite translations but certainly orally, influenced the *Iliad* and the *Odyssey*.[20] Bits of fifteenth-century BCE Luwian song may even have found their way into the *Iliad*.[21]

Much of this interplay of orality and writing will be pertinent to the discussion of the Old Testament narrative books. But, like the Old Testament, the *Iliad* as we have it is not from "Homer's hand." Just as there are text-critical variants between *written* manuscripts of the Hebrew Bible, so too there are many divergent texts of Homer. This is not entirely a separate issue from oral tradition. In the case of Homer, for example, a summary of the Trojan War found in the then-oral Greek Epic Cycle is also found in a single manuscript of the *Iliad* (Venetus A).[22] The implications for the Old Testament could be significant, if variant textual tradi-

---

14. Scodel, *Listening to Homer*, 29.

15. Davies, "The Reliability of the Oral Tradition," 97.

16. Scodel, *Listening to Homer*, 31, 43. Nevertheless, when performers hear each other perform the same song, their versions will tend to become similar (ibid., 50).

17. Martin, "Epic as Genre," 16.

18. Edmunds, "Epic and Myth," 34–35; Burgess, "The Epic Cycle," 345.

19. Edmunds, "Epic and Myth," 36.

20. Ibid., 34; Henkelman, "The Birth of Gilgameš," sec. 1.3.1.

21. Sherratt, "Archaeological Contexts," 139.

22. Burgess, "The Epic Cycle," 346.

tions—in Judges 1–3, for example—might reflect variant oral traditions, and a written *Urtext* being nonexistent.[23]

Icelandic Saga[24]

Icelandic sagas present the interplay of written and oral literature. Icelandic sagas, or specifically the Icelandic family sagas I am interested in, "are anonymous prose stories. They are not heroic epics, folktales, chronicles, or romances but plausible vernacular tales."[25] They are set in the period from the settlement of Iceland in the 980s until about 1030, but were written more than one hundred fifty years later.[26]

Biblical scholars have a long history of interest in the Icelandic sagas, and with good reason.[27] As with Israel the Israelite context, the original context of composition and recitation of the Icelandic material are lost to us, reconstructible only through scenes created in the text itself much later than the material's origin.[28]

As with the Old Testament narrative books, there has been a century-long debate between those who argued for primarily written origins of the sagas, and those who maintained that they were in essence orally derived, written versions of oral tradition.[29] In 1913, Andreas Heusler named the former, "Bookprosists," and the latter, "Freeprosists."[30] By

23. Carr makes the same conclusion in "Torah on the Heart," 33; as does Niditch in "The Hebrew Bible," 14.

24. Herein, I normalize fictional names according to English conventions, with *d* for *ð* and *th* for *þ* except in the titles of ancient works (and in direct quotations). Following modern Icelandic convention, I use *ö* for *ǫ*, except in quotations. I preserve the nominative ending on names: thus, Thorgrímr, not Thorgrím.

25. Byock, "Saga Form," 153. Shorter family sagas are technically known by the term *þættir;* Lindow, "*Þættir* and Oral Performance," 180, 182.

26. Beard, "The Berserkir in Icelandic Literature," 99.

27. E.g., Alt, "The Origins of Israelite Law," 131. It must be admitted that the fascinating contents of these marvelous tales accounts for some of their constant appeal (Mitchell, "Reconstructing Old Norse Oral Tradition," 203). For an early observation of similarities between Icelandic saga and the Homeric poetry, see Phillpotts, *The Elder Edda*, 35.

28. Ross, *A History*, 66. Gísli Sigurðsson notes that at one time these accounts were taken at face value ("Orality and Literacy in the Sagas of Icelanders," 288–89).

29. Jónas Kristjánsson, "*Íslendingadrápa* and Oral Tradition," 77.

30. Heusler, *Die Anfänge der isländischen Saga*. The nineteenth century had its share of each, also, Jónas Kristjánsson, "*Íslendingadrápa*," 82.

the 1960s, Bookprosists like Sigurður Nordal (founder of the so-called Icelandic School),[31] Einar Sveinsson, Bjarni Einarsson, Walter Baetke, and, much later and with some qualifications, Carol Clover, seemed to have prevailed.[32]

With the rise of Oral Formulaic theory, Norsists did not rush to "prove" orality as classicists did.[33] Many argued that Parry and Lord's work was irrelevant for Norse literature, while others condemned this insularity.[34] Some tried their hand at Lordian statistical analysis of formulaity.[35] Still, the work of several Freeprosists in the 1970s that reopened that debate (e.g., Jónas Kristjánsson, Haukr Valdísarson, Óskar Halldórsson) did not employ Oral Formulaicism in its arguments.[36]

In this debate, Gísli Sigurðsson took a rather Goody-Ong position that brought him to somewhat Bookprosist conclusions. That is, he believes that while oral tales were no doubt the precursors of the sagas, the advent of writing so transformed them that the written sagas no longer reveal anything about the prior tradition.[37] He warns that we must be careful not to misread oral stylistics that are the work of writers imitating an oral style in order to guarantee a certain reception of their text.[38] Yet such an illusion would surely be hard to sustain; textuality usually becomes clear from the borrowing of structures from written texts, and while such structures are clear in some sagas, like *Völsunga Saga*, they are absent in many others.[39]

Without entering into these debates and pretending to say anything about a field in which I am very much an outsider, I venture that the state of the question seems to be like that of the question about the narrative books of the Old Testament (as will be shown herein). The sagas are writing drawing on written *and* oral literature, which itself drew on writing,

---

31. Jón Aðalsteinsson, *A Piece of Horse Liver*, 84.

32. Byock, "Saga Form," 153; Finlay, "Skalds, Troubadours, and Sagas," 105.

33. Andersson, "From Tradition to Literature in the Sagas," 7.

34. See discussion in Gísli Sigurðsson, "Orality Harnessed," 20.

35. E.g., Acker, *Revising Oral Theory*; Mitchell, "The Sagaman and Oral Literature," 407, 415.

36. Byock, "Saga Form," 157. E.g., Jónas Kristjánsson, "*Íslendingadrápa*," esp. 90.

37. Gísli Sigurðsson, *The Medieval Icelandic Saga*, 37, 48, 328–30.

38. Würth, "The Rhetoric," 103–4.

39. Ibid., 105–6, 109.

too.[40] The Icelandic family sagas or *Íslendingasögur* drew on both oral poems and written stories, many of them from continental Europe.[41] Several important sagas are shaped according to episodes of the *Nibelungenlied*.[42] *Njáls Saga* has a structure largely the work of its own author but with episodes based on earlier traditions, and some of these traditions were clearly written.[43] Njáls even borrows from the writings of St. Gregory the Great.[44] Lars Lönnroth, the best authority on *Njáls Saga*, at first concluded that such Latin influence was great on other sagas, as well. In this, he has been criticized.[45] The work of Jónas Kristjánsson and others, followed later by Richard Perkins, shows on internal evidence that the sagas cannot be the work of a writer drawing solely on other writers.[46] Statistical analysis of the sagas indicates that even writers deeply indebted to written material and written literary structure were "still dependent to a reasonable extent on oral tradition."[47] This oral tradition, however, can be just as "imported" as the written. It can be just as readily from outside the Norse world. Michael Chesnutt proved that *Njáls Saga* incorporates oral tradition from the Baltic Finns.[48] The interplay of oral and written sources and performances for *Njáls Saga* can be viewed graphically in this figure by Lönnroth:[49]

40. Byock, "Saga Form," 163. There is a vocal "New Bookprosist" movement identified with Baldur Hafstað, Berljót Kristjásdóttir, and Svanhildur Óskarsdóttir, but it concludes written origin from the historical unreliability of the sagas. "It is simply a false premise to assume that because a saga is not factual it is not oral" (Byock, "The Sagas and the Twenty-First Century," 71–72, 78–81.

41. Vésteinn Ólason, "Family Sagas," 113.

42. Wolf, "Zur Rolle des Epischen im mittelalterlichen Norden," 252, 254, 257–58.

43. Lönnroth, *Njáls*, 34.

44. Hermann Pálsson, *Oral Tradition and Saga Writing*, 77; Lönnroth, *Njáls*, 39. The story of Flosi's dream in chapter 133 comes from one of Gregory's *Exempla* (Lönnroth, *Njáls*, 121).

45. Chesnutt, "Popular and Learned Elements in the Icelandic Saga-Tradition," 30, 2.

46. Perkins, "Objects and Oral Tradition," 241.

47. Margaret Clunies Ross, *A History*, 187; Chesnutt, "Popular," 34.

48. Chesnutt, "Popular and Learned Elements," 34.

49. Lönnroth, "New Dimensions and Old Directions," 60.

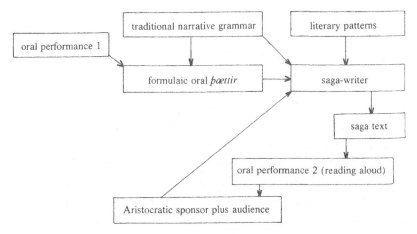

Figure 3.1 Interplay of Oral and Written in *Njáls Saga*

This figure should not minimize the compositional skills of the "sagaman" himself, whom Stephen Mitchell likens to a medieval Poul Anderson or Michael Creighton.[50]

But we must also reckon with the possibility of an oral tradition in which stories were told about the *same events* as those narrated in written texts.[51] That is, in the oral+written model I am developing here, the pool of tradition available to writers and oral tradents is quite wide, and we should nowise think of a linear progression from oral tale to written text. Taking into account the secondary nature of its evidence, *Þorgils Saga* describes a saga writer orally performing a saga he has just created for the king of Norway and also bringing a physical copy of the saga along with him.[52]

The Icelandic family sagas will therefore be used as a foil for the biblical material in what follows, to suggest performance contexts, and in the discussion of the shape of oral Israelite literature. To provide an example of how such sagas read, I conclude this section with a tiny excerpt from *Hrafnkels saga Freysdóa*, the *Saga of Hrafnkel Frey's Godi* (1; trans. by Terry Gunnell): "Halfred built a farm. During the winter, a foreign slave-woman named Arnthrud died there, and that is why it has been

50. Mitchell, "The Sagaman," 413.

51. Gísli Sigurðsson shows this to be the best explanation for a number of phenomena, such as the variant careers of Thorkell Geitisson ("Orality and Literacy," 294).

52. Torfi H. Tulinius, "Sagas of Icelandic Prehistory," 450.

called Arnthrudarstadir [Arnthrud's place]. In the spring, Halfred moved his farm north across the heath, and built a new home at a place called Geitdal."[53]

Arabic Epic Poetry

When the two kinds of literature coexist, not only do oral works get written down, but written tales become the source of oral productions, while other things are composed in writing precisely for oral consumption. This complex interplay can be seen at work with the Arabic *siyar* (sing. *sīra*).[54] The *sīra* is a sung epic, a collection of narratives told in alternating prose and poetry.

Siyar appear in manuscripts as early as the 1100s AD.[55] The only *sīra* still in oral tradition is the *Sīrat Banī Hilāl*, which chronicles the massive migration of the Bani Hilal Bedouin tribe from Arabia across Egypt to their conquest of North Africa. The events from which the epic is spun date to 900–1200 CE, and the *sīra* is attested as early as Ibn Khaldun (1332–1406 CE).[56] The *sīra* continues to be performed orally even to this day, and the wide variation in its performance mode allows it to be variously dubbed epic, saga, romance, cycle, or legend.[57] The song cycle is known throughout North Africa, in Egypt, Sudan, and Chad, in Nigeria, in Jordan, and among Palestinians.[58]

Although there is some improvisation, the key elements of the story line and certain dramatic songs remain constant, in line with the modified Parry-Lord vision of John Miles Foley, described earlier.[59] The *Sīrat*

53. Gunnell, "The Saga of Hrafnkel Frey's Godi," 438.

54. Reynolds, *Heroic Poets, Poetic Heroes*, 6; Finnegan, *Literacy and Orality*, 113–20. Some of these *siyar* are quite lengthy narratives; Reynolds, *Heroic Poets, Poetic Heroes*, 5, 7, 8.

55. Reynolds, "Sīrat Banī Hilāl," 82.

56. Connelly, *Arab Folk Epic*, 26; Schippers, "An Episode in the Life of a Hero," 347.

57. Reynolds, "Sīrat Banī Hilāl," 81. On similarities with Homer, see ibid.," 86; Connelly, *Arab Folk Epic*, 267; Honko, "Comparing the Textualization of Oral Epics," 7–8. This material too has had its oral formulaicists: Zwettler, *The Oral Tradition of Classical Arabic Poetry*, ix, 5, 41, 63, 189; Susan Slyomovics, "The Death-Song 70–71.

58. Connelly, *Arab Folk Epic*, 194, 219. The *sīra* can be heard in live performance at http://www.nyu.edu/projects/mednar/file.php?id=7.

59. Reynolds, "Sīrat Banī Hilāl," 85; Reynolds, "Epic and History in the Arabic Tradition," 404.

Banī Hilāl is both an oral tradition one can hear and a book one can buy. The singer may or may not have recourse to a written text while singing. Even if he does not, he may have referred to a written text earlier. But in no case does the sung performance reproduce any written text. Moreover, a written *Sīrat Banī Hilāl* one might buy is most definitely based on an oral predecessor. And yet it reproduces no specific performance.[60] In all of these ways, as will be shown further, the *Sīrat Banī Hilāl* is a valuable analogue for the narrative books of the Hebrew Bible.

Also similar to the biblical case, if one goes back into the origins of the oral *Sīrat Banī Hilāl*, one again finds *written* antecedents. Like those behind the *Njáls Saga*, the oral composers of the *sīra* drew on written materials, such as the sixth-century-AD *Ayyām al-ʾArab*, along with oral poetry of Jahiliyya (pre-Islamic) Arabia.[61] Thus in all periods of its existence, the *sīra* blurs the margins of orality and literacy.[62]

Mention should be made briefly of the *Sīrat ʿAntar ibn Shaddād*, which resembles the *Sīrat Banī Hilāl* in many ways but survives only in writing.[63] In spite of this, while seemingly everyone in the Arab world knows its story, very few have ever actually read any of it.[64] Similarities between this text and the Bible were pointed out over a century ago, and the *Sīrat ʿAntar ibn Shaddād* will be important in the final section of this book.[65] Here is an excerpt from ʿAntar 36.89, translated by Peter Heath: "And there arose toward them from the heart of the land a dust cloud. And it rose up and filled the countryside. And in short time the dust cloud dissipated and lifted for a while and revealed beneath it in the flash of chainmail and the gleam of helmets and men—Sudanese—beyond number."[66]

60. Reynolds, "*Sīrat Banī Hilāl*," 93.

61. Garcin, "*Sīra*/s et Histoire," 47.

62. Connelly, *Arab Folk Epic*, 268.

63. Heath, "A Critical Review of Modern Scholarship on *Sīrat ʿAntar ibn Shaddād* and the Popular *Sīra*," 19. It was in oral performance as recently as the 1850s and possibly even the 1940s (Heath, *The Thirsty Sword*, 32–34). Heath cautiously attempted a careful Oral Formulaic analysis of ʿAntar in ibid.; see esp. 105.

64. Ibid., 25.

65. "Antar," 1–35, esp. 12.

66. Heath, *The Thirsty Sword*, 135.

Gobbets

Literary authors of written work in antiquity composed mentally and then *aurally*, by dictation, as late as the patristic period.[67] "Transmission [is] through the interaction or combination of the concurrent oral and written versions."[68] What is "passed down" varies in nature from society to society, although chapter 5 will make some tentative suggestions. Yet in all cases, the traditional modules or "gobbets," as I would call them, are intentionally crafted *aides-mémoires* that are constitutive for narration and function as generic markers.[69] In general, they include story lines (or story patterns, structural pathways for the action, characters, etc.),[70] textual elements such as images of situations (like the scenes, which are the basic units of Icelandic saga composition),[71] and some traditional phraseology (which may or may not be formulaic)[72]—what Foley calls a "register."[73]

Is this, then, merely Lord's formulas and themes resurrected?[74] No, the difference is that these recurrent patterns are culturally, historically, and generically specific, not only in their content but in their form, as well.[75] And the registers are far more flexible in expression than formulas.[76]

The tradition is made up of these gobbets, usually in some sort of semi-rigid, easily reconstructable order.[77] In the Israelite case, the "stream

67. Griffiths, *Religious Reading*, 56–57; Shear, *Kingship in the Mycenaean World*, 94.

68. Finnegan, *Literacy and Orality*, 172; Shear, *Kingship in the Mycenaean World*, 94; Griffiths, *Religious Reading*, 55.

69. Assmann, *Religion*, 8–9; Baines, *Visual and Written Culture*, 152; Harvilahti, "Textualising an Oral Epic," 3. Lauri Honko calls these "multiforms" (Honko, "Oral and Semiliterary Epic," 2; and Honko, "The Quest for the Long Epic," 200).

70. Foley, "Analogues: Modern Oral Epics," 202.

71. Byock, "Saga Form," 161.

72. Russo, "Oral Theory," 14.

73. Foley, *The Singer of Tales in Performance*, 50. Symbolic/pictorial images can also serve as such *aides-mémoires* (Calvet, *Tradition orale*, 73; Harvilahti, "Textualising an Oral Epic," 4).

74. Seybold refers to these gobbets as "Thema" (Seybold, "Zur mündlichen," 147).

75. Finnegan, *Oral Traditions and the Verbal Arts*, 117.

76. Amodio, *Writing the Oral Tradition*, 43.

77. Ásdís Egilsdóttir, "From Orality to Literacy," 219; Ilmari Soisalon-Soinen, "Der Charakter der ältesten alttestamentlichen Erzähltraditionen," 139. The *Sīrat Banī Hilāl*, however, is rarely sung in the same order; Reynolds, "Sīrat Banī Hilāl," 87n.7.

of tradition," as Oppenheim dubbed it, is not coterminous with the Bible. We should not think of merely an "oral tradition" that lies behind the Bible. This will be treated in more detail in the next chapter, but let us tentatively postulate a plethora of songs, myths, cultic instructions, heroic poems, and the like in ancient Israel, not all of which entered the "stream of tradition" that moved them from their context of origin into what David Carr describes as "a context of ongoing oral-written education."[78] This educational context is then another ongoing section of the same stream.[79] Secondarily, not all of that oral-written literature entered into the canon of Second Temple Judah that became the Old Testament.[80]

But let us return to the "'tradition pool' (the wealth of traditions shaping Israel's perceptions of its past)"[81] and the "stream of tradition" (oral and written) leading out of it. The distinction of the two—pool and stream—should not be pressed too hard. The stream is still quite wide and "pool-like." Since a lasting insight of Parry and Lord is a degree of composition-in-performance, we cannot return to an image of "stemma-like lines of progeny between the variants of oral song," and must instead "postulate a theory of a 'pool of tradition' where not so much the songs or tales as such but their basic elements [pass down] to be activated in a particular situation of performance"[82]—or to be activated in a particular oral-written educational context,[83] or to be activated in a particular written text.

The Gunkel model of tradents who could be traced back to tradents before them in continual lines back to hoary antiquity cannot hold. The literary critic Slavica Ranković is worth quoting at length in this regard:

> What we hoped to be a "string" (something one can actually fol-
> low) would immediately start splitting at its tip, shooting innu-

---

78. Carr, "The Rise of Torah," 40, 45; Renz, "Die vor- und ausserliterarische Texttradition," 73. The use of the term "education" should not suggest absence of an element of performance.

79. Schier, "Einige methodische Überlegungen," 112; Finnegan, *Oral Traditions and the Verbal Arts*, 179.

80. Yassif, *The Hebrew Folktale*, 33. One might note the use of "as it is written" in Ezra-Nehemiah that often refers to material found nowhere in the Bible (Stern, "'One of These Things'").

81. Campbell and O'Brien, *Rethinking the Pentateuch*, 7; Jensen, "Performance," 49.

82. Honko, "The Quest for Oral Text," 1.

83. Renz, "Vor- und ausserliterarische," 73.

merable threads both horizontally / synchronically toward other singers [i.e., tradents] . . . The texture of this network is hardly as regular as that of a fishing net or a sweater: there is no way of telling how many filaments each singer-node will sprout and of what thickness these will be, that is, not all relationships between the nodes/singers will carry the same weight, some will be more important/influential than others. There is no regularity in the way of sprouting, or the intervals in the progression of branching; the threads would not always depart from one another—some would occasionally merge into one and the same point (for example, two different singers shared the same "teacher"), some would also have to loop back into the point from which they started (such would be the ones relating to a particular singer's own applications of the same line in other songs from his repertoire, that is, he has also learned the usage of the line from himself, placing it in different contexts), while some would still split further, at different speeds, entwining, converging and diverging, entering ever more complex interrelationships.[84]

Tradition (or, if you prefer, folklore) entails the invoking of a context that is enormously larger and more echoic than the text of work itself.[85] This will be key when chapter 6 addresses identifying the oral in the narrative books of the Old Testament. But the attempt should be made (and will be, in chapters 5 and 6), for, as Foley writes: "Even when the process becomes one of making oral-derived texts, traditional phraseology and narrative patterns continue to provide unique ways for the poet to convey meaning, to tap the traditional reservoir. Poets do not persist in employing traditional structures after the advent of literacy and texts out of a misplaced antiquarianism or by default, but because, even in an increasingly textual environment, the "how" developed over the ages still holds the key to worlds of meaning that are otherwise inaccessible."[86]

84. Slavica Ranković, "Who Is Speaking in Traditional Texts?" 298.

85. The pool of tradition extends over a period of two or even three millennia and the whole area of Mesopotamia and the eastern Mediterranean (Jensen, "Performance," 49).

86. Foley, "The Implications of Oral Tradition," 34.

4

Literacy and Orality in Preexilic Israel

Some biblical scholars knew many of these recent insights long before Parry and Lord taught otherwise.[1] In Scandinavia, Ivan Engnell, Helmer Ringgren, Alfred Haldar, and Aage Bentzen all held that "oral tradition and literacy worked hand in hand from a very early time onwards"[2] and that traditions history should be applied to both.[3]

One of the earliest of this "school," H. Nyberg stressed in 1935 that even after a text had been committed to writing, oral transmission remained the normal way of perpetuating and using a text,[4] while writing served an "accessory [*accessoriskt*]" role.[5] Harris Birkeland concurred in 1938: "Kein Gegensatz besteht zwischen schriftlicher Fixierung und mündlichem Vortrag. Normalerweise gehen beiden nebeneinander her."[6] Engnell wrote, "Certain parts of the Old Testament were undoubtedly written down early . . . However, in actual use and in application to the 'life situation,' undoubtedly remembrance and oral transmission . . . were predominant, all along."[7] So also, Ringgren: "Oral and written transmis-

---

1. The parallels between the Scandinavian school and postformulaic thought have been noted by Ska, "Le Pentateuque," 100.

2. Haldar, "Tradition and History," 32.

3. Knight, *Rediscovering the Traditions*, 263, 282, 317. E.g., Koch, *Growth of the Biblical Tradition*, 84.

4. Nyberg, *Studien zum Hoseabuche*, 7.

5. Nyberg, *Muntlig Tradition*, 70.

6. Birkeland, *Zum Hebräischen Traditionswesen*, 13. Translation: "There is no opposition between textualization and oral proclamation. Normally both operate alongside each other."

7. Engnell, *A Rigid Scrutiny*, 6.

sion should not be played off against another: they do not exclude each other."[8] Birger Gerhardsson argued in 1960 against the rigid assignment of folktales to oral cultures and "literature" to literate ones, well in advance of Finnegan's evidence that would support his argument.[9]

Many of the insights of these preformulaic scholars can be recovered for a full understanding of the oral-written nature of the biblical text, and will be in chapter 6. The portrait of the Hebrew Bible's narrative books presented at the end of the previous chapter, albeit somewhat broad, draws on the insights of folkloristics in general and the three index cases in particular. In order to be more specific, to illuminate particular parts of the Hebrew Bible narrative books as orally derived and speak intelligently about their genesis, the extrabiblical traditions will provide more suggestive parallels. Yet, "conclusions about the role of tradition in composition and in conveying meaning must take into account factors that delineate similarities and differences among the traditions compared."[10] John Miles Foley presents five criteria necessary for such cross-cultural comparison: 1) a written, textual tradition; 2) its oral basis; 3) common genre; 4) a dependence on tradition; and 5) both synchronic and diachronic variability.[11]

The first of these parameters is self-evident: there is a tradition of texts subsumed under the rubric "Hebrew Bible." Skipping the second parameter for the moment, there is reason to challenge the assumption that like genres must be compared with like. Certainly this was Parry's assumption, a fact that was ubiquitously overlooked. Nevertheless, when we separate oral/traditional literature into metaliterary categories based on content and call these, "genres" (e.g., epics, tales, sagas, legends),[12] this kind of generic distinction is not helpful, especially as it confuses the genre labels assigned by linguistic characteristics (e.g., poetry, prose, aph-

8. Ringgren, "Oral and Written Transmission," 34.

9. Gerhardsson, Review of *Mündliche und schriftliche Tradition*, by A. H. J. Gunneweg, 179–80. Outside of Scandinavia, too, it is worth noting Albright's observation that "Even in such literate regions as . . . Iran, India, and China, literary composition was mostly oral, and a surprisingly high proportion of the most important literary works (especially in India!) was composed and transmitted orally, often with no use of writing" (Albright, "Some Oriental Glosses," 164.

10. Hayes, *The Earth Mourns*, 221.

11. Foley, *Traditional Oral Epic*, 5–11; Foley, *Immanent Art*, 14–16.

12. Edmunds, "Epic and Myth," 31.

orisms, dialogues) and ignores the nature of performance or reception.[13] But is it even necessary to compare poetry with poetry, prose with prose? Biblical scholars since Robert Lowth have assumed that the Bible must contain the major literary categories of "prose" and "poetry," but have famously differed on what constitutes which. Does parallelism constitute poetry, or, as Michael O'Connor argued, do syntactical patterns?[14] James Kugel argues that the distinction of poetry and prose is completely meaningless for the Hebrew Bible.[15] In traditional literature in general, Richard P. Martin argues that "the invention of 'genre' as a system of categories . . . only occurs when the oral-traditional performances of the archaic period are reduced to writing."[16] While this seems a bit extreme, it is necessary only to have a very general generic correspondence between the biblical material and the comparand (e.g., poetry to poetry, prose to prose).

We turn now to the fourth and fifth parameters, which can be dealt with briefly. The tradition-dependence of the Hebrew Bible has long been known. Particularly in Genesis, the Psalms, Isaiah, and Job there are abundant examples of the dependence of Israelite literature on Mesopotamian and Canaanite oral-written literature, language, and themes. These have been thoroughly expounded in the work of John Day, Nicolas Wyatt, and others.[17] Within the biblical tradition itself, the prevalence of traditional *forms*, so dear to form criticism, is another evidence of tradition-dependence.[18] The fifth criterion, the synchronic-diachronic variability, is best seen in the very doublets that gave birth to Old Testament source criticism centuries ago.[19] There is a better way to understand these in light of the present study, and this will be outlined further in this chapter.

What remains is the criterion of orality. This is not the time to revert to oral-formulaic tests or Romantic assumptions. The question is whether oral literature was a major part of ancient Israel's society and, if so, whether the Hebrew Bible has some relation to that oral literature. In the model

13. Gunnell, "Narratives, Space and Drama," 20; Todorov, *The Poetics of Prose*, 218. Causse recognized this long ago (Causse, *Les plus vieux chants de la Bible*, 35 n. 1).

14. O'Connor, *Hebrew Verse Structure*.

15. Kugel, *The Idea of Biblical Poetry*.

16. Martin, "Epic as Genre," 15. See also Niditch, "Epic and History," 86.

17. Day, *God's Conflict with the Dragon and the Sea*; Day, *Yahweh and the Gods and Goddesses of Canaan*; Wyatt, *Space and Time*; Wyatt, *The Mythic Mind*.

18. Hayes, *The Earth Mourns*, 230.

19. Ibid., 232.

I am proposing, that question is further whether oral *and* written literature were simultaneously a part of ancient Israel's society and related to
the Bible. The discussion of this question below, largely in dialogue with
William Schniedewind, Susan Niditch, and John Van Seters, is grounded
in an understanding of Israelite literacy, which will be treated first.

Israelite Literacy

From the dawn of Israel's existence, the Early Iron Age (1200–1000 BCE),
there are almost no epigraphic remains. Iron I texts are minimal. The
most significant is a supposed abecedary inscribed on a wheeled storage
jar found at Izbet Sartah. It consists of five lines of eighty-three letters total, written left to right and epigraphically dated to the twelfth to eleventh
centuries.[20] Given the possibility that the inscription has no relation to
Hebrew—Naveh thought it a Greco-Canaanite Philistine and there was
abundant Philistine pottery on the site[21]—it is best to remove it from the
discussion.

Other than this, there is a potsherd from an Iron I burial cave at
Manahat inscribed *lšdḥ*[22] and a potsherd inscribed *šmn*, "oil," from the
tiny village of Khirbet Tannin near Tell el-Farah North.[23] The "Ahilud" inscription from Khirbet Raddanah appears now to be a find without stra-
tigraphy, quite possibly not from Iron I, and should not be considered.[24]

This is in marked contrast to the scribal cultures of the Late Bronze
(LB) and Iron II periods, and to continued Iron I scribalism at neighboring
Aphek, Beth Shemesh, Taanach, and elsewhere.[25] Ryan Byrne concludes
that scribalism survived from LB to Iron II through elite patronage, private instruction, and as a luxury commodity during Iron I.[26] This probably underplays cases where writing was reserved for a ritual function (cf.

20. For recent discussion, see Miller, *Chieftains of the Highland Clans*, 106.

21. Naveh, "Some Considerations on the Ostracon," 35; on the pottery, see Finkelstein,
ʿ*Izbet Sartah*, 91.

22. Stager, "Inscribed Potsherd," 45–52.

23. Lemaire, "Notes d'épigraphie nord-ouest sémitique," 54.

24. Lederman, "An Early Iron Age Village."

25. Byrne, "The Refuge of Scribalism," 2–3.

26. Ibid., 3, 6, 22–23.

Deut 31:26)[27] and bypasses the trend in similar societies for literature to be oral even among the literate.[28] The most curious factor is the restriction of written texts to small, obscure sites: Izbet Sartah, Khirbet Tannin, and Manahat. Why no inscriptions from Shechem, Dothan, Shiloh, Tell el-Farah North, Ai, Bethel, Gibeon, Gibeah—if scribalism was, indeed, an indulgence of the elite?

Since the discovery of the Tel Zayit Abecedary, there has been much discussion about literacy in the tenth and ninth centuries BCE. The Tel Zayit Abecedary is an inscription of a portion of the alphabet, eighteen letters carved in the first line and at least two in the second line with two terminating symbols. It and the Gezer Calendar become the best examples of writing from this period,[29] and enters an ongoing debate between those confident that writing was common practice in Israelite society (André Lemaire, Aaron Demsky, Joseph Naveh, Alan Millard) and those who minimize the place of literacy.[30]

Let us be clear about the definition of literacy. I adopt Christopher Rollston's working description: "Substantial facility in a writing system, that is, the ability to write and read, using and understanding a standard script, a standard orthography, a standard numeric system, conventional formatting."[31] "The capacity to scrawl one's name" or even decipher a receipt is not literacy.[32] Under this definition, the adjective "literate" applies

27. Sherzer, *Verbal Art in San Blas*, 123. Nevertheless, the scroll discovered under Josiah in 621 receives no particular veneration (Silver, *The Story of Scripture*, 62–66).

28. Keesing and Keesing, *Elite Communication in Samoa*, 168.

29. Hess, "Writing about Writing," 342. At the time of writing, it remains to be seen if the five-line Hebrew inscription from tenth-century Khirbet Qeiyafa sways this discussion; Yosef Garfinkel and Saar Ganor, "Khirbet Qeiyafa," 8; essays by Haggai Misgav, Ada Yardeni, Aron Demsky, and Shmuel Ahituv in Amit et al., *New Studies in the Archaeology of Jerusalem and Its Region*, in Hebrew; essays by Haggai Misgav, Yosef Garfinkel, Saar Ganor, Ada Yardeni, Greg Bearman, and William A. Christens-Barry in *Khirbet Qeiyafa*, vol. 1, ed. Garfinkel and Ganor. The affinities of the inscription are stronger to the Philistine Qubur el-Walaydah Inscription and the Tell es-Safi Sherd than they are to the Israelite Tel Zayit Abecedary. Given the many questions raised about the Qeiyafa ostracon by Christopher Rollston, Yitzhak Sapir, Edward Cook, and others, I do not include it as evidence in my discussion.

30. Van der Toorn, *Scribal Culture*, 10–11; Rollston, *Writing and Literacy*, 132.

31. Rollston, "The Phoenician Script," 61; Rollston, *Writing and Literacy*, 127.

32. Rollston, "The Phoenician Script," 61–62; Rollston, *Writing and Literacy*, 127; van der Toorn, *Scribal Culture*, 11; Jaffee, *Torah in the Mouth*, 15; contra Rabinowitz, *A Witness Forever* 27.

to individuals, not to societies. The importance of this will be clear in what follows.

Richard Hess concludes from the location of Tel Zayit that the abecedary is proof that "literacy could be found in rural areas."[33] Adding to his evidence the Tel Dan inscription, the Mesha Stele, the Tell Fekhariyah inscription, and the Philistine text from Tel Miqne/Ekron (wrongly dubbed "Tel Ekron"), he goes on to conclude that "a significant number of people could read."[34] "There is evidence that throughout Iron Age 2, and extending back to Iron Age 1 (c. 1200–1000 BCE), every region and every level of society had its writers and readers."[35]

These "marvellous romantic" conclusions are far too sweeping.[36] The Tel Zayit Abecedary, while evidence of some literacy in the region, "certainly cannot be used" to prove such a claim.[37] First, the Tel Zayit inscription is an abecedary; it has no lexemes, morphemes, or syntagms, provides no orthographic data, no information about phonological isoglosses.[38] One cannot even say what "language" it is; it merely shows an alphabet of twenty-two consonants, with only one example each.[39] Second, old assumptions about the ease and speed of learning to read and write alphabetic scripts are simply false.[40] There is no evidence of widespread literacy in alphabetic ancient Greece or Italy, and data on Israeli children learning modern Hebrew as their first alphabet (surely the closest example) show a long process of years.[41] Third, of the mass of nearly two hundred seals and seal-impressions from tenth- and ninth-century Tel Rehov and Jerusalem, not a single seal bears the owner's name—in sharp contrast to the abundant Hebrew-inscribed seals of the eighth and seventh centuries.[42]

33. Hess, "Writing about Writing," 343.

34. Ibid., 344.

35. Ibid., 345.

36. Rollston, *Writing and Literacy*, xvi, 130.

37. Rollston, "The Phoenician Script," 63.

38. Ibid., 63–66.

39. Rollston, "The Phoenician Script," 66.

40. Ibid.; Rollston *Writing and Literacy*, 92.

41. See exhaustive evidence in Rollston, "The Phoenician Script," 70–71; and Rollstein, *Writing and Literacy*, 93, 113, 128.

42. Sanders, "Writing and Early Iron Age Israel," 103. A similar situation obtains in the Nordic world. In the 1000s AD, runestones begin to appear throughout east central

There is considerably more evidence for literacy in the late preexilic period.[43] In spite of Ian Young's insistence that a literate few composing large amounts of material does not constitute literacy,[44] percentages of literate individuals remained low even in China and Japan, with their great production of literature.[45] There are three pieces of evidence for Israelite literacy in the late preexilic period: numerous administrative seals (e.g., *LMLK* seals), vulgar script, and writings by military officers and landlords (e.g., Lachish letter 3).[46] The occurrence of inscriptions increased dramatically from the mid-eighth century on.[47] There is also substantial evidence in this period for scribal schools—that is, a mechanism that facilitated formal, standardized scribal education for a segment of the population.[48] The synchronic consistency of Hebrew palaeography, sophisticated, consistent, and meticulous morphology (even between the semi-formal cursive used on ostraca and the cursive employed on stone), consistent orthography, and the use of the complicated Egyptian hieratic numeral system all attest to "sophisticated knowledge of trained professionals."[49] Christopher Rollston's thorough assessment of the data concludes there was "formal, standardized scribal education" that could only have been

---

Sweden. They are a form of literacy, but their short, fixed sentences repeated on rune-stone after runestone are not a medium for communication but a "monumentalization" typical of oral societies (Brink, *"Verba Volant,"* 85). Brink dubs this kind of quasi-literacy "Runacy." A very few scholars speculate that oral poetry was transmitted by runes, and this theory gained some support from the discovery in recent decades of a few rune staves in the port of Bergen, Norway, preserving poetry (Harris, "The Performance of Old Norse Eddic Poetry," 227). Rune staves are said to preserve poetry in *Grettis saga* and in the poem *Sonatorrek*. It is tempting to relate such phenomena to the instructions for writing on the doorposts in Deuteronomy 6; cf. Gandz, "Oral Tradition," 255.

43. Na'aman, *The Past That Shapes the Present*, 73; Schaper, "Theology of Writing," 103.

44. Young, "Israelite Literacy . . . Part I," 240.

45. Wilcke, *Wer Las und Schrieb in Babylonien und Assyrien?*

46. Yairah Amit, *History and Ideology*, 26–27; Carr, *Writing on the Tablet of the Heart*, 166; Schniedewind, *How the Bible Became a Book*, 98–106. While noting the literacy of the military officers, Young dismisses such "craftsman's literacy" (Young, "Israelite Literacy, . . . Part I," 242; Young, "Israelite Literacy . . . Part II," 411).

47. E.g., Arad, Horvat cUza, Mesad Hashavyahu;. Coogan, "Literacy and the Formation of Biblical Literature," 47–48; Carr, *Writing on the Tablet of the Heart*, 166; Rollston, *Writing and Literacy*, 95, 133.

48. Rollston, *Writing and Literacy*, 95, 113.

49. Rollston, "Scribal Education," 53, 60–61, 66; Rollston, *Writing and Literacy*, 91, 96, 107–9, 113.

fostered by the state.[50] Cross-culturally, the rise of literacy is often a tool of the state, in administrative uses first but then for textual glorification of rulers' exploits and documentation of noble genealogies.[51] At the same time, "a corporate strategy found in some archaic states aims, instead, to restrict writing and literacy" as an "exclusionary political strategy."[52] This may be why widespread narrative writing only develops when the Israelite state authority is removed in the exilic period.

As van der Toorn writes, "Determining the level of literacy in the ancient Near East is not a matter of merely accumulating percentages and figures. In the absence of incontrovertible evidence, estimated literacy rates fluctuate according to the motives, bias, and personal assumptions of modern scholars."[53] We should not expect incontrovertible evidence and should not need it if Foley is correct that it is a "quite misleading matter of whether or not writing was 'available' to the poets and audiences."[54] Epigraphic remains from Palestine are primarily ostraca. Most ostracon texts are ephemeral letters or economic documents that might be kept for a short time before being transcribed, if at all, on to something archival.[55] *Belles lettres* could not be accommodated by ostraca, and there are only two examples of ink-written West Semitic literary texts, the Ahiqar papyrus and the Deir Allah wall plaster. It is possible that chalked or waxed wooden boards were used but have not survived.[56] It is more than likely that literature, *even* in the late preexilic period, was oral literature.[57]

William Schniedewind

Schniedewind affirms that "literacy was quite restricted" in the ancient Near East.[58] Yet he reads the epigraphic evidence as indicating "a spread of writing through all classes of society by the seventh century BCE in

---

50. Rollson, "Scribal Education," 67–68; Rollston, *Writing and Literacy*, 91, 113.

51. Blanton, "Beyond Centralization," 161.

52. Ibid.

53. van der Toorn, *Scribal Culture*, 10.

54. Schniedewind, *The Singer of Tales in Performance*, 72.

55. Jaffee, *Torah in the Mouth*, 15.

56. Sasson, "Comparative Observations," 217.

57. Much of the last paragraph derives from a discussion among Frank Polak, Peter T. Daniels, and myself on the ANE-2 listserv in July 2009.

58. Schniedewind "How the Bible Became a Book."

Judah."[59] He adds to this epigraphic evidence a belief that it is difficult to imagine "how the exile could have provided a social setting where such an enormous literary project could be carried out—that is, if it were not substantially complete already,"[60] and so the bulk of Israel's *literary* composition must have taken place before 586 BCE. Since the world of the exile, Persian, and Hellenistic periods was dominated by the Aramaic *lingua franca,*[61] Schniedewind can only explain the linguistic problem of a *Hebrew* canonical literature by ascribing its composition to before that time.[62]

If Schneidewind is correct, then the orality criterion of Foley is in jeopardy. That is, in Schneidewind's reconstruction, ancient Israel was a "literate society" for much of the Iron II period, and that is when the bulk of the Old Testament was composed.[63] In that case, we cannot engage in the comparison undertaken here.

But there are several problems with this reconstruction. The epigraphic evidence has been discussed above and shows literacy only substantial in the late preexilic period. Nothing in Schniedewind's other observations excludes oral transmission of the literature in question. Schniedewind finds it difficult to imagine "how the exile could have provided a social setting where such an enormous literary project could be carried out—that is, if it were not substantially complete already."[64] I find it much harder to imagine the exiles transporting to Babylon (at a pace of fifteen kilometers per day for five hundred kilometers)[65] large scrolls that

59. Ibid.

60. Schniedewind, "Orality and Literacy," 330.

61. And earlier, Winter, "Royal Rhetoric," 30; Janowksi and Gernot, *Staatsverträge,* 312–13; Dirk Schwiderski, *The Old and Imperial Aramaic Inscriptions,* 2:1.

62. Schniedewind, "Orality and Literacy," 329.

63. Kawashima reaches a similar conclusion, that the Bible is a wholly literate product of a literate society; *Biblical Narrative,* 14. Yet his conclusion is not based on epigraphic or historical evidence but on a Goody-Ongian view of the nature of oral vs. literate discourse (*Biblical Narrative,* 163, 168, 186, 210) and a Parry-Lord understanding of what oral literature should look like (*Biblical Narrative,* 175–85).

64. Schniedewind, "Orality and Literacy," 330. He writes also: "It is hardly credible that the exiles working on Babylonian canal projects wrote or even valued literature" ("How the Bible Became a Book"). There is simply no evidence for such forced labor in the Babylonian exile, and the Murashu banking archives of a century later suggest quite another situation.

65. Angelika Berlejung, "Assyrians in the West," paper presented at the XX International Organization for the Study of the Old Testament, Helsinki, 2010.

the Babylonians generously allowed them to collect before departure. As Martin Jaffe puts it, "Long books made for long, heavy scrolls."[66] Only with caution should we take the Bible's own assumptions about literacy, its "as it is written" phrases, as attesting to textualization in the seventh century.[67]

Susan Niditch

Niditch's reconstruction is much the reverse of Schniedewind's. Her ancient Israel is an oral society with oral literature. For her, even epigraphic texts of the eighth and seventh centuries are clearly those of an oral society. Seals are evidence of "how few people wrote."[68] Even the Siloam Tunnel inscription is "writing in the oral mode."[69] As for the written texts of the Hebrew Bible, "all, I would argue, evidence the use of traditional-style registers of varying kinds and degrees."[70]

It might seem that she underestimates the increase of literacy as much as Schniedewind overestimates it. Her treatment is more sophisticated than such a caricature and encroaches on my own. She rejects, for instance, an evolutionary view of orality leading into writing of the Bible.[71] In a certain sense, it is true that "the oral world lives in the words of scripture."[72] She argues, for example, that biblical references to divine record-keeping emphasize the oral nature of society.[73] In fact, Joachim Schaper is no doubt correct that this is evidence for a literate bureaucracy in the seventh century.[74] Epigraphic evidence shows that by that time, many people used writing extensively. As Carr points out, we actually have more evidence for widespread literacy in terms of abecedaries and other school exercises for preexilic Israel than we do for ancient Greece.[75]

---

66. Jaffee, *Torah in the Mouth*, 16.
67. As per William Schniedewind, *Society and the Promise to David*.
68. Niditch, *Oral World and Written Word*, 50.
69. Ibid., 54–55.
70. Niditch, "The Hebrew Bible," 7.
71. Niditch, *Oral World and Written Word*, 134.
72. Ibid., 2.
73. Ibid., 81.
74. Schaper "Exilic and Post-Exilic Prophecy," 329.
75. Carr, "Torah on the Heart," 23.

Also important are the standardized scripts of the sort seen as early as the Tel Zayit inscriptions, letter forms that must have been taught in some kind of educational system.[76] As David Carr explains, "Sometime in the Iron Age, however, scribes in Israel and surrounding areas began to develop a standardized 'inland' script that built on Phoenician prototypes but diverged in regular ways, thus suggesting the existence of an increasingly independent scribal-education system."[77] The direct evidence for this is the epigraphic remains from the eighth and seventh centuries, but there are two indications that this "inland" scribal system originated earlier. The first is the common script tradition of both the northern and southern kingdoms, which at the very least suggests a shared scribal tradition, and perhaps imposition by one of the two kingdoms on the other.[78] The second is the presence of similar script (and sometimes phraseology and language) in the Mesha Stele and other Edomite and Philistine inscriptions.[79] All this suggests precisely the interplay of orality and literacy in the tradition pool/stream outlined at the end of chapter 3.

John Van Seters

There remains another possibility that would exclude the ability to compare the Bible with Homer, the sagas, or the *siyar*. Perhaps Israel was exactly the sort of "oral-and-literate society" outlined here, producing a tradition pool and stream as described, but the Bible has no connection with this. That is, the Bible is the product of literate composition of the exilic or postexilic period that is not connected to the Iron II "oral-written educational" context or the oral-and-written literature of preexilic Israel and Judah, whatever that may have been. This is, in essence, the argument of John Van Seters.

Van Seters does not exclude the possibility that there was oral prose narration of the traditions that appear in parts of the Hebrew Bible.[80]

76. Carr, "The Tel Zayit Abecedary," 114. The Iron I textual remains are quite different; Carr, "Tel Zayit," 115.

77. Ibid., 120.

78. Ibid., 120–21.

79. Ibid., 121.

80. Van Seters, "Oral Patterns," 140; Van Seters, *The Life of Moses*, 457. In this he is roundly criticized by Thomas L. Thompson, who says the texts are perfectly explainable by scribal traditions alone: there is no oral *Grundlage* (Thompson, "Why Talk about the Past?" 7, 9, 11).

But as Gísli Sigurðsson does for the Icelandic sagas, he does not think anything that appears in the Bible looks like the text of an oral bard or storyteller.[81] Most of the "traditional language" found in the Bible can be accounted for by literary invention or by the borrowing of written language from, for example, the Assyrian world.[82]

This is really two different things. Borrowing from written language is certainly part of the oral-and-written process I am outlining, as illustrated in Lars Lönnroth's diagram. Nevertheless, what Maria Pretzler says of Pausanias holds true for the Priestly writer: "The thought of Pausanias heading for the local library to copy down any special written accounts seems unrealistic in a world where even asking for access to local books would have involved conversations with people who were likely to volunteer plenty of information."[83] But it is a different matter to suggest that a story in antiquity might be a literary product with *no* tradition behind it.[84] Van Seters argues "that the stories are the product of literary composition."[85] Some of the stories are a "great mythic fantasy."[86]

Such composition is extremely unlikely in societies where much of "literature" was oral, which was surely the case in the Babylonian exile and in the Persian period. An author in such a society "never creates from a blank page"[87] All authors in such societies remain in dialogue with other stories of similar kind, with the traditional folklore. The "distributed author" is not a Romantic illusion as Van Seters claims,[88] but an insight of Bakhtin.[89] "In the case of epic, . . . normally the story is known to the audience already."[90] "Historical epic, whether composed

81. Van Seters, "Oral Patterns," 141.

82. Ibid., 142.

83. Pretzler, "Pausanias," 245.

84. As Van Seters, "Oral Patterns," 148; Van Seters, *The Life of Moses*, 458. Van Seters does not claim that *all* the stories of J, for example, have no traditions behind them: "It is a work of ancient antiquarian historiography that takes up the extant traditions, written or oral" (Van Seters, *Life of Moses*, 147). My concern is that for a great many stories he believes this was *not* the case.

85. Van Seters, "Oral Patterns," 151 n. 10.

86. Van Seters, *The Pentateuch*, 174.

87. Ranković, "Who Is Speaking?" 304.

88. Van Seters, "The Origins of the Hebrew Bible," 94.

89. Ranković, "Who Is Speaking?" 304; Ross, *A History*, 233.

90. Jensen, "Performance," 48.

orally or in writing, worked by telling people what they already knew."[91] Anthropologically, it would be quite difficult to explain a single erudite author inventing a learned tale that was then able somehow, en masse, to enter the performance-educational tradition.[92] As Adolphe Lods knew a half century ago, the Israelite writers were neither rote copyist-editors nor from-scratch authors, but writers with powerful personal originality working in a long oral-written tradition.[93] And it is quite improbable that an exilic or postexilic audience could be disengaged from its own past cultural heritage (which Van Seters regards as beyond our ken) and attached to a new one of an author's invention.[94]

One matter should be foregrounded. Van Seters is convinced that Homer is *not* the product of oral tradition and that this was a Romantic, nineteenth-century view long abandoned in classical scholarship.[95] He makes this claim repeatedly,[96] and always without citing a single classicist. As has been shown in chapter 3, the opposite is the case. "The oral-derived, traditional status of the *Iliad and Odyssey* is not disputed."[97] No one today denies that the Homeric epics, especially the *Iliad*, are the offspring of an oral society and a wide pool of tradents.[98]

Van Seters is correct that we cannot simply assume an oral epic lies behind the Primary History.[99] But undergirding Van Seters's denial of the Bible's connection with the oral literature of preexilic Israel are the premises that there is no early poetry in the Hebrew Bible,[100] that the Hebrew language cannot be linguistically dated even to the scale of

91. Sherratt, "Archaeological Contexts," 125.

92. Armistead, "Epic and Ballad," 384–85 refutes such a notion for Spanish epic and balladry.

93. Lods, *Histoire de la littérature hébraïque et juive*, 128. Lods identified the proto-Van Seters view that it was impossible to reconstruct an oral precursor to the Bible with Bernhard Luther; Lods, "Rôle de la tradition," 59. Rofé believes that if the authors of the Pentateuchal sources were not writing from scratch, "they must have been significantly constrained in their work" (Lods, *Introduction*, 89).

94. Pasayat, *Oral Tradition, Society, and History*, 7.

95. Van Seters, "The Origins of the Hebrew Bible," 90, 94.

96. Van Seters, "The Role of the Scribe," 113; Van Seters, *The Edited Bible*, 133–84.

97. Greenwood, "Sounding Out Homer," 507.

98. Skafte . "In What Sense," 19; Bakker, "Homer, Hypertext, and the Web of Myth," 159; Foley, "Reading Homer," 1, 4; Foley, "Plenitude," 113.

99. Van Seters, "The Origins of the Hebrew Bible," 93.

100. Ibid., 94.

pre- vs. postexilic,[101] and that the present text of the Primary History cannot be explained by an unproven editorial process.[102] He interprets the epigraphic data in a minimalist way along the lines of Niditch, so as to conclude, "among the populace there was no more literacy in Josiah's day than in the preceding period."[103]

Such views are radical in the extreme and would merit the most careful scrutiny. It is not Van Seters's dating of texts that is at issue here. It is the view that the biblical text did not result from an oral-written tradition pool but emerged (with the introduction of broader literacy?) from new compositional principles (borrowed from Herodotus and Hallinucus),[104] motivated not by the Persian government (another theory Van Seters rejects), but merely by aesthetic principles. This view furthermore implies abrupt disruptions in the traditions stream. "And it would carry with it the responsibility to produce reasons for believing in such disruptions, and also for addressing the question of the sources of these new compositional principles. These are questions that anyone with [Van Seters's] professed concern for the cultural context would want to address at once."[105]

Finally, ethnographically, "behind most epics, whether oral or literary, lies a long 'prehistory' of subject matter which feeds directly into them."[106] "Can we really suppose that Israel alone had no singers of tales?" asks Frank Cross.[107] Jean-Louis Ska asks, "Mais pourquoi? Faut-il donc imaginer qu'à l'époque biblique il n'existait que l'information écrite?

---

101. Ibid., 95.

102. Van Seters, *The Edited Bible*, chap. 5.

103. Van Seters, "The Origins of the Hebrew Bible," 96. Hess would no doubt agree, but for the opposite reason!

104. Van Seters, *The Life of Moses*, 457.

105. Treitler, "Sinners and Singers," 156, speaking of Peter Jeffery. The proposals of Peter Jeffery for Medieval chant and Van Seters for the Hebrew Bible are remarkably similar and should be rejected for similar epistemological reasons, above and beyond the evidence marshaled above.

106. Sherratt, "Archaeological Contexts," 135. As with the authentic pre-1400 BCE elements lurking in the *Iliad* and *Odyssey* (e.g., Ajax's shield, Penelope's palace; Sherratt, "Archaeological Contexts," 135), relics of the Iron I and Iron II period in the narratives and poetry of the Hebrew Bible cannot be mere archaizing. They are too infrequent, too contradictory, and would hardly be noticeable to an epic audience (Sherratt, "Archaeological Contexts," 136).

107. Cross, "Telltale Remnants of Oral Epic," 87.

Ne faut-il pas supposer, au contraire, que l'écriture était l'apanage d'un cercle restreint et que la tradition orale était le canal d'information le plus habituel?"[108]

Israel and the Bible: Orality and Literacy

All three of these reconstructions minimize the extent to which Israel was always a society of oral literature full of literate individuals. As David Carr laments, "Though scholars decades ago deconstructed the idea that there was a 'great divide' between orality and literacy, a remarkable number of high quality publications still work with a strong distinction between the two, or at least a 'continuum' with orality at one end and literacy at the other."[109]

The great majority of the people of biblical Israel both before and after the exile received the message of the "text" aurally. Just as much as the boundary between orality and literacy needs to be removed, so too the boundary between orality and aurality.[110] In short, in the model I have proposed for biblical literature, written texts circulated in spoken form by recitation long after they were committed to writing. And those recited forms begat oral forms that were not in writing, or were not put in writing for some time afterwards.[111] Oral texts that circulated from bard to audience or bard to bard could be recorded in writing, could be consulted by writers, could be consulted by bards of other stories.[112]

---

108. Ska, Review of *The Life of Moses*, by John Van Seters, 421. Translation: "But why? Must we therefore imagine that the biblical period had nothing but written information? Should we not suppose, on the other hand, that writing was prerogative of a restricted circle and that oral tradition was the most common channel of information?" "The absence of surviving poems," as Matthew Townsend writes of lost York-Dublin Viking poetry, "constitutes no reason to doubt that such poems once existed." As in his case, the hints of a shared poetic culture with the ancient Near East, extant scraps of early Hebrew poetry, and textual references to orality, "For all these reasons, therefore, . . . it seems reasonable to conclude that there was also at one time a considerable body of poetry . . . which has neither survived nor left any trace of its former existence. Townsend, "Whatever Happened to York Viking Poetry?" 60.

109. Carr, "Torah on the Heart," 18.

110. Khamis, "From Written through Oral," 203. This boundary is insisted upon by Izre'el, "Study," 155.

111. So also, Carr, "Torah on the Heart," 18–19.

112. Béré, "*Auditor in fabula*—la Bible dans son contexte oral," 1102.

Older models viewed the literary process as linear.[113] First, there were oral stories that circulated among bards or storytellers. Eventually, these were written down. Those texts, perhaps as soon as they were written, were recited or chanted orally to the illiterate masses, a process that continued through the Masoretic vocalization,[114] and on into the Mishnaic period (*b. Šabb.* 96b; *B. Meṣ.* 92; see chapter 2, above).[115] This process was sometimes called "re-oralization"[116] or "text brokering."[117]

This model should be abandoned.[118] The process is not nearly so linear and cannot be in a society where writing was known long before the twelfth century BCE and oral literature common long after the fifth.[119] In Ugarit, literary texts are among the latest written, long after the advent of writing.[120] Even in the Mishnaic period, rabbinic writers drew amply from the oral folk tradition, writing texts that were immediately passed on orally (e.g., Rabbi Bechai [Bahyee ibn Paquda]'s *Duties of the Hearts*, eleventh century CE).[121]

We should instead appropriate the insights of Antony Campbell.[122] He views much of the biblical narrative as "neither the record of the oral telling of a story nor the skilled fashioning of a story as a work of literary art,"[123] but as written outlines for oral elaboration (or for omission in performance).[124] Ancient editors were intelligent; they included several alternatives and options, perhaps to be chosen from by the bards.[125] Do we really think they did not see the contradiction between Genesis 1 and

---

113. E.g., Gandz, "Oral Tradition," 248.

114. The vocalization attests to previous oral tradition at the same time as it somewhat removes the necessity of oral transmission (Rothenberg, "2 July 1975").

115. Gómez Aranda, "Transmisión Oral," 254–55.

116. Mills, "Domains of Folklore Concern," 232.

117. Stern, "One of These Things."

118. So too says Heda Jason, "The Study of Israelite," 75.

119. Sanders, "Writing and Early Iron Age Israel," 108.

120. Vidal, "King Lists and Oral Transmission," 561.

121. Jason, "The Study of Israelite," 72.

122. Campbell, "The Reported Story," 77–85.

123. Ibid., 77, 80.

124. Campbell and O'Brien, *Unfolding the Deuteronomistic*, 6–7; Campbell and O'Brien, *Rethinking the Pentateuch*, xiii–xiv, 6–7, 15–19. See chapter 6, below, on "performance."

125. Campbell and O'Brien, *Rethinking the Pentateuch*, 6, 16.

2? The multiple times Moses goes up the mountain in Exodus 24? Why did they accept such duplication and inconsistency? Ancient editors were intelligent; they include several alternatives and options. For Campbell's "User Theory,"[126] the texts are starting points for oral literature.[127] Martin Jaffe has proposed much the same thing—the narratives of the Hebrew Bible had to be "rendered orally by reciters" in interpretive contexts supplied by tradition, choosing from alternatives and options[128]—and now, David Carr has, as well, calling these options "memory variants."[129] The details of the story—descriptions of settings, for example—are provided by the storyteller in performance, based on the skeleton of the gobbets.[130] The gobbets are the "oral building blocks . . . varied at will according to the needs of the moment, and modified to suit new purposes and places," such as the darkening of the sun and the conquest of Simurrum in Akkadian literature, which appear in different order in different manuscripts of the Sargon texts and also (for the former) find their way into the Epic of Gilgamesh.[131]

This is exactly what has been observed with the Arabic *siyar* and deduced for the Homeric material.[132] Using the *aides-mémoires* (the gobbets), one tells a tale that the written text enables to be told.[133] The Sumerian case has already been discussed. Jean-Marie Durand believes much of Akkadian literature seems to serve the same function, requiring oral "actualization."[134] John Baines views some fully syntactic Egyptian texts as "inscribed versions of something that would be differently realized

126. Ibid., 17 n. 10.

127. Ibid., 2, 5. I am not endorsing Campbell and O'Brien's entire model. User Theory will not work as ubiquitously as they believe. It cannot explain large texts (e.g., the Joseph story), legal texts, or all doublets. In using their theory here, I say nothing about the final form of the Pentateuch or the process of literary composition of the Primary History.

128. Jaffee, "The Hebrew Scriptures," 326, 328; also Davidson, *Intricacy, Design & Cunning*, 370–72. So too did Lods, "Rôle de la tradition," 58. Alan Dundes, of course, agrees, but to an excess (Dundes, *Holy Writ*, 115).

129. Carr, "Torah on the Heart," 33.

130. Minchin, "Spatial Memory," 19.

131. Westenholz, "Historical Events," 30.

132. Reynolds, *Heroic Poets, Poetic Heroes*, 19; Thomas, *Literacy and Orality*, 91–92; Finnegan, *Literacy and Orality*, 169.

133. Ethnographically, the common practice in oral epic is for bards to perform part of what we would consider the entire tale (Foley, "Analogues: Modern Oral Epics" 204).

134. Durand, "Écrit et parole," 52.

when spoken."[135] It seems to be a maxim of oral literature that traditions are "a store of obligatory, alternative and optional textual possibilities to be accepted or rejected by the singer at the moment of performance" or textualization.[136] It should also be noted that "the repertoire includes not only a number of variations but also rules for producing them."[137] As was stated earlier, the bard or writer is not free to invent things out of whole cloth, except as such invention follows guidelines from which he cannot deviate. Still, the author has created *something*. It is a new piece of literature, but one that depends on those different antecedents for much more than formulae and themes—and yet much less: no formulaic language need be repeated at all. "Antecedents" is of course not the best term, as it implies a linear relationship when the relationship is far more skein-like (see figure 3.1, above). "The narrative remains in constant dialogue with its versions."[138] "The interrelations are not simple, and can be explained neither by postulating a closed circle, whereby the primacy of neither the written nor the oral tradition can be ascertained (the 'chicken-and-egg' question), nor by adopting a priori the primacy of one of the two traditions."[139] And it is important to remember the issue of textual variants, not addressed in this monograph. In the end, there is no "Hebrew Bible"; there are no autographs, and we will eventually have to abandon the image of textual variants derived from some fixed, authorized text we can discover by sifting through the competing readings.[140]

It seems odd to ask for reasons *why* the literature remained oral, when a similar situation obtained in ancient Greece, Rome, and elsewhere (viz. Plato, *Phaedrus,* 275C–D, 276D; Pliny, *Natural History* 2: Bk. VIII, XV, #88, 565). Some suggest that the act of oral delivery guaranteed the authenticity of a written text.[141] It remains a fact that "the dominance of

135. Baines, *Visual and Written Culture*, 155; Redford," Scribe and Speaker," 194; Assmann, *Religion*, 108. So too Icelandic Eddic poetry contains many interchangeable lines, not the mark of a conscious, creative *writer* (Gunnell, "The Play of Skírnir," 22).

136. Honko, "The Quest for Oral Text," 1. Thomas suggests a connection between texts of the User-Theory sort and a desire to keep power in the hands of professional performers (Thomas, "Performance Literature," 3).

137. Oesterreicher, "Types of Orality," 209.

138. Ranković, "Who Is Speaking?" 297.

139. Jason, "The Study of Israelite," 72.

140. Amodio, *Writing the Oral Tradition*, 45; Jason, "Folk Literature in Its Cultural Context," 89.

141. Jaffee, *Torah in the Mouth*, 26.

oral/aural interaction with sacred texts has been the rule rather than the exception for the vast majority of persons and communities throughout history."[142] I am not sure this explanation is necessary for antiquity.[143]

And yet, ancient Israel was never without writing.[144] Even given the collapse of the scribal culture of the Late Bronze Age, some forms of writing continued in all periods of Israel's existence. The majority of the narrative books of the Hebrew Bible were written in times of substantial scribal activity in Israel and Judah and under domination of highly literate foreign cultures from the Assyrians on.[145]

142. Graham, *Beyond the Written Word*, 159. Most such interaction has been liturgical; Graham, *Beyond*, 161.

143. Cooper, "Babbling On," 105.

144. Seybold, "Zur mündlichen," 141; Schaper, "Exilic and Post-Exilic Prophecy," 337.

145. Schaper, "Exilic and Post-exilic," 334. Note how writing plays a major role in exilic and postexilic prophecy; ibid., 333.

5

What Lies behind the Written

Even in the heyday of the oral-formulaic method, discussion of oral literature in ancient Israel usually resorted to speculation. Since the only literature we have is written literature, once the scholar goes beyond statements about which parts of that literature are orally derived and attempts to speak about the oral "stage" of the literature, only conjecture is available. Such conjecture has, unfortunately, been largely based on what seems logical, on common sense, on assumptions, and in all honesty, imagination. In order to avoid the inevitable failure of our imaginative powers, we shall presently apply our intellect to the issue.

In chapter 3, several focal analogies were presented for the orally derived material in the Hebrew Bible's narrative books. These were the Homeric epics of *Iliad* and *Odyssey*, the Icelandic sagas, and the Arabic *siyar* epics. In the previous chapter, John Miles Foley's five criteria for effective comparative work were presented and satisfied for the biblical material. In chapter 6, we will examine actual texts of the narrative books of the Old Testament that might qualify as orally derived. In this chapter, however, the focus is on what such orally derived texts would have been derived from. That is, in the oral-and-written model of Israelite literary production elucidated in chapter 3 and in the last chapter, what was the oral component? Rather than assume or guess, the comparative material will be used, particularly the Icelandic and Arabic material. For both the Icelandic sagas and the *Sīrat Banī Hilāl* exist in written form. They are orally derived from something else that is not exactly the saga or even the *sīra*. The Homeric epics, too, have a "'prehistory' [that] consists of bodies of hexameter heroic songs and cycles of songs,"[1] but these are not as accessible as the other two cases.

The Eddic and Skaldic poetry and the Arabic *suwālif* are probably the nearest approximations to the oral literature of ancient Israel. We can conclude that the prose and poetic repertoire of the bards of Israel, especially prior to the seventh century BC, resembled such as these.

Eddic Poetry

Some members of the "Icelandic School" (see above) "repeatedly tell us that we can never know" what oral sources lay behind the Icelandic sagas.[2] Most, however, look to Old Norse poetry.

Old Norse poetry is divided into two categories, called Eddic and Skaldic. While there is some medieval support for this division,[3] no one criterion divides the two categories from each other. The origin of the term "Eddic poetry" is a historical accident. In 1643, an Icelandic bishop acquired a small medieval codex of poems. Recognizing similarities between the poems and the well-known treatise on poetics and mythology by Snorri Sturluson known as the *Edda*, he falsely concluded that Snorri had quoted some of these poems in his own *Edda*. He further surmised that the codex contained poems compiled by a late eleventh-century Icelandic historian that Snorri had used. From that time, the title *Elder Edda* or *Poetic Edda* has been applied to this poetic anthology, to distinguish it from Snorri's *Younger* or *Prose Edda*, although there is no evidence that the codex comes from the eleventh-century historian or was ever called *Edda*. The codex is now properly known as the Codex Regius, and it dates to the late thirteenth century.[4]

The meters of the poems of the Codex Regius are found in other early Icelandic poetry, and poems in those meters are therefore known as "Eddic poetry." All Eddic poetry "is likely to have been first composed and then recited orally."[5] There are several pieces of evidence for this.

1. Sherratt, "Archaeological Contexts," 135.

2. Chesnutt, "Popular and Learned Elements," 44. I use the term "behind" only for convenience; the progression from oral to written in the sagas is not linear.

3. Ross, *A History*, 6.

4. See detailed history in ibid., 7.

5. Ibid., 69; Gunnell, "The Performance of the Poetic Edda," 299; Gunnell, "Eddic Poetry," 83. There were, of course, oral formulaicists who tried to prove this statistically:

First, the Latin prosimetria (a medieval genre of prose intertwined with poetry) of Saxo Grammaticus (1150–1220) shows that he had access to an Old Danish alliterative poetic tradition akin to the Eddic poetry, which also shows parallels with Old High German and Old English poetry.[6] Second, a portion of the written sources of the Codex Regius can be traced back to about 1200. Yet the poems are clearly masterpieces of the pre-Christian era (before 1000) in Iceland. Most are "archpagan masterpieces . . . and even in the younger heroic peoms there is no certain allusion to Christianity. So even without the evidence of language and the realia alluded to, most of which reflect the Viking Age and not the High Middle Ages, there would be a gap to be explained."[7] This is a gap of two centuries.

This gap potentially replicates the biblical situation. The dating of the various texts of the Old Testament is always contentious and beyond the scope of this study. But a growing consensus assigns most of the composition of the so-called Primary History (Genesis through 2 Kings) to the exilic period or thereafter.[8] And yet, not only does the text claim to treat events of centuries earlier, but it is certain that events, idioms, phrases, structures, and other "gobbets" or "registers" must come from the eighth century BCE and earlier.[9]

Sagas regularly include poems, and in some sagas most of the poetry is in the so-called Eddic meters.[10] "Eddic-style" poetry seems to have been recognized by saga writers and their presumed audiences as generically appropriate to include in sagas, just as Snorri Sturluson quoted Eddic poetry in the mythological section of his *Edda*.[11] The saga writers must have had access to the oral Eddic repertoire, otherwise the Germanic parallels,

e.g., Kellogg, "The Prehistory of Eddic Poetry," 187–99; Gísli Sigurðsson, "On the Classification of Eddic Heroic Poetry," 245–55.

6. Ross, "Poetry and *fornaldarsögur*"; Online: http://www.dur.ac.uk/medieval.www/sagaconf/clunies.htm/.

7. Harris, "Performance," 226.

8. See, *inter alia*, Person, *The Deuteronomistic School*; Wilson, "Deuteronomy, Ethnicity, and Reform," 109–12, 116.

9. For the eighth century, see Miller, *Covenant and Grace in the Old Testament*. For far earlier periods, see Miller, *Chieftains*.

10. Ross, "Poetry and *fornaldarsögur*." The main manuscript of Eddic verse outside of Codex Regius is the *Íslendingadrápa* (Kristjánsson, "*Íslendingadrápa*," 80). It is unlikely that the author of this work used *any* written source material (ibid., 90).

11. Ross, "Poetry and *fornaldarsögur*."

including Saxo's, make little sense.[12] It cannot be that Snorri and other thirteenth-century authors made up Eddic-like poetry from scratch and, in unrelated manuscripts, all attributed them to the exact same poets.[13] Thus, Eddic poetry represents one aspect of the "oral precursors" of the Icelandic sagas.[14]

The poems of the Codex Regius fall into two divisions: mythological poems and those with historical themes. They use three different meters, which go by the names *fornyðislag*, *ljóðaháttr*, and *málaháttr*. The first is probably the oldest, as it is used in poems found in runic inscriptions and, in fact, translates as "old-lore meter."[15]

Outside of the Codex, *fornyðislag* verse was deemed "appropriate to subjects that either narrated the events of prehistory or reconstructed a prehistoric world."[16] In the twelfth and early thirteenth centuries when the Eddic poems were committed to writing, both in sagas and in such manuscripts as Codex Regius, Iceland (and much of Europe) was undergoing "a number of cultural initiatives [having] to do with a redefinition of individuals and the societies to which they belonged in terms of a re-imagined and reinterpreted past, with which people claimed direct though often attenuated links."[17] Here, again, there are parallels to the biblical situation. In the exilic and especially postexilic periods, a profound focus of the intellectual and cultural "initiatives" that produced the Hebrew Bible were engaged in precisely such a forging of direct links with a reinterpreted past.[18]

Eddic poetry will be an essential analogue for constructing a description of oral literate life in ancient Israel in chapter 6, below. The following is an example of Eddic poetry, from W. H. Auden's translation of *Völundarkviða*:

12. Ibid.

13. Ibid.

14. Harris, "Proverbs in Saxon and in the Sagas"; Kristján Árnason, "Perennial Purism: The Case of Icelandic"; Thorvaldsen, "Eddic Form," 152.

15. Phillpotts, *The Elder Edda*, 25; Gunnell, "The Play of Skírnir," 23.

16. Ross, "Poetry and *fornaldarsögur*"; Tulinius, "Sagas," 448.

17. Ross, "Poetry and *fornaldarsögur*."

18. P. F. Esler, "Ezra-Nehemiah as a Narrative," 413–26; Albertz and Becking, *Yahwism after the Exile*.

1

Three maidens through Mirkwood flew,
Fair and young, fate to endure:
Winged maidens by the water's edge
Peacefully retted precious flax.

2

Olrun was the first; she took Egil for lover.
Swanwhite the second: she took Slagfidur.
Hervor the third; she threw round
Völund's White neck wanton arms.

3

So they sat for seven winters,
Then in the eighth for home they longed,
In the ninth their dooms drove them apart:
Three maidens through Mirkwood flew,
Fair and young, fate to endure.[19]

Skaldic Poetry

As stated previously, the line between Eddic and Skaldic poetry is not easy to draw. While Skaldic poetry is typically of a much more complex and artificial meter than Eddic, a great deal of Skaldic poetry is actually composed in *fornyðislag* verse.[20] Several Eddic poems show the influence of the language and imagery of Skaldic poems.[21] Characteristic of Skaldic poems is the extravagant, unlimited use of kennings of every variety and complexity,[22] something to which we will return in a later chapter.

Skaldic poetry takes its name from the *skald* or poet/bard (the English word "scold" is related), so "Skaldic poetry" is poetry composed by West Norse (mainly Icelandic) skalds of the ninth to fourteenth centuries.[23] Almost none of it was written down before 1200, yet it is only

19. Taylor and Auden, trans., *The Elder Edda*, 108.

20. Ross, *A History*, 13.

21. Gunnell, "Eddic Poetry," 94.

22. Word clusters that stand for other more mundane terms: "swan's road" for "the sea," "dispenser of rings" for "prince."

23. Ross, *A History*, 13; Townsend, "Norse Poets and English Kings," 271.

known today from written texts, primarily within the sagas.[24] So Skaldic poetry is another example of orally derived text, yet considerably less "derived" than the sagas and closer to the poetry's oral form. "Skaldic poems are the only witnesses of Old Norse-Icelandic literature that was definitely produced in preliterary times, and that was definitely performed and transmitted orally."[25]

Skaldic poetry, too, found its way into sagas, including into *Njáls Saga*.[26] Some Skaldic verses in *Njáls Saga* are also found in *Kristni saga*, probably indicating that both drew on one oral source.[27] Skaldic verses "remain the most distinctly oral legacy in the written sagas of the thirteenth and fourteenth centuries, perhaps the only authentic voices in the text."[28] That is, "most scholars accept that the written versions of this kind of skaldic verse are likely to represent their oral ancestors faithfully."[29] But the Skaldic poems also provide a view of the sagas' own prehistory. There are Skaldic poems that treat events recounted in sagas that are *not* quoted within the saga in question.[30] The sagaman "had a choice whether or not to quote from such poems, or to imitate them, or to refer to them, or be otherwise influenced by them."[31]

In content, Skaldic poems sing the praises of kings and nobles (and always the skald himself).[32] Mythological themes are minimal. In sagas, Skaldic verses are often inserted into narratives, serving as the dialogue between the characters of the saga (e.g., Thorkel's poem in *Gísla saga Srssonar*, 9).[33] The relationship between the Skaldic poetry and the surrounding saga prose is quite fluid: "The different saga accounts of the incident thought to be authenticated by the stanzas seem in their shifting

24. Ross, "From Iceland to Norway," 58; Ross, *A History*, 69. There is a skaldic verse on the Karlevi stone in Sweden from 1000 (Ross, *A History*, 233; Townsend, "Norse Poets," 270).

25. Würth, "Skaldic Poetry and Performance," 263.

26. Wolf, "Zur Rolle des Epischen," 258. Many sagas are actually *about* skalds; Vésteinn Ólason, "The Icelandic Saga as a Kind of Literature," 34–35.

27. Nordal, "The Dialogue between Audience and Text," 187.

28. Nordal, "The Art of Poetry and the Sagas of Icelanders," 220.

29. Jesch, "Skaldic Verse," 193.

30. Jesch, "Sagas and Scaldic Poetry," 12.

31. Ibid., 10.

32. Nordal, *Tools of Literacy*, 7; O'Donoghue, *Skaldic Verse*, 5.

33. O'Donoghue, *Skaldic Verse*, 12, 16.

perspectives to serve as touchstones for the regulation of oral speculation, not as permanent fixatives."[34] Skaldic verses comparable to saga narratives in several striking ways would have suggested themselves unconsciously to saga audiences because they formed a part of their shared cultural knowledge.[35] On the other hand, some Skaldic poems appear to have been composed by the sagamen themselves when they composed the surrounding prose.[36] Yet the latter cannot account for all or even most of the Skaldic poems, whose independent existence is confirmed by runic inscriptions.[37] As Judith Jesch writes, "I have not yet come across any scholar who seriously believes or, more importantly, is able to demonstrate that all of the hundreds of stanzas quoted in the kings' sagas, for instance, were composed by Icelandic prose writers in the twelfth and thirteenth centuries. Why would they bother?"[38]

The following is an excerpt from the Skaldic poem *Höfuðlausn* ("Head Ransom," translated by Hermann Palsson and Paul Edwards), which is found in *Egils saga*.

> When swords anoint
> What man is saved?
> Who gets this point
> Is deep engraved:
> And men like oak
> From Odin's tree,
> Few words they spoke
> At that iron-play.[39]

34. Frank, "Skaldic Poetry," 175.

35. Ross, "From Iceland to Norway," 62. On similarities of Skaldic poetry to Homeric, see Hollander, *The Skalds*, 26.

36. Poole, "Composition Transmission in Performance," 42.

37. Ibid.; contra Bjarni Einarsson. Alison Finlay has shown that attempts to prove dependence on thirteenth-century continental troubadours are mistaken (Finlay, "Skalds," 106–7, 118, 150).

38. Jesch, "Sagas," 9.

39. Palsson and Edwards, *Egil's Saga*, 159.

Arabic *Suwālif*

This section engages in a bit of conjecture that the present author has little place undertaking. Clearly the long, epic *siyar* cannot have originated orally in their extended form. The *sīra* is an extensive oral production that takes days to present in its entirety (something that rarely happens). Is it not likely that there were shorter building blocks of oral literature that worked their way together to form the long epic song? Poems on the theme of the Bani Hilal Bedouin migrations are attested by Ibn Khaldun,[40] and these written "gobbets" must have had oral counterparts.

There is an oral historical narrative genre in Arabia called *suwālif* (sing. *sālfih*). Not to be confused with *suwālīf* (sing. *sūlāfih*), which are tall tales or "old wives'" tales, *suwālif* deal with supposedly real events or social circumstances in the past.[41] Nevertheless, the *suwālif* are not always related in chronological order, a small detail or tangential digression may easily develop into a full episode, dialogue may be invented, and the storyteller/bard is really "transforming the historical event into an artistic product."[42] Incidental elements of one *sālfih* can easily become the impetus for launching into an entirely different story; when this happens in performance and is then repeated that way by the next bard, a conflation results.[43] *Suwālif* are preserved orally and passed down from generation to generation.[44] Some modern *suwālif* narrate events of nearly two hundred years ago.[45]

Like the Icelandic sagas, *suwālif* are interspersed with poetry that is used to corroborate the narrative.[46] Sometimes the story serves merely as the background for the poems, but no story is thought to be complete without a poem.[47] As with Parry and Lord's original insight (and somewhat like Campbell's User Theory), "the flexible structure and the unfixed language of the *sālfih* can give rise to the proliferation of versions," none

---

40. Connelly, *Arab Folk Epic*, 26.

41. Sowayan, "The Bedouin," 66.

42. Ibid., 66–68.

43. Ibid.," 69. This is called *as-suwalif tijīb as-suwālif*, "stories bring to mind other stories."

44. Ingham, "The *Sālfah* as a Narrative Genre," 6.

45. Sowayan, *The Arabian Oral Historical Narrative*, 5.

46. Sowayan, "The Bedouin," 71; Ingham, "*Sālfah*," 7.

47. Ingham, "*Sālfah*," 13.

of them telling the full story.[48] For each new bard creates anew the composition and actual wording of the narrative.[49] There will be variations of length, style, even point of view.[50] And yet, "specific turns of phrase describing important phases of the action [gobbets] do recur in separate renderings,"[51] "even though these might violate the intention of the speaker or the context of the event somewhat"[52] The embedded poetry does not change from performance to performance.[53]

Bruce Ingham has suggested that *suwālif* are sometimes the building blocks of *siyar*.[54] Although true *suwālif* are confined to central Arabia and the Syrian desert,[55] there are links between the two Arabic genres. Some Bedouin renderings of the Bani Hilal stories are not different in character from the *sālfih*.[56] I am not aware if possible links between the two have been explored in any detail and am certainly not qualified to add my support to Ingham. Yet it will be worthwhile to consider *suwālif* as an auxiliary to Eddic and Skaldic poetry in the comparisons that follow. The following is an excerpt from a Shammari *sālfih*, translated by Sowayan:[57]

> Low flying vultures circled over us,
> Certain to gorge themselves on our enemy's flesh.
> There lies Rija in the field of the valiants.
> No reward except winds blowing dust over him.
> Such is the reward of a man who hastens to meet us
> Risking his life to get the stallion or our camel mounts.
> And there was Muhammad, blood flowing from his right side.
> The shield of fair maidens had knocked him down.

48. Sowayan, "The Bedouin," 73; *The Arabian Oral Historical Narrative*, 13.

49. Kurpershoek, *Oral Poetry and Narratives from Central Arabia* 1:60.

50. Sowayan, *The Arabian Oral Historical Narrative*, 13.

51. Ingham, "Sālfah," 6, 28; Kurpershoek, *Oral Poetry*, 1.25–26.

52. Sowayan, *The Arabian Oral Historical Narrative*, 57.

53. Ingham, "Sālfah," 7.

54. Ibid., 10.

55. Ingham, "Sālfah," 6.

56. Ibid., 10.

57. *Arabian Oral Historical Narrative*, 127.

6

Towards Identifying the Oral in the Old Testament

From Hermann Gunkel to Theodor Gaster, biblical scholars customarily argued for the oral origin of biblical text by pointing out the use of a standard mythological vocabulary drawn from ancient Near Eastern prototypes (*Stoffgeschichte*).[1] Most recently, this has been the argument of Yair Zakovitch.[2] While Israel did borrow, reuse, rephrase, and respond to Canaanite (and Mesopotamian) myths abundantly,[3] one cannot simply assume the epic roots of biblical narrative and an oral means of their importation from the Canaanite and Mesopotamian world.[4]

It was also common to enumerate supposed characteristics of oral style that originated in the scholar's own "common sense": "introductory clauses giving the setting in time,"[5] repetition,[6] rhythmic diction,[7] and deictic expressions that "would be intelligible only if accompanied by a gesture on the part of the speaker."[8] For Ivan Engnell, "analysis of tradition technique, the combination of different complexes according

---

1. Gaster, *Myth*, xxviii.

2. Zakovitch, "Yes, There Was an Israelite Epic," 20, 24.

3. See Miller, "The Origin of the Zion Hymns," 667–75. Less discussed are the interrelations between Jewish and other Aramaic literatures from ca. 500 BCE to 1000 CE; Jason, "A Study of Israelite," 95.

4. Thompson, "Why Talk?" 4. Rofé considers oral "legends that solely expressed wonder at heroic deeds that were accomplished by *human strength*, without even a suggestion of any divine role in the events" (Rofé, *Introduction*, 130–31; italics original).

5. Gaster, *Myth*, xliv.

6. Ibid., xlvii.

7. Causse, *Plus vieux*, 16.

8. Gaster, *Myth*, xlviii.

to particular cognate words and similar themes . . . is often conclusive for determining whether the transmission is oral."[9] More recently, Claus Westermann stressed simple, memorable forms of preliterate usage.[10]

Frank Polak's work is uncommon in its continued attempt to identify orally derived texts in the Hebrew Bible by linguistic criteria.[11] Polak suggests a number of linguistic features that distinguish oral prose language from written, including a scarcity of embedded subordinate clauses, the scarcity of long noun strings relative to the number of clauses, and infrequent use of references by independent pronouns and deictic particles.[12] While he may be correct that such features characterize earlier Hebrew language,[13] his conclusion that they are also telltale signs of orality is conjectural (see chapter 1, above).[14] Purely linguistic criteria should be used with great caution, as the oral-formulaic movement discovered. "Indeed, it is very difficult to identify material which may be very close to oral performance."[15] In fact, Skaldic poetry is so intricate and turgid that "if we were not sure for other reasons that most skaldic verse was composed and received orally in preliterary times, the style and manner of the verse would suggest that it was literary and meant to be read."[16]

Some evidence particular to the biblical text itself suggests oral derivation. One piece of evidence is the sometimes sloppy competition between traditions in a given section of the Bible.[17] "Many texts, such as Exod 3–6, remain wholly unreadable as story."[18] If we decide that the final editors of the Bible are anything other than copyists bound to include what they have received in writing, then the "as many as five different accounts tumbl[ing] over each other, trying to find their place in the

9. Engnell, *A Rigid Scrutiny*, 5.

10. Westermann, *Das Mündliche Wort*, 56; so too Causse, *Plus vieux*, 21.

11. Polak, "Style Is More than Person," 38–103. Ivan Engnell had earlier explored psychological aspects of Hebrew tenses as signs of orality (Engnell, *Rigid Scrutiny*, 4).

12. Polak, "The Oral and the Written," 59, 86–87.

13. Ibid., 78, 100–101.

14. Niditch, "The Challenge of Israelite Epic," 281; Niditch, *Judges*, 16–17.

15. Culley, "Five Tales of Punishment," 26.

16. Faulkes, *Poetical Inspiration*, 25.

17. Lods, *Histoire de la littérature hébraïque*, 129.

18. Thompson, "Why Talk about the Past?" 14.

tradition . . . collected and interpreted, and the tradition is still arguing theologically about its variants," could be signs of orality.[19]

There are several examples of the opposite extreme—where there is not a surplus of competing congeries of traditions but a strange lack of traditions, with only tantalizing soupçons left to us in the written text. Some such exiguous examples include the nonstory of Nimrod (Gen 10:9), or of the giants Sheshai, Ahiman, and Talmai, who fought Caleb at Hebron (Num 13:22; Judg 1:8).[20] These are at least allusions to other stories, stories that cannot all have been in the "stream of tradition" solely in writing. But they are probably also individual components for story-tellers, short stories of only a few sentences, which connect occasionally to cycles—that is, bare gobbets.[21] These occur in the Eddic poetry, also, as in the elusive reference to Odin hanging on a tree in *Runatals þáttr Óðins* (*Hávamal*, 140–41). As in the Norse tradition, such "*disjecta membra* testify to the much fuller forms that these poems must have assumed once."[22]

On a somewhat related note, David Carr cites "a number of indicators that point to probable Northern origins for early pentateuchal traditions,"[23] most notably the parallels between Moses and Jeroboam,[24] that suggest the stream of tradition between the stories' origins and their writing. Finally, we might observe verses (from the Pentateuch?) that appear again and again throughout the Bible without identification of source, such as "The LORD, the LORD, a God merciful and gracious, slow to anger and abounding in steadfast love and faithfulness" (Exod 34:6; Pss 86:15; 103:8; 145:8; Joel 2:13; Jon 4:2; Neh 9:17).

Nevertheless, one could counter, as Thompson does, that *all* of these things are merely evidence of intertextuality, and not of orality. They show that the biblical text drew on many traditions and reworked those traditions, but in no way do they prove that those traditions were oral. The northern sources, untold stories, competing traditions, and stream of tradition could have been all in writing—either a late writing tradition as Thompson supposes or an early one as do Hess and others. There

---

19. Lods, "Le Rôle de la tradition," 62. The quote is from Thompson, "Why talk?" 14.

20. Lods, *Histoire de la littérature hébraïque*, 130. See below.

21. Seybold, "Zur mündlichen," 143.

22. Townsend, "Norse Poets and English Kings," 269.

23. Carr, "The Rise of Torah," 46.

24. Miller, "The 'Biography' of Moses."

is abundant evidence that editorial activity took place after stories were conscribed to writing, evidence ranging from the *Epic of Gilgamesh*'s extensive incorporation of the actual texts of its intertexts to the editorial activity evident in the Samaritan Pentateuch and Dead Sea Scrolls.

There are two "internal" suggestions of orality that are not subject to this criticism. The first of these is cases of variant readings that cannot be graphic, that is, errors or mistakes in the Hebrew text that cannot be the result of textual confusion (like the mistaking of a *resh* for a *dalet*), but that must be the result of mistakes in hearing.[25] A famous modern example is the corruption of *L'Enfant de Castile* into the "Elephant and Castle" pub in England. There are examples from orally transmitted Arabic literature,[26] and numerous examples found by Redford in orally derived Egyptian literature.[27]

Helmer Ringgren catalogued a number of these in the variants between Psalm 18 and 2 Samuel 22. For example, in v. 32 (of each), Psalm 18 has מבלעדי, while 2 Sam 22 has זולתי.[28] So, too, the variant in v. 38 of ואשיגם and ואשמידם.[29] Ringgren lists several other examples. On the other hand, the difference in v. 11 between וידא and וירא is clearly graphic.[30] Similar oral variants occur between Isa 37:22–35 and 2 Kgs 19:21–34; Isa 37:24's מרום and 2 Kgs 19:23's מלון.[31]

Still, one might argue that these might be merely *aural* variants. They only prove that the text was being dictated aloud; they say nothing about oral tradition. Ringgren cites a number of other variants between these pairs of passages[32] that "give us the impression that they must be due to mistakes within an oral transmission of a text,"[33] but these prove no more than any other doublets in the Bible. They could very well be the product of variant written traditions.

Several other options remain for us. First, some ethnographic generalizations about oral literature from various cultures could be

25. Ringgren, "Oral and Written Transmission," 36.

26. Ibid.

27. Redford, "Scribe and Speaker," 211.

28. Ringgren, "Oral and Written Transmission," 44.

29. Ibid.

30. Ibid., 43.

31. Ibid., 54.

32. Ibid., 43–45, 54.

33. Ibid., 57.

offered as characteristics to look for in the narrative books of the Hebrew Bible. If we wish to remain within the overall tradition of the Hebrew Bible, we might note that keys to oral transmission of the Mishnah included brevity,[34] singing (*t. Ohol.* 16.8; *t. Para* 4.7; *Meg.* 32a), systematic arrangement by numbers (*y. Šeqal* 5.1; e.g., *Yebam.* 1.1; *Ker.* 1.1; *Ṭohar.* 1.1; *B. Qam* 1.1; *Šabb.* 7.2), and literary clichés (e.g., *Meg.* 1.4–11; *Nazir* 9.2–4; *ʿArak.* 2.1; 3.1–5; *Nid.* 6.1–10). If we prefer to remain in the ancient Near East, Baines notes in Egypt repetitive stanza forms, organized but not narrowly repetitive language, and highly formed prosodic organization.[35]

If no cultural or chronological limits are demanded (and the ethnographic method does not demand them), then we might note that by and large oral poetry tends to be rigorously formalized, replete with markings of a very evident structuration, especially "in the most widely held opinion of ethnologists, the constant and perhaps universally definitive feature of oral poetry is the recurrence of diverse textual elements: every type of parallelism."[36] Cross-culturally, parallelism is often an indicator of orality, as among the Navajo, Zulu, and the Acholi of Uganda.[37] The *Song of Ullikummi* is replete with parallelism (as well as rhythm and formulaicism) in both Hittite and Hurrian.[38] Indeed, the parallelism of Hebrew poetry has regularly been considered a sign of its oral origin.[39]

Oral literature tends to be replete with apparent grammatical problems like event-heavy sentences, ambiguous references,[40] inconsistent deictic orientation (like Gaster's deictic gestures but contra Polak),[41] and other illogical imperfections that betray a lack of textual editing.[42] Stories that are the result of oral retelling tend to be humorous[43] and have few

---

34. Zlotnick, "Memory," 229.

35. Baines, *Visual and Written Culture*, 158–59. These are similarly indicated for Homer by Honko, "Text as Process and Practice," 19.

36. Zumthor, *Oral Poetry*; Jensen, "Performance," 47; Foley, *The Singer of Tales in Performance*, 86.

37. Kratz, "Persuasive Suggestions and Reassuring Promises," 42–67; Joubert, *The Power of Performance* 76, 138.

38. Archi, "Orality," 222–23.

39. Birkeland, *Zum Hebräischen*, 19; Engnell, *A Rigid Scrutiny*, 8.

40. Gordon, "Oral Tradition and the Sagas of Poets," 70.

41. Oesterreicher, "Types of Orality," 200.

42. Russo, "Oral Theory," 16.

43. Barber and Barber, *When They Severed*, 158.

characters, since the actions of the minor characters are eventually attributed to the major ones.[44] The actual instruction, "Hear!" can be meant quite literally, according to D. H. Green's extensive study of medieval oral literature.[45]

In the writings of Pausanias, indications of oral tradition include "connections between history and specific places, . . . stories that are connected to a peculiar aspect of local culture, such as unique customs or festivals or a special feature of the memorial landscape, for example peculiar monuments, works of art with special iconographic details, or unusual place names."[46] Such are the etiologies of the Hebrew Bible (e.g., Gen 19:15–22, on the name of the city Zoar; Exod 17:1–7 on the names "Massah" and "Meribah"; Num 11:3, 34 for "Taberah" and "Kibroth-hattaavah").[47] Many of the etiological explanations of names, for example, are so bad that the name cannot possibly have given rise to the story. When Baal's devotees come to kill Gideon, Gideon's father says, "Don't fight Baal's battles for him. If Baal is wronged, 'Let Baal Contend' with Gideon." And, with that, Gideon is renamed "Let Baal Contend," or Jerubbaal. Yet this meaning for Jerubbaal is impossible. Nowhere else does *yarub* occur as the jussive form of the Hebrew root ריב, "let him contend." Any Hebrew reader could see that the name would mean "May Baal contend *for* him," or if the root is instead רבב, "May Baal show himself great." Gideon's father, Joash, is interpreting precisely the opposite of what this form of name would have meant to someone who did not know the story.[48] The name cannot have given rise to the story; an existing folk motif (gobbet) must have been hung on an existing name.[49] But when does this "hanging" take place—in an oral or writing community? Presumably at a time when the object or place existed.[50] Particular locations are used in the *Iliad* as mnemonic

44. Ibid., 124–25.

45. Green, *Medieval Listening and Reading*, 81–82, 174.

46. Pretzler, "Pausanias," 246. For such in the *Iliad*, see Minchin, "Spatial Memory," 26.

47. Lods, *Histoire de la littérature hébraïque*, 130.

48. Block, "Will the Real Gideon Please Stand Up?," 359–60; Mobley, *The Empty Men*, 123.

49. Leson, "The Function of Etiological Legends"; Treitler, "Sinners and Singers," 144; Calvet, *La Tradition orale*, 81.

50. Niesiołowski-Spanò, "Two Aetiological Narratives in Genesis," 369.

devices, spatial memory clues for the oral storyteller.[51] And what is the antiquity of the etiological tales themselves?

We turn now to the second option that remains after our discussion of supposed internal evidence of orality. We might limit the comparative approach just provided to the two analogous cases outlined in this monograph: the Icelandic and the Arabian. We will consider the hallmarks of the oral language in the *suwālif* and its derived *sīra*, and of the Eddic and Skaldic poetry and derived sagas.

Redundancy occurs in the *suwālif* in several forms, including doubling the demonstrative pronoun, framing clauses by two identical independent pronouns referring to the same object, and adding the independent subject pronoun to the verb even where the verb's conjugation makes the subject perfectly clear.[52] Deictic particles are used preceding almost any kind of clause (e.g., *wlawinnah*).[53] The imperative is used regularly instead of the perfect or imperfect.[54] Paronomasia or punning (Arab. *zhar* or *jinās*) seems to be characteristic of the Arabian oral tradition.[55] Printed texts of the *Sīrat Banī Hilāl* contain few examples of paronomasia, while they are ubiquitous in oral versions.[56] Paronomasia is also found in Icelandic Skaldic poetry[57] and in ancient Egyptian oral literature (e.g., *Ipuwer*).[58] Paronomasia is found in the Ugaritic Baal Epic, while significantly less so in *Keret* and *Aqhat*.[59] It generally operates on the level of *sound* and so involves at least aurality.[60]

51. Minchin, "Spatial Memory," 10, 18.

52. Sowayan, "The Bedouin," 70–71; Sowayan, *The Arabian Oral Historical Narrative*, 49.

53. Ingham, "*Sālfah*," 23.

54. Sowayan, *The Arabian Oral Historical Narrative*, 47.

55. Connelly, *Arab Folk Epic*, 120.

56. Slyomovics, "The Death-Song," 63; Slyomovics, *The Merchant of Art*, 9; Reynolds, "*Sīrat Banī Hilāl*," 92; Canova, "Il Poeta Epico," 94; Schippers, "An Episode," 352–53.

57. Brink, "*Verba Volant*," 109. Cf. Russo, "Oral Theory," 13. One must be careful, however; there is abundant paronomasia in the Tell el-Amarna editions of *Adapa and the South Wind* and *Nergal and Ereshkigal*, both composed in writing (e.g., *EA* 356.29–32); Izreʾel, "The Study of Oral Poetry," 159–72, who also provides examples from *Macbeth*. These are, admittedly, signs of aurality.

58. Redford, "Scribe and Speaker," 207; Loprieno, "Puns and Word Play in Ancient Egyptian," 4, 8, 11.

59. Watson, "Puns Ugaritic Newly Surveyed," 117, 133.

60. Reckendorf, *Über Paronomasie*, 1, 19–23; Gliick, "Paronomasia in Biblical

In some of the Icelandic sagas, there are variant traditions of the same stories.[61] These are similar to the doublets and competing traditions discussed by Thompson and Ringgren. One particular example illustrates how some further precision might be added to Thompson and Ringgren's method. The account of the murder of Thorgrímr is found in both *Gísla saga* and *Droplaugarsona saga*. The account in *Gísla saga* preserves the variant that Thorgrímr was slain while engaged in (or about to engage in) the marital act with his wife Thordís. This is not merely "the residue of a tradition about the slaying of Thorgrímr,"[62] but a scene from a pre-Christian Icelandic pagan fertility rite. A variant tradition has Thorgrímr slain in the performance of this rite.[63] While the death of Thorgrímr was forty years before the conversion of Iceland in 1000, and before the advent of writing in Iceland that accompanied it, the sagas are from the twelfth century. The variant cannot be other than an oral tradition that survived the century and a half.

The pagan tradition is inconsistent with the Christian environment of the saga's writing. We might, therefore, look not merely for doublets in the Hebrew Bible (such as Abraham and Isaac with Abimelech at Gerar), but for variant traditions that preserve gobbets that are awkward in the religious and cultural environment of their written setting. The residue of Canaanite mythology that Gaster and others used as proof of orality is half of what is needed, just as Thompson and Ringgren's variants are half. The fullest evidence would be *variant* traditions that preserve gobbets of Canaanite mythology. From the "pagan side" of the oral tradition black box, we can predict that outright "heathen worship of individual gods" is not as likely to survive into canonical Israelite texts as would more innocuous elements "in happy accord with the concepts of folktales."[64] From the biblical side of this black box, we will not be looking for blatant polytheism (nor, fortunately, for mere veiled allusions), but for its non-threatening accessories.

Another way of looking at variant traditions would be noting cases where two versions of the same tale share *no* common orthography or

---

Literature," 50; Immanuel M. Casanowicz, "Paronomasia in the Old Testament," 105–6.

61. There are also variants between manuscripts of the same saga that, like Ringgren's, must at least be aural (Mitchell, "The Sagaman," 409).

62. Jón Aðalsteinsson, *A Piece of Horse Liver*, 98.

63. Ibid., 99.

64. Ibid., 111.

phraseology.[65] Such cases would not be likely from multiple *written* traditions; an oral explanation seems best.[66] Such variants must have lived within the stream of tradition orally "and altered in accordance with local vocabulary and traditions."[67] And if the variants go back to the prenormative religious period, so much the better.

Etiologies, too, can be important. Etiologies are attached to "phenomena from the past that contaminate the present."[68] Folk motifs are "hung" on these phenomena or their names (like the Arnthrudarstadir in *Hrafnkels saga Freysdða*, cited above). So too in Icelandic sagas, hooks for prose oral traditions included both Skaldic (and Eddic) poetry[69] and such "phenomena" as place-names,[70] or manmade objects or man-used natural objects that were thought to have had a history in the preliterate pagan past.[71] Some of these items never existed at all (e.g., the sword Jardhússnautr in *Flóamanna saga*).[72] Many were things that could be seen "unto this day" (e.g., the beaks of Thórir Skeggjason's ship in *Landnámabók*, or the stone at Raufarnes that Skalla-Grímr used as an anvil in *Egils saga*).[73] Perhaps items like King Og's bed in Ammon-Rabbah (Deut 3:11) are comparable: "For only Og the king of Bashan was left of the remnant of the Rephaim. Behold, his bed was a bed of iron. Is it not in Rabbah of the Ammonites? Nine cubits was its length, and four cubits its breadth, according to the common cubit."[74]

65. Mitchell, "The Sagaman," 410.

66. Mundal, "Oral or Scribal Variation," 220.

67. Gunnell, *"Grýla, Grýlur, Grøleks* and *Skeklers"* Online: http://jol.ismennt.is/english/gryla-terry-gunnell.htm/.

68. Leson, "The Function of Etiological Legends."

69. Perkins, "Objects and Oral Tradition," 242; Andersson, "From Tradition," 14.

70. Gunnell, "Narratives, Space and Drama," 18; Gunnell, "Legends and Landscape," 308.

71. Perkins, "Objects and Oral Tradition," 243.

72. Ibid., 243–44.

73. Ibid., 244. Similar, too, is the use of Skaldic verse in the sagas themselves. They are often put into the mouths of various characters. Such poems may or may not have existed at the time of the character, and if they did, may or may not have been spoken by the character. And some Skaldic poems were composed about artifacts (ibid., 260 n. 8; Gordon, "Oral Tradition and the Sagas of Poets," 71–72).

74. Whether or not this has analogies to Assyrian war trophies, it reads as an etiology. Maria Lindquist interprets it as a piece of anti-Assyrian resistance literature (written by a seventh-century author who knew iron was "like gold" in the thirteenth century) (Lindquist, "King Og's Iron Bed").

We might also look at the content of the Icelandic material in question. "Things that tend to be placed on record are those things which are out of the ordinary."[75] A "denial of authorship" is also common, claiming that words are the words of another.[76] These are also present in orally derived ancient Egyptian literature.[77] Some of these "denials of authorship," or designation of passages as the words of other individuals, can be phrased as if the quote in question were a "residual object" like the beaks of Thórir Skeggjason's ship or King Og's bed, as in the *sālfih* "*The Slave of the Sharif*" line, "*That* was when the Sharif said, 'What news, Bais?'"[78] This is much like 1 Sam 10:11–12 (and 19:24), "*That* was when it was said, 'Is Saul also among the prophets?'"

As stated previously, one of the main characteristics of Skaldic poetry is its use of kennings. In some ways, this is a subset of the Skaldic diction's fluency in paraphrasing by long lists of nouns.[79] Often these kennings contain the most archaic and obsolete words, many of them *hapax legomena*, such as are also found in some Eddic poetry.[80]

Moreover there is a development in the nature of the kennings.[81] If one visualizes the two (or more) contrasting elements of a kenning (e.g., "fish" and "valley" in "fish valley" = sea), the outcome can be bizarre to varying degrees.[82] The more bizarre the image, the easier it is to remember.[83] In fact, "one of the original functions of the images of the contrasting kennings, and indeed the system of kennings in general, must have been a mnemonic one."[84] "Various imagery and metaphors were drawn from the mnemonic technique, with its ingenious visual and pictorial methods."[85] The kennings of the oldest Skaldic poems (seventh and eighth

75. Gunnell, "*Grýla, Grýlur,* and *Grøleks.*"

76. Ranković, "Who Is Speaking?," 296.

77. Redford, "Scribe and Speaker," 214.

78. Ingham, "*Sālfah*," 15.

79. Nordal, *Tools of Literacy*, 5.

80. Brink, "*Verba Volant*," 107. There are some kennings in the Hebrew Bible, such as in Qoh 12:1–7, where in v. 3, "keepers of the house" means arms, "strong men" legs, "those that look out the window" eyes. The rest of the verses probably contain more kennings it is impossible to decipher.

81. Birgisson, "What Have We Lost by Writing?" 165.

82. Ibid., 166.

83. Ibid., 167, 176.

84. Ibid., 167; Foley, "Analogues: Modern Oral Epics," 203.

85. Ásdís Egilsdóttir, "From Orality to Literacy," 219.

centuries) are the most bizarre and also require the most visualization to understand: "fire-wolf," "house-thief in fire-stockings."[86] The kennings from the Christian skalds of later periods are different, less blended: "wolf of the tree" (for a bat), for example.[87] The "cognitive archaism" disappears in the written, literate world.[88] The use of similarly bizarre, "blended," "cognitively archaic" picturesque expressions is characteristic of *suwālif*.[89] We are thus looking for the uniquely *visualizable* in biblical metaphor.[90]

The Texts

This section is the most tentative part of the present book. We should be very wary of identifying orally derived bits in the Hebrew Bible. Yet in a study of this sort it is condign to do so. Sufficient conclusions have been drawn in the foregoing chapters to predict the features of such material and apply these predictions to the biblical text, not as some novel nostrum to replace the oral-formulaic test for orality, but as a cumulative set of attributes whose association is suggestive of orally derived literature.

This list is dependent on the comparative material amassed hitherto. We cannot simply assume that, for example, "certain phrases may even be markers of an Israelite ethnic genre comparable to 'epic.'"[91] There is little to suggest that temporal markers like "In those days" "mark tales of olden times" or "reveal certain linguistic markers of heroic and perhaps 'epic' material."[92] Nevertheless, the presentation of this section is exploratory; sciolism is not my intent.

We are looking for "gobbets," intentionally crafted *aides-mémoires* that are constitutive for narration. These will include storylines, textual elements such as images of situations, and some traditional phraseology. Some of these will be *disjecta membra*, fragments of unpreserved tales. The traditional phraseology may employ cliché, systematization by numeric schemes, uniquely visual metaphors, and parallelism. We will

86. Birgisson, "What Have We Lost by Writing?" 167–70.
87. Ibid., 170–71.
88. Ibid., 184.
89. Ingham, "*Sālfah*," 13, 18.
90. Béré, "*Auditor in fabula*," 1091.
91. Niditch, *Judges*, 14.
92. Ibid., 14–15.

look for ambiguous references, inconsistent deictic orientation, and other illogical imperfections. The contents might include humor, few characters, etiologies (such as of manmade objects "still visible," as Deut 3:11 says of Og's bed), and variant traditions that preserve Canaanite heritage or its nonthreatening elements. On a linguistic level, we will look for paronomasia, doubling the demonstrative pronoun (this does not occur in Hebrew, but there are similar constructions as we shall see), framing clauses by two identical independent pronouns referring to the same object, adding the independent subject pronoun to the verb even where the verb's conjugation make the subject perfectly clear (this is actually very common), and deictic particles preceding almost any kind of clause.

Let us begin with a brief discussion of paronomasia, since it, like parallelism, is so characteristic of oral literature worldwide. There are two basic kinds of paronomasia—rhetorical and grammatical;[93] the difference is that the latter requires a semantic relationship of the two words (verb + infinitive absolute, or verb + cognate accusative).[94] These may have nothing to do with orality,[95] although the nuances of their meaning are beyond the scope of this study.[96]

Rhetorical paronomasia "often contains a subtle and recondite *double entendre* which keeps the reader [listener] in suspense until its significance emerges into the light of day at the end of the oracle or enigmatic saying."[97] Rhetorical paronomasia can be further broken down into six categories. Equivocal puns are based on homonyms (double meaning of a single word or root), as in Jer 12:4 where the earth "mourns" or "is parched," both meanings of אבל. Such puns work fairly well in writing and will strike even a silent reader. They are common in late prophecy.[98] Metaphonic puns are nearly the same, the only change in the word necessary to produce the second meaning being a different vowel pointing.[99]

93. We may exclude the "accidental" paronomasia, where the coincidence was unavoidable, as, e.g., Ps 1:1 "אֲשֶׁר־הָאִישׁ־אַשְׁרֵי"; Casanowicz, "Paronomasia in the Old Testament," 105.

94. Lunn, "Paronomastic Constructions," 33–38, 45.

95. Casanowicz, "Paronomasia in the Old Testament," 105.

96. See Joüon, *Grammaire de l'hébreu biblique* (Rome: Pontifical Biblical Institute, 1923), 373, 486; Waltke and O'Connor, *An Introduction to Biblical Hebrew*, 584.

97. Guillaume, "Paronomasia in the Old Testament," 286.

98. Gliick, "Paronomasia," 53; Rendsburg, "Word Play in Biblical Hebrew," 182–85, 192.

99. Gliick, "Paronomasia," 61–66; Rendsburg, "Word Play in Biblical Hebrew," 157.

For example, Ps 49:13 refers to man as "in splendour" בִּיקָר, v. 21 as "cattle," בְּקָר. Associative puns would also work in writing. These are puns that involve mixed metaphors or similar plays on words.[100] The remaining three types depend on hearing the words aloud. Parasonancy involves rhymes (Job 17:10 אֻלָּם . . . כֻּלָּם); assonance/alliteration must hit the ear for effect (1 Sam 28:16–17 עָרֶךָ . . . לְרֵעֶךָ); and farrago is when the sound of the words itself evokes an image (e.g., Gen 1:1 "tohu wa bohu"; Isa 8:1 "Maher-shalal-hashbaz").[101] It is these types of paronomasia that we are looking for, particularly examples where the written text does not suggest what the ear will detect, as when _tet_ is alliterated with _tav_, _het_ with _kaf_, and so on.[102] That many of the biblical puns also preserve archaic words further supports the traditional nature of such material.[103]

Of the many suggestions presented earlier in this chapter, the strongest potential oral texts are the disconnected gobbets: the non-story of Nimrod (Gen 10:9), and the giants Sheshai, Ahiman, and Talmai (Num 13:22; Judg 1:8). These seem much more likely than Northern origins, doublets, and other potential inter-textual cases. Here we have examples of the gobbets upon which oral literature depends. But the gobbets alone are preserved. They are bare and bereft of narrative content.

In Gen 10:8–12, a genealogy is interrupted by the brief account of Nimrod: "Cush fathered Nimrod; he was the first on earth to be a mighty man. He was a mighty hunter before theLORD. Therefore it is said, "Like Nimrod a mighty hunter before the LORD." 10 The beginning of his kingdom was Babel, Erech, Accad, and Calneh, in the land of Shinar. From that land he went into Assyria and built Nineveh, Rehoboth-Ir, Calah, and 12 Resen between Nineveh and Calah; that is the great city." Scholars have long tried to identify Nimrod with some historical person (Tukulti-Ninurta I and even Amenhotep III have been suggested) or non-Israelite deity (Marduk and Ninurta are common).[104] This quest seems oddly literalistic in the context of Genesis 1–11. Two aspects of the story are of interest for our purposes. First, the identification of Nimrod as the son of

---

100. Gliick, "Paronomasia," 72–74.

101. Ibid., 66–71, 75; Rendsburg, "Word Play in Biblical Hebrew," 198.

102. Casanowicz, "Paronomasia in the Old Testament," 107–8.

103. Ibid., 121.

104. Van der Toorn and Van der Horst, "Nimrod," 1–14; Levin, "Nimrod the Mighty," 356–59.

Cush in v. 8 makes little sense in light of the overwhelming Mesopotamian nature of the rest of his character. Rather than seek a Mesopotamian Cush (Speiser, Lipiński, Levin) or a North African Nimrod (Eduard Meyer, Kurt Sethe), it is more likely that the free-floating story of Nimrod has been artificially inserted into the genealogy and the first two words of Gen 10:8, יָלַד וְכוּשׁ, have been added in an attempt at a mortise and tenon joint.[105] The second item is in v. 9: "Therefore it is said, 'Like Nimrod a mighty hunter before the Lord.' This is the kind of displacement of authorship exemplified by the *sālfih* "*The Slave of the Sharif*" line, "*That* was when the Sharif said, 'What news, Bais?'" noted above. Nimrod traditions abounded in later Jewish tradition (e.g., 1QapGen 31), perhaps as early as Judith 5:6–8.

Sheshai, Ahiman, and Talmai are described as "sons of Anak," or Anakim, that is, giants, and appear multiple times in Numbers and Judges. They are first met by the Israelite spies at Hebron in Num 13:22: "They went up into the Negeb and came to Hebron. Ahiman, Sheshai, and Talmai, the descendants of Anak, were there." In Judg 1:20, they are driven out of Hebron by Caleb, a datum also found in Josh 15:13–14. But in Judg 1:10 it is said that the tribe of Judah defeated them. And this is in spite of the statement in Josh 11:21 that no Anakim remained in the land after Joshua. Rather than see this as different views of the same event—conflicting contemporary accounts by different groups who wanted to take credit,[106] it is best to see these as distinct gobbets, isometric but separate story kernels.[107] They circulated independently in the Israelite tradition, all of them alluding to more substantial stories not preserved in the Hebrew Bible.[108] Only the name Sheshai occurs outside of the Hebrew Bible, as the name of one of the first Hyksos pharaohs of Egypt, Šš'. Curiously, the seeming successor to this pharaoh was Meruserre Yaqub-har or Ya'qub-Ba'al, who will reappear in discussion of further texts below.[109] It is also worth noting that the slaying of three giants (or oc-

---

105. I thank my graduate student Timothy Snow for this insight. Early scholarship assigned the Nimrod pericope to J and the rest of the chapter to P, but this makes no difference for the current discussion (Levin, "Nimrod," 355). A recent reading of the passage as integral to Genesis 10–11 is Hom, "'A Mighty Hunter,'" 68.

106. Bowman, "Narrative Criticism," 29.

107. In this, the older commentaries were correct: Moore, *Judges*, 49; Hertzberg, *Josua, Richter, Ruth*, 152–54.

108. Van Seters, "The Terms," 74–75.

109. Ryholt, *The Political Situation in Egypt*, 99–100; Edwards et al., *The History of the*

casionally a three-headed giant) is a standard folklore motif throughout the world.[110]

For larger pericopes, we can begin with some comparative Norse material. In each of the examples that follow, I provide first a Norse text, without comment. This is intentional. If gobbets are handed down, then we risk fragmentation of literary context if we do not gain a conceptual overview of a whole gobbet.[111] I make no claims about the applicability of the texts Norse chosen in each case; it is a subjective choice, based on an integralist reading of both it and the biblical comparand. Detailed discussion of the biblical pericope then follows.

The following is an excerpt from the Eddic poem *Atlakviða* (4–5), as translated by William Morris and Eirikr Magnusson:

4

Shield shall ye have there
And spears ashen-shafted,
Helms ruddy with gold,
And hosts of the Huns;
Saddle-gear silver gilt,
Shirts red as blood,
The hedge of the warwife,
And horses bit-griping.

5

And he saith he will give you
Gnitaheath widespread,
And whistling spears
And prows well-gilded,
Might wealth
With the stead of Danpi,
And that noble wood
Men name the Mirkwood.[112]

Middle East and the Aegean Region, 1800–1380 BC, 59–60.

110. Stephenson, *The Jack Tales*; Davis, *Jack Always Seeks His Fortune*, 83–98, 119–31; Moore, *The Folk-Lore of the Isle of Mann*, 97.

111. Rosenblatt, *The Reader, the Text, the Poem*, 36–50; Kuiken et al., "Forms of Self-Implication," 171–203.

112. Morris and Magnusson, *The Story of the Volsungs*, 1152.

To this let us compare Genesis 49, Jacob's final blessing, specifically vv. 9–12 and 22–25 (my own translation, with minimal textual notes provided):[113]

> Judah is a lion's cub;
> from the prey, my son, you have gone up.
> He crouches, he lies stretched out as a lion
> and as a lioness; who dares rouse him?
> The scepter shall not depart from Judah,
> nor the commander's mace from between his feet,[114]
> until he comes to Shiloh;[115]
> and to him shall be the obedience of the peoples.
> Binding his male donkey to the vine[116]
> and his purebred ass to the ripe vine,[117]
> he has washed his garments in wine
> and his vesture in the blood of grapes.
> His eyes will be dull with wine,
> and his teeth whiter than milk.
> Joseph is the son of a fruit-bearer,[118]
> a fruitful bough by a spring;
> his daughters[119] have climbed over the wall.
> The archers bitterly attacked him,
> shot at him,[120] and harassed him severely,
> yet his bow remained steady;
> his arms were agile
> by the hands of the Mighty One of Jacob
> by the name of the Shepherd,[121] the Stone of Israel,
> by the God of your father, who will help you,
> by Shaddai, who will bless you

---

113. Gunkel considered this oral literature, but that has no bearing on my choice of it here. See Herman Gunkel, *Genesis* (2nd ed.) 420–21; Gunkel, *Genesis* (3rd ed.), 477.

114. "Feet" being a common euphemism for genitals.

115. Since the verb is masculine, this seems the best translation of the Masoretic Text (MT).

116. The archaic third-person masculine singular ending on "donkey."

117. The idiom for "purebred ass" is known from Mari (Held, "Philological Notes," 32–40).

118. Or, "one of [lit., 'a son of'] the פֹּרָת [fem. of פֶּרֶ =ʽonager']." I take the word to be a Qal active participle of פרה.

119. Or "wild asses"; cf. Arab. *banāt saʿdat*.

120. Assuming the root is רבב and not ריב.

121. Revocalizing following *Targum Onqelos*.

with blessings of heaven above,
blessings of Tehum lying beneath,
blessings of the breasts and of the womb.

The formal similarities are the first suggestions that this passage should be considered for orally derived features. On a linguistic level, parallelism is abundant. Were we to consider the entire poem, paronomasia is found, first in v. 8: יְהוּדָה ... יוֹדוּךְ.[122] Verse 16 provides an etiology of the name "Dan": דָּן יָדִין, "Dan shall *dîn*"; this is also paronomasia. As for content, there is a great deal of illogical and ambiguous syntax. How can you tie a donkey to a grape vine? Why wash a garment red in wine? What is being said about Joseph's daughters?

There also seems to be a great deal of Canaanite baggage here.[123] First, the title "Mighty One of Jacob," translates אֲבִיר יַעֲקֹב being a word that is frequently used of bulls and in Ugaritic means "bull" (*UT* 3.39). The "bull of Jacob" is related to Jeroboam's cultic bulls at Dan and Bethel, and in light of the association of the bull with El (*KTU* 1.12:I.4–8) and Baal (KTU 1.5:V) at Ugarit, and Hyksos scarabs with Yaʿqub-Baʿal, it makes sense to consider this a "Canaanite holdover," or at least, "non-normative Yahwism that is contiguous with the Late Bronze age."[124] The name Yaʿqub-Baʿal occurs several times at Ugarit, but it is also the name of the Hyksos pharaoh otherwise known as Meruserre Yaʿqub-har, discussed above.[125]

Another such example is the reference to "breasts and womb" in v. 25. This is a euphemism for Athirat and Anat in Ugaritic literature.[126] There is paronomasia between the "breasts," שָׁדַיִם, and the name of God, שַׁדַּי, in the same verse. If the etymology of the divine name Shaddai has anything to do with breasts,[127] this is also a "non-expunged vestige." The

122. Casanowicz, "Paronomasia in the Old Testament," 132.

123. I make no claim about the age of the text. It has been "almost unanimously considered to be old"; Raymond de Hoop, *Genesis 49*, 55. De Hoop has challenged this early dating (ibid., 62, 78).

124. Rose, "Names of God in the Old Testament," 1004–11; cf. Whitley, "Archaeological Evidence for Conceptual Metaphors," 21–22, on religious continuity over multiple ethnolinguistic groups.

125. Dijkstra, "Jacob," 459–61.

126. Korpel, *A Rift in the Clouds*, 31, 588; Moor, *An Anthology*, 257–58, no.218.

127. Biale, "The God with Breasts," 240–56; Lutzky, "Shadday as a Goddess Epithet," 15–36.

entire context of vv. 10–13 and 25 link the ruler to ensured fertility, which is another non-normative religious notion.[128]

Finally the insertion of the poem into the narrative at this point is somewhat artificial. While the narrative requires some blessing from Jacob here, the poem only occasionally appears to be such a thing (vv. 4, 8, 26).[129] The relationship of the poem to the surrounding "saga" is congruent to that of the Skaldic poem in an Icelandic saga: "The accounts of the circumstances purportedly prompting these and other *lausavísur* sometimes seem suspiciously ex post facto."[130]

There is abundant evidence therefore to consider Genesis 49 an orally derived text.[131]

Next we consider a Skaldic poem, the *Höfuðausn* or "Head Ransom" of Egil Skallagrímsson, stanzas 1–2, 8–9, in W. C. Green's translation:

1

I launched my floating oak
When loosening ice-floes broke,
My mind a galleon fraught
With load of minstrel thought.

2

A prince doth hold me guest,
Praise be his due confess'd:

8

Breast-plates ringing crashed,
Burning helm-fire flashed,
Biting point of glaive
Bloody wound did grave.
Odin's oaks (they say)
In that iron-play

128. Keel, *The Symbolism*, 285.

129. Hylander, *Der Literarische Samuel-Saul-Komplex*, 194. De Hoop's (*Genesis 49*, 79) argument that the poem can only be read in the context of the surrounding narrative is circular: "The isolation of Genesis 49 from its literary context is mainly based on a form-critical classification instead of on literary-critical arguments. Theoretically this is impossible because form criticism is not a method developed for this application."

130. Poole, "Composition Transmission," 57.

131. De Hoop's assembly of ancient Akkadian and Egyptian and modern Arabic analogies neither adds to nor detracts from this conclusion; *Genesis 49*, 258–69, 281–82, 314.

Baldric's crystal blade
Bowed and prostrate laid.

9

Spears crossing dashed,
Sword-edges clashed:
Glory and fame
Gat Eric's name.

To this compare the following excerpts from Numbers 21:

14 Therefore it is said in the Book of the Wars of the Lord,
"Waheb in Suphah, and the valleys of the Arnon,
15   and the slope of the valleys
      that extends to the seat of Ar,
      and leans to the border of Moab."
16 And from there they continued to Beer; that is the well of which
the Lord said to Moses, "Gather the people together, so that I may
give them water." 17 Then Israel sang this song [שִׁירָה]:
      "Spring up, O well!—Sing to it!—
18   the well that the princes made,
      that the nobles of the people dug,
      with the scepter and with their staffs."
27 Therefore the ballad singers [הַמֹּשְׁלִים] say,
      "Come to Heshbon, let it be built;
let the city of Sihon be established.
28   For fire came out from Heshbon,
flame from the city of Sihon.
      It devoured Ar of Moab,
and swallowed the heights of the Arnon.
29   Woe to you, O Moab!
You are undone, O people of Chemosh!
      He has made his sons fugitives,
and his daughters captives,
to an Amorite king, Sihon.
30   So we overthrew them;
Heshbon, as far as Dibon, perished;
and we laid waste as far as Nophah;
fire spread as far as Medeba."

The narrative surrounding these poems indicates both written and
oral preservation.[132] The second poem (vv. 17–18) was certainly not com-

132. Christensen considers vv. 14–15 to be the opening lines of the "narrative poem"

posed by the author of the prose for the occasion, as it bears little resemblance to the narrative of v. 16. The third poem (vv. 27–30) also alludes to traditions nowhere preserved in the prose: the fire from Heshbon, Ar, and Nophah.[133] Yet these place-names may serve as spatial memory cues for those traditions. Verse 29 reappears minus its final clause embedded in an oracle of Jeremiah in Jer 48:46, which might be evidence of a free-floating gobbet.[134]

Parallelism is readily apparent. The designation of Moab as "People of Chemosh" seems uncharacteristic of normative Yahwism. While the association of Moab and Chemosh is common (Jer 48:13; 1 Kgs 11:33), the designation of Moab as "his people" is more reminiscent of Jephthah's speech in Judg 11:24: "Will you not possess what Chemosh your god gives you to possess? And all that the LORD our God has dispossessed before us, we will possess." It is, like the death of Thorgrímr, a pagan tradition inconsistent with the environment of the surrounding saga's writing. The invocation to the well itself in vv. 17–18 is likewise a bit animistic.[135] Antonin Causse cited two similar modern Arabic chants:[136]

> *Jaillis, onde, coule à flots!*
> *Puisse Allah t'abreuver, ô puits*
> *Avec la pluie en abondance!*

Grôttasöngr is an Eddic poem from outside of the Codex Regius. Its stanzas 18–19, translated by W. H. Auden and P. B. Taylor read:

18
The hands shall hold handles hard, bloodstained weapons.
Wake up, Frode! Wake up, Frode,
If you would hear our songs and our sayings of long ago.

19
Fire I see burning east of the fort;
Call up the couriers, call for the beacons!

Book of the Wars of the Lord, but his reconstruction and translation of the text is amazingly speculative (Christensen, "Numbers 21:14–15," 359–60).

133. The translation here, which is the English Standard Version, follows the Septuagint and Samaritan Pentateuch for the final line, which in the Hebrew is, "Nophah, which is as far as Medeba."

134. Schmitt, "Das Hesbonlied," 30–31.

135. Causse, *Plus vieux*, 16.

136. Ibid., n. 1.

A warrior horde shall o'errun this place
And burn the Budlung's [King's] dwelling.

To this we might compare Balaam's fourth oracle in Numbers 24, especially vv. 17–19:

> 17 I see him, but not now;
> I behold him, but not near:
> a star shall come out of Jacob,
> and a scepter shall rise out of Israel;
> it shall crush the corners of Moab
> and break down all the sons of Sheth.
> 18 Edom shall be dispossessed;
> Seir also, his enemies, shall be dispossessed.
> Israel is doing valiantly.
> 19 And one from Jacob shall exercise dominion
> and destroy the survivors of cities!"

Of course, there is again parallelism. The contents are very ambiguous, especially in v. 17. There is deictic orientation (but not deictic particles) in v. 17, and that is also inconsistent. There are many "broken connections, obvious gaps, and repetitions."[137] Were we to continue another verse, into v. 20 ("I have taken him to bless; if he has blessed, I cannot revoke it"), the identification of the first-person elements is quite uncertain, since considering it to be Balaam presents many problems.[138] The metaphorical images are bizarre, as the scepter and star rise out of Israel to crush Moab's "corners." In 23:21, the cliché אָוֶן . . . עָמָל (cf. Hab 1:3; Ps 55:1; Isa 59:4; Job 15:35) is used.[139] Although there is no paraonomasia in this oracle, there is in the third oracle. In 24:8, there is וְחִצָּיו יִמְחָץ, seemingly intentional since a plural is expected, referring to צָרִים.[140] In the fourth oracle (24:15–19), there is no clear addressee at all. It might be Jacob, Moab, or Balak.[141] The Balaam oracles overall evince almost no independent use of the preterite verb, while the imperfect yaqtul (and not the participle) is used archaically for simple present and immediate future.[142]

137. Albright, "The Oracles of Balaam," 226.
138. Notarius, "Poetic Discourse," 63.
139. Casanowicz, "Paronomasia in the Old Testament," 124.
140. Ibid., 136.
141. Notarius, "Poetic Discourse," 65.
142. Ibid., 85.

Of course, there are late linguistic usages in the Balaam oracles (although the archaic elements are used quite consistently),[143] but I am suggesting nothing about the dating of these texts by suggesting oral derivation.[144] The Balaam texts from Deir 'Allah attest to the widespread circulation in writing and, since the Israelite author was not copying from the plaster of Deir 'Allah, oral tradition of stories about Balaam the prophet. There are other *disjecta membra*, fragments of unpreserved tales about Balaam in the Bible itself, as the passage in Num 31:16 that says Balaam had instigated the idolatry at Peor. Finally, the very appearance of a non-Israelite prophet who really hears the word of the LORD seems awkward in the religious and cultural environment of the written setting.

The next comparative text to present is the Eddic poem, *Helgakviða Hundingsbana in Fyrri* I, translated by Lee M. Hollander, from which are these excepts:

1

'Twas in olden times, as eagles screamed
and holy streams flowed from the Heaven-Fells,
when in Brálund Borghild bore to the world
a hero highhearted, Helgi by name.

11

Then Hunding's sons for hoard and rings
swiftly summoned King Sigmund's son,
thirsted, forsooth, to repay the thane
for their father's fall and wealth from him taken.

32

Asked then Guthmund, of goodly kin:
"Who the highborn hero, leading
these hosts hither to harry on us?"

---

143. Ibid., 86. For discussion of the dating of the text, see Schmitt, "Das Hesbonlied," esp. 28, 34; Gass, "Modes of Divine Communication," 19.

144. Hylander, *Literarische Samuel-Saul-Komplex,* 194.

Judges 5, the Song of Deborah,[145] presents a complex interplay of various poems, perhaps not originally related to each other.[146] If the poetry is divided according to the number of words per stich (colon), there is first a song with tetralexic (four-word) stichs in vv. 2–3, 5, 26b, 28, and 30. A second song with trilexic stichs is present in vv. 4, 26a, and 29. There is a very archaic snippet in tetralexic distichs, a form found in Ugaritic texts (e.g., *Aqhat KTU* 1.17.ii 27–29; 1.17. v 4–5, 13–15, 33–35), in v. 25. The enclitic *mem* coordinating the two lines here is similarly used in Ugaritic and Phoenican (e.g., Karatepe inscription; CIS 119.2 = *KAI* 59; KI 37.2 = KAI U8). There are marginal notes, probably completely unrelated, in vv. 6a and 31. The remainder of the chapter varies from the untranslatable v. 8 (and vv. 15a and 21b nearly so) to the clear vv. 17b–18.

I present some portions of the Song of Deborah here, deliberately chosen to reflect *Helgakviða Hundingsbana* I. First, here is the opening portion of the tetralexic-stich song, in my translation. The translation of much of Judges 5 is dubious, and each translation choice will not be defended here:

> When the Pharaohs ruled in Israel[147]
> When the people volunteered
> Bless the LORD
> Hear, O kings. Give ear, O rulers:
> I, of the LORD I will sing,
> I will sing about the LORD, the God of Israel

Here is a portion of the "main text" of Judges 5:

> Then down came the remnant of the nobles
> The people of the LORD came down for me
> Among the champions
> From Ephraim is their ancestry, in Amalek,
> Following you, Benjamin, with your kin;

145. A Parry-Lord examination of Judges 5 was undertaken by Heda Jason (in modern Hebrew) in "Deborah and Barak; and by Robert Kawashima in "From Song to Story," 155. Kawashima's construct has an oral original in which "Deborah and Barak" are actually theophanies, God's lightning (cf. Ps 18:15) and "bees" (Deut 1:44) (Kawashima, "From Song to Story," 161–62). Most of the events of Judges 4 are inventions of the writer as he works with the song (ibid., 166–68).

146. For discussion, although a different division scheme than mine, see Echols, "*Tell Me, O Muse*"; H.-D. Neef, *Deboraerzählung und Deboralied*, a redactional analysis of Judges 4–5, neglects many issues and contributes little original.

147. Miller, "When Pharaohs Ruled," 650–54.

From Machir the lictors[148] came down
And from Zebulon those who carry
The scribe's fasces.[149]

Finally, here is a portion from late in the tetralexic-stich song:

She looked down through the window,
Wailing,[150] the mother of Sisera, through the lattice.
"Why is his chariot late in coming;
Why do the hoof-beats of his chariot tarry?"

Judges 5 is replete with parallelism. It is also filled with ambigui-
ties, even when the translation is clear. Who chose new gods in v. 8?
Who are the arrow-makers between the reservoirs in v. 11? What city
gates are meant in v. 11b? Cliché is used in v. 5, with the expression
"the mountains melted," found in Ps 97:5; Isa 34:3; Mic 1:4; etc. Several
examples of paronomasia are present. The most significant is in v. 12:
מְחָקָה רֹאשׁוֹ וּמָחֲצָה .Verse 26 shows עוּרִי עוּרִי דְּבוֹרָה עוּרִי עוּרִי דַּבְּרִי־שִׁיר.[151]
The extended paronomasia in v. 4, יהוה בְּצֵאתְךָ מִשֵּׂעִיר בְּצַעְדְּךָ מִשְּׂדֵה bears
some relationship to Ps 68:8: אֱלֹהִים בְּצֵאתְךָ לִפְנֵי עַמֶּךָ בְּצַעְדְּךָ.[152]

The prose "saga" into which the Song of Deborah has been placed
treats Judges 5 as the victory hymn of Deborah and Barak.[153] JudgES
5:10–11 indicate oral transmission. Antonin Causse cites a similar victory song of Chief ʿAwdeh Abu Tayih of the Howeitat Bedouin after raids
on the Shararat of southern Transjordan.[154] The surrounding narrative of
Judges 4 is almost a Lordian "theme," a type-scene where the male general
will not go into battle without the brave woman taking the lead (Judg
4:9), to which *Eiríks saga rauða* 11 is quite comparable: "Why do you flee
such miserable opponents, men like you who look to me to be capable of

---

148. Cf. Gen 49:10.

149. Not "pen."

150. Piel of בבי, an Aramaism, with adverbial use of the prefixing ("imperfect") form.

151. Casanowicz, "Paronomasia in the Old Testament," 131, 141.

152. Ibid., 153.

153. Contrary to the assertion by Kawashima that "Without the story to prop it up,
much of the song's underlying fabula would be lost" (*Biblical Narrative*, 20; the quote
reappears in Kawashima, "From Song to Story," 154), I do not believe much of the song
has much to do with the story of Judges 4. Kawashima is forced to argue that "the prose
historian misreads the song" to explain the differences (Kawashima, *Biblical Narrative*,
23; Kawashima, "From Song to Story," 152, 164).

154. Causse, *Plus vieux*, 47.

killing them off like sheep? Had I a weapon I am sure I would fight better than any of you."[155]

Last, consider some further Skaldic poems of Egil Skallagrímsson, in Lee M. Hollander's translation. From his *Arinbiarnarkviða*, 11:

> Arinbior,
> Of all men best,
> Who saved me
> From the sea-king's wrath—
> The king's friend,
> Who failed me not.
>
> In the fell
> Folkwarder's hall.[156]

And from his *Sonatorrek*, 4:

> For my kin
> Hath come to an end,
> Like a tree
> O'erturned by the storm.
> Unblithe he
> Who bears the corpse
> Of dear kin
> From his dwelling place.[157]

To this we can compare David's lament over Saul and Jonathan in 2 Sam 1:19–27.[158] Here are vv. 23–25:

> Saul and Jonathan, beloved and lovely!
> In life and in death they were not divided;
> they were swifter than eagles;
> they were stronger than lions.
> You daughters of Israel, weep over Saul,
> who clothed you luxuriously in scarlet,
> who put ornaments of gold on your apparel.
> "How the mighty have fallen
> in the midst of the battle!
> Jonathan lies slain on your high places!"

155. The context is a pitched battle between the Vikings and Lenape Indians on what is now Manhattan Island.

156. Hollander, *The Skalds*, 80

157. Ibid., 91.

158. Causse considered this to be a written composition (*Plus vieux*, 64).

Linguistically, like in all Hebrew poetry, parallelism is abundant here. The use of parallelism is quite sophisticated, as seen in v. 22.[159] Nissim Amzallag and Mikhal Avriel have now comprehensively analyzed the macro- and microstructures of this poem, and there is no need to repeat their thorough work here.[160]

Arvid Bruno identified a sustained meter through the entire song.[161] There is paronomasia between vv. 19, 20, 23, 24a, and 25c of the song, בָּמוֹת . . . בְּנוֹת . . . פֶּן . . . בְּמוֹתָם . . . בְּנוֹת . . . מָבוֹת.[162] Some of the puns are pointed double entendres. In v. 21, it is the (leather) shield of Saul that is "no longer anointed," but it is, of course, Saul himself who had become "no longer anointed" as king, because shield and king had become נִגְעַל, meaning both "defiled" and "rejected."[163]

While the contents do not appear in any way "Canaanite," Mark Smith has shown how much language here is drawn from the Ugaritic *Lament over Baal* (e.g., v. 19 and *KTU* 1.15.iv 6–7; 1.5.vi 8; v. 21 and *KTU* 1.19.i 44–46; etc.).[164]

The dual "performance" instructions given in 2 Sam 1:18 will be discussed in the section that follows. The incorporation of the song into the surrounding "saga" resembles the use of the Skaldic poems in the Icelandic sagas.[165] That is, while it certainly fits the occasion, the poem could have been inserted early by the author, late by the Deuteronomistic Historian, or even inspired the prose narrative itself.[166]

These, then, are some examples of what gobbets of oral literature look like in the written narrative books of the Old Testament. But by no means are these or passages like them the only orally derived texts in those books.[167] The Old Testament narrative books, it may be repeated, were part of the oral-written stream of tradition throughout their his-

159. Linafelt, "Private Poetry and Public Eloquence," 511.

160. Amzallag and Avriel, "Complex Antiophony in David's Lament," 6–12.

161. Bruno, *Das Hebräische Epos*, 23, 92.

162. Smith, "Warrior Culture." Interestingly, there is paronomasia in the Septuagint of v. 20, ἐν Γεθ καὶ μὴ εὐαγγελίσησθε; Casonowicz, "Paronomasia," 131.

163. Linafelt, "Private Poetry and Public Eloquence," 519. On the many double entendres in this text, see Vermeylen, "Comment sont tombé les héros?," 111.

164. Smith, "Warrior Culture."

165. Cf. Hylander, *Literarische Samuel-Saul-Komplex*, 35.

166. Linafelt, "Private Poetry and Public Eloquence," 510n.32.

167. Yassif, *The Hebrew Folktale*, 9.

tory. Just as the Skaldic and Eddic poems are not the only orally derived Icelandic texts, but the sagas themselves often show both oral and written sources, weaving in and out of writing in the course of their passage through the generations (see figure 3.1), so, too, the narratives of the Old Testament employ gobbets oral and written.[168]

Kirkpatrick argues that the Jacob stories are wholly written compositions.[169] Yet the saga *Bolla Þáttur Bollasonar* looks no different (e.g., par. 2: "The story now turns to Thord who returned home to learn of the slaying of his son, for whom he grieved deeply"; cf. Jacob's learning of the "slaying" of Joseph in Gen 37:33–35).[170] Gideon's angelic visitor in Judg 6:11–12: "Gideon was beating out wheat in the winepress to hide it from the Midianites. And the angel of the LORD appeared to him and said to him, 'The LORD is with you, O mighty man of valor'" looks remarkably like Hallfred's in *Hrafnkels saga Freysdoða* 1: "He dreamed that a man came to him and said, 'There you lie, Hallfred, and rather careless, too. Move your farm away, west across Lagarflot river. There is where your luck is.'"[171] And the formulaic start of the David and Bathsheba story in 2 Sam 11:1: "In the spring of the year, the time when kings go out to battle, David sent Joab, and his servants with him, and all Israel," is much the same as the similar incipit of *Gunnlaugs saga ormstungu* 9: "Gunnlaug arrived in Uppsala around the time of the Swedes' Spring Assembly."[172]

With this in mind, we might venture one more biblical example, although the current form of this passage is far less like poetry than the previous examples and is now locked into a literary context more firmly. The account of Ben-Hadad's siege of Samaria in 2 Kgs 6:24—7:20 contains several vignettes. The first scene is in Samaria:

> And there was a great famine in Samaria, as they besieged it, until a donkey's head was sold for eighty shekels of silver, and the fourth part of a kab of dove's dung for five shekels of silver. Now as the king of Israel was passing by on the wall, a woman cried out to him, saying, "Help, my lord, O king!" And he said, "If the LORD will not help you, how shall I help you? From the threshing floor, or from

168. Hylander, *Literarische Samuel-Saul-Komplex*, 146. For this phenomenon in East Africa, see Khamis, "From Written through Oral," 203.

169. Kirkpatrick, "The Jacob-Esau Narratives," 17

170. Jacob and Laban's grazing contest complements *Króka-Refs Saga* 2.

171. Gunnell, "The Saga of Hrafnkel Frey's Godi," 438.

172. Attwood, "The Saga of Gunnlaug Serpent-tongue," 577.

the winepress?" And the king asked her, "What is your trouble?" She answered, "This woman said to me, 'Give your son, that we may eat him today, and we will eat my son tomorrow.' So we boiled my son and ate him. And on the next day I said to her, 'Give your son, that we may eat him.' But she has hidden her son." When the king heard the words of the woman, he tore his clothes—now he was passing by on the wall—and the people looked, and behold, he had sackcloth beneath on his body.

The second scene is at the home of Elisha:

> Elisha was sitting in his house, and the elders were sitting with him. Now the king had dispatched a man from his presence, but before the messenger arrived Elisha said to the elders, "Do you see how this murderer has sent to take off my head? Look, when the messenger comes, shut the door and hold the door fast against him. Is not the sound of his master's feet behind him?" And while he was still speaking with them, the messenger came down to him, and he said, "This trouble is from the LORD! Why should I wait for the Lord any longer?"

And the final scene is outside Samaria, where four lepers wander into the Aramean camp and find it abandoned, the Arameans having thought they heard the sound of an army and concluding that hitherto unknown Hittite and Egyptian allies of Israel had arrived (2 Kgs 7:3–20).

There are many vivid images in this story. There are several numeric references, some that serve the story such as the various costs given in 6:25 and 7:1, and some that seem to serve none such as the fact that there were four lepers. The story has several humorous elements. The thought of purchasing horse heads and dove's dung,[173] Jehoram's sackcloth underwear, keeping the king's captain at bay by holding the door shut, the rather comic lepers, an army that flees from a noise, and even the dark comedy of the trampled Israelite captain in 7:20.[174] One might even allow a morbid comedy in the focus on the selfishness of the one cannibal mother and not on the cannibalism itself.[175]

---

173. Regardless of whether these terms really designate plants, the humor is in their plain sense; cf. Cogan and Tadmor, *II Kings*, 79.

174. Lasine, "Jehoram," 40.

175. Ibid., 28, 31.

While the double demonstrative is unknown in Hebrew, 2 Kgs 6:33 uses the "tautological demonstrative," הִנֵּה־זֹאת.[176] The relative particle -שׁ appears in 7:12, and has been considered by some to be a sign of northern Hebrew, even by Schniedewind in his balanced appraisal of supposed "Israelianisms," in light of its occurrence in Phoenician and Ammonite.[177] The same verse contains in the kethib בְּהַשָּׂדֶה, a preposition plus definite article, which Burney, Rendsburg, and Davila suggest is also northern. Schniedewind is rightly more skeptical on this latter identification, since the list of distribution of this feature in the Hebrew Bible does not seem uniquely northern (1 Sam 13:21; Ps 36:6; Qoh 1:7; 6:10; 8:1; Ezek 40:25; 47:22; etc.).[178] But were at least the ־שׁ to be northern, perhaps some of this story circulated orally from the time of the northern kingdom in the manner discussed by Carr, above. In 7:10 appears the stock pairing of אָדָם and אִישׁ (cf. Isa 2:9; Jer 2:6).[179] There may be more cliché here, as well, or at least phrasing that becomes standard, in that the captain's retort in 7:2: "If the Lord himself should make windows in heaven, could this thing be?" repeated in 7:19, sounds very similar to Mal 3:10: "And thereby put me to the test, says the LORD of hosts, if I will not open the windows of heaven for you and pour down for you a blessing until there is no more need."

The transition from 6:32 to 33 is abrupt and apocopated; the listener is left to figure out just what happened, or the storyteller is left to fill it in.[180] It is not even really clear who is speaking in v. 33, the messenger or Elisha.[181] There is some directional ambiguity in 7:5–8, in that the lepers arrive "at the edge of the camp" in 5b, and then arrive at the edge of the camp in v. 8. In between, we have the narrator's interruption that explains why the camp was empty. This analepsis is aimed only at the hearer and disrupts the narrative in the interests of the storyteller's voice.[182] It dramatizes the divine causality that makes fun of both the lepers and the king.

---

176. Muraoka, *Emphatic Words and Structures*, 81–82.

177. Schniedewind and Sivan, "The Elijah-Elisha Narratives," 328–29.

178. Ibid., 317.

179. Again, I am not arguing that the text is early. There are many late elements, such as the appearance of the "seah," a postexilic "translation" of a preexilic "ephah" (Powell, "Weights and Measures," 94).

180. Cogan and Tadmor, *II Kings*, 80.

181. Satterthwaite, "The Elisha Narratives," 22.

182. Long, "Framing Repetitions," 394.

The repetition of the prophet's prediction in 7:20, the only such repetition in the entire Elisha cycle, acts as an inclusio (the elements actually appear in chiastic order) to remind the audience of the story's message.[183]

The reference to "Hittites and Egyptians" makes no sense in the story or in historical context. It is probably an old literary image, itself a cliché from the broader ancient Near East.[184] It occurs repeatedly in the Hittite "Plague Prayers of Murshili II" (A obv. 13'–34'; *CTH* 378). LaBarbera argued that the expression "threshing floor and winepress" in 6:27 is a motif from Ugaritic literature, although he cites no texts in support.[185] It is a cliché from the Hebrew Bible, occurring in Num 18:30; Deut 15:14; 16:13; Hos 9:2–4. The episode of the two cannibal women and the king is clearly a parody of the judgment of Solomon in 1 Kgs 3:16–28.[186] This might be a literary allusion, of course, although the judgment of Solomon is a story even today easily transmitted orally. So ubiquitous is it in folklore in general that it occurs almost exactly as in 1 Kings 3 with the young Buddha as the judge in the *Jataka* (300 BCE–400 CE), the only variation being that the imposter mother wants to actually eat the baby, as in 2 Kings 6.[187] Parents resorting to eating their children during siege and famine is a common folkloric motif.[188]

While these vignettes related to the siege of Ben-Hadad fit the surrounding narrative of 2 Kings, there is no evidence of historical accuracy. Ahab was allied with the Arameans from Year 6 to Year 18 of the Assyrian king Shalmaneser.[189] The siege is not likely to have taken place.[190] At the same time, there is nothing to suggest they are retrojections of, say, experiences of the Neobabylonian siege of Jerusalem. They seem, rather, to be pieces of folklore, the episode of the cannibal mothers in particular, used metaphorically to express violent social distrust.[191]

---

183. Cogan and Tadmor, *II Kings*, 83–84.

184. Ibid., 82, 85.

185. LaBarbera, "The Man of War and the Man of God," 646.

186. Satterthwaite, "Elisha Narratives," 22; Lasine, "Jehoram," 41.

187. Fausbøll, *Buddhist Birth-Stories*, xiv–xvi.

188. Lasine, "Jehoram," 34–36.

189. Evidence includes the Kurkh Monolith and the Kurba'il Statue; Thiel, "Erwägungen zur Aramäisch-Israelitischen Geschichte," 126.

190. Cogan and Tadmor, *II Kings*, 84.

191. Lasine, "Jehoram," 45.

This suggests that some of the material of 2 Kings 6–7 existed orally before it entered the book of 2 Kings, even if some of it did not, at that stage, concern Elisha. Many oral gobbets that circulated in the ancient Near East entered the stories of Elijah and Elisha, including gobbets that entered the myths of neighboring lands.[192] Second Kings 6–7 cannot be definitively called "orally derived," but we must recognize that cycles of tales like the Elijah-Elisha material are the most common literary context for orally derived literature in general.[193] The Bani Hilal cycle or the Völsung Cycle or Tyrfing Cycle—cycles of multiple sagas each are examples. Nevertheless, with material as episodic as this, it is much more speculative to distinguish the orally derived from the literary. But the two categories are, in the terminology of the sociologist Max Weber, ideal types. That is, they are deliberate simplifications, perhaps oversimplifications, of how ancient authors composed. In an oral-written culture like ancient Israel, the line between these types is porous. The two are mixed, and that is reflected as well in the larger cycles of stories.

Performance

There is a larger issue here. The Skaldic poems and their biblical counterparts are remnants of performances. A mode of thought distinct from the literary mode was operative in employing them in ancient Israel. As Paul Béré has noted,[194] for oral biblical material we need a distinct set of tools to investigate this material, a form of performance criticism.[195] We would not imagine a musicologist who only studied scores, or a scholar who studied ancient Greek dramas never seeing them performed. "The poem is everything-that-happens: and if it is, then to insist that it is only part of it (the words), is to mistake the event, to miss that total presence."[196] And

192. Yassif, *The Hebrew Folktale*, 18.

193. Ibid., 30–31. The comparison between parallel stories *within* the Elijah-Elisha cycle is further evidence of this (Ibid., 36).

194. Béré, "*Auditor in fabula*," 1091.

195. Giles and Doan, "Performance Criticism of the Hebrew Bible," 273; Finnegan, *The Oral and Beyond*, 78; *Oral Traditions and the Verbal Arts*, 93. Admittedly, among some folklorists, "Performance" (which became important in the 1960s) is already "out" (Fine, *The Folklore Text*, 45, 47; Harvilahti, "Textualising," 3). Joubert (*The Power*, 67) disparages its focus on the aesthetic mode of experience; cf. Fine, *Folklore Text*, 58.

196. Rothenbert, "2 July 1975"; Khamis, "From Written through Oral," 215.

"*all* folk narratives (whether or not they involved role play) should be seen as a form of 'dramatic' performance."[197]

Performance criticism would use semiotic theory to investigate address, implicit audience, and projected identity, and the way they weave together to constitute a "Performative Scheme," itself determined by social and cultural conventions familiar to the original performer and audience.[198] "The narrative is often closely and deliberately connected to the immediate performance space in which the story is told."[199] This means performance criticism would eventually lead us to history, to *Sitze im Leben* (and so, also, because location was significant in the ancient setting of performance). Governing conditions of performance determine the kinds of Performative[200] Schemes a society will generate. Linguists and anthropologists recognize that texts emerge in contexts in which they were actually employed and that these contexts are not dictated by social environment but emerge in negotiations between participants in social interactions.[201] In short, performance is anchored in and inseparable from its context of use.[202]

"The Oral Poetic text, insofar as it engages a body thru the voice that carries it, rejects any analysis that would dissociate it from within its social function and from its socially accorded place—more than a written text would."[203] But while form criticism focused on literary genres (which we now know have no identity other than within their cultural context), types, and the *Sitze* in which they were used, performance criticism must focus on the event or the dynamic complex of action of a performance, which includes sound and gesture[204]—although semiotics will still pro-

197. Gunnell, "Narratives, Space and Drama," 9.

198. Giles and Doan, "Performance Criticism," 273; Schieffelin, "Problematizing Performance," 196; Foley, "Analogues: Modern Oral Epics," 200–201; Foley, *The Singer of Tales in Performance*, 8; Jason, "The Study of Israelite," 92.

199. Gunnell, "Narratives, Space and Drama," 13.

200. I use this term broadly, without direct allusion to J. L. Austin; cf. Phelan, "Narrative and Performance," n.p.; Katz, "Oral Tradition in Linguistics," 261. Würth ("Skaldic Poetry," 270) applies Austinian theory to the Skaldic poetry.

201. Finnegan, *The Oral and Beyond*, 87; Foley, *The Singer of Tales in Performance*, 9, 49; Giles and Doan, "Performance Criticism," 279–80.

202. Pelias and Vanoosting, "A Paradigm for Performance Studies," 219.

203. Zumthor, *Oral Poetry*; Finnegan, *Oral Traditions and the Verbal Arts*, 43; Giles and Doan, "Performance Criticism," 276.

204. O'Keeffe, "The Performing Body," 53; Greenwood, "Sounding Out Homer," 503.

vide much of the analytical method that allows us to go beyond historical study.

Performative Schemes operate within a system of culturally determined conventions.[205] To describe these patterns, we need to ask what kinds of presentations were needed. What were the contexts for these acts of presentation?[206] What political and religious forces shaped these acts?[207]

"The performance is not a citation of the text. The ceremony deploys the text—and much else—as part of an elaborate reiteration of a specific vision of social order: the meaning of the performance depends on the citation not of the text but of the regimes of socialization, on the interplay among a specific text, individual performers, the materiality and historical density of performance, and the web of performance practices that constitute the performance as a meaningful citation."[208] The audience/spectator co-creates the oral traditional work.[209]

But for the ancient past we cannot look at a real spectator, and if we want to avoid merely casting *ourselves* in that role, we will construct an "ideal spectator" using ways to deal with spectatorial practices that are of necessity located in the contingent realities of actual performances.[210] Ethnography will be chief among these ways.[211] "The only way out of this dilemma seems to be more and better empirical studies on living oral epic traditions, a careful comparison of the results and their cautious application to other epics whose performance contexts will always remain poorly known but may be elucidated with the help of comparisons."[212]

There is abundant evidence of the actual performance contexts for the *Sīrat Banī Hilāl*.[213] Yet since these ethnographic case studies are from the twentieth century, where even in Egypt the storytellers were radio

205. Joubert, *The Power*, 75; Richard Bauman, "Verbal Art as Performance," 39–40.

206. Joubert, *The Power*, 126.

207. For Homer, see Bakker, "Epic Remembering," 67.

208. Worthen, "Drama, Performativity, and Performance," 1093–1107.

209. Foley, "Implications of Oral Tradition," 43–44; Fine, *The Folklore Text*, 87.

210. Zerubavel, *Time Maps*, 29.

211. Foley, "Analogues: Modern Oral Epics," 199.

212. Honko, "Comparing the Textualization," 2; Thomas, "Performance Literature and the Written Word," 5. Cf. the opposition to comparative use of modern oral societies by Sasson, "Literary Criticism, 81.

213. Slyomovics, *The Merchant of Art*.

listeners and newspaper readers, thoroughly exposed to Western society for generations, the applicability of the observations to a radically different world of medieval Arabia or ancient Israel is questionable. We might at least note that interaction between the poet and audience is integral to the composition-in-performance features of the oral text.[214] This is surely true of earlier periods, as it is generally of oral literature. Moreover, various contexts render the *Sīrat Banī Hilāl* into different genres—at times poetry, at times song, at others spoken prose that is sometimes rhymed and sometimes not.[215] This also seems ancient, and reinforces the decision made earlier in this study to minimize the importance of genre in the study of oral literature. When the *Sīrat Banī Hilāl* is sung, it is accompanied by either a large tambourine (*ṭār*), which is considered to be more traditional, or a *rabāba*, a sort of viola with coconut body, membrane belly of fish skin, and horsehair strings.[216]

The *siyar* have professional storytellers—bards, minstrels, or however we decide to call them. The *suwālif* do not; there are no specialists in the art, although some people are recognized as better at it than others.[217] As with the *siyar*, there is an interaction of audience and performer with *suwālif* that helps mold the tale.[218]

With Eddic and Skaldic poetry, there are obviously no ethnographic accounts of their performance.[219] We have accounts of performances (of the sagas too) found in some of the sagas, but these must be used cautiously as they reveal only the sagaman's perceptions of performance.[220] Nevertheless, what is evident in such saga descriptions is the same in-

214. Ibid., 8; Connelly, *Arab Folk*, 67; Reynolds, "Epic and History," 405. From old accounts, this seems to have been true of the *Sīrat ʿAntar ibn Shaddād*, as well; Heath, *Thirsty Sword*, 38.

215. Reynolds, "*Sīrat Banī Hilāl*," 85.

216. Canova, "Poeta Epico," 90, 96, 101.

217. Sowayan, "The Bedouin," 68.

218. Ibid.

219. Gunnell, "The Performance of the Poetic," 300.

220. Mitchell, "Reconstructing," 203; O'Donoghue, *Skaldic Verse*, 15; Jones, "Where Now the Harp?" 487. Stefanie Würth is particularly skeptical about learning anything from such testimonies (Würth, "Skaldic Poetry," 266). The situation is similar to the performances depicted in Anglo-Saxon sources. While they are not a reliable picture, they attest to a literate audience's perception of an oral situation that is clearly identical to real ancient Germanic oral practice (Niles, "Myth," 12, 37; also Amodio, *Writing the Oral Tradition*, 39).

terplay of audience and bard visible in the Arabic examples. The poet/
skald is encouraged in his own reconstitution of the saga by the audience's
interaction.[221] Even Skaldic poems may have been constructed in performance from the linking of earlier, shorter poetic verses.[222] We might
envision such a process lying behind the assembly of Judges 5 from "free-
standing poems—perhaps as situational lyrics or dramatic monologues
. . . metrical realizations of episodes in a more extensive body of story
material rather than truly isolated lyrics in troubadour style."[223] "These
verses would later have been inherited by the person who compiled the
total [Deborah] saga as part of the mass of heterogeneous story materials.
The compiler then dovetailed the verses together with prose, using the
same skills as were evolving to cope with the dove-tailing of diverse prose
elements."[224]

We must again distinguish between the two main Eddic meters,
fornyðislag and *ljóðaháttr* (*málaháttr* is considerably less common).
Fornyðislag is probably the older, attested in runes also. It, in turn, provided the structural basis for the most common meter of Skaldic poetry
(*dróttkvæt*).[225] This meter is also the one used for epic narrative works,
especially those dealing with ancient heroes, while *ljóðaháttr* is more
commonly used for mythology.[226] *Ljóðaháttr* is a dialog form, and Terry
Gunnell has convincingly argued for a dramatic or ritual-dramatic performance context for its origin.[227] Bernt Thorvaldsen has proposed similarly, noting that the performative effects of the text "could be the same
if the text was performed from a manuscript, or from memory based
on reading, as long as the text is spoken by a person and listened to by

221. Gordon, "Oral Tradition," 73; Lindow, "*Þættir*," 184.

222. Poole, "Composition Transmission," 42.

223. Ibid., 56.

224. Ibid., 57.

225. Suzuki, "On the Emergent Trochaic Cadence," 77.

226. Gunnell, "The Performance of the Poetic," 301; Gunnell, "'Til holts ek gekk
. . .,'" 238. There are exceptions, *Völuspá* is mythological and *fornyðislag*. A few Eddic
poems are in more than one meter: *Reginsmál, Fáfnismál, Sigrdrífumál,* and *Hamðismál*
(Dronke, *The Poetic Edda*, 1:176).

227. E.g., Gunnell, "Play of Skírnir," 23–32; Gunnell, "*Til holts ek gekk*," 239. A more
"Cambridge Ritualist" dramatic performance origin was suggested for the *Sagas* much
earlier by Phillpotts, *Edda and Saga*, 143, 161.

others."[228] This is an important insight and clearly alien to oral formulaicism. It makes the application to the biblical material less tenuous.

Yet *fornyðislag* should be considered a better analogy for the biblical material. The biblical subject matter is more akin to the heroic epics, except in Genesis 1–11. Additionally, little if anything in the Bible (outside of the Wisdom literature) bears a dialogical form. Finally, the demise of the early twentieth-century "Myth-and-Ritual" school rightly illustrates the implausibility of reconstructing ritual dramatic contexts for anything in the Old Testament outside of the Psalms.[229] All the Eddic poems used for comparative purposes in the previous section are in *fornyðislag* meter.[230]

The poems in *fornyðislag* had a different performance setting than those in *ljóðaháttr*.[231] Gunnell writes, "Those in *fornyðislag* might have been performed as Norna-Gestr presents his poems (although it must remain somewhat questionable whether harps were commonly used in Scandinavia in the early Middle Ages) . . . the *fornyðislag* poems could have been performed anywhere, although one can expect an indoor setting."[232]

The tale of *Norna-Gestr* recounts the arrival of an anonymous stranger (*Gestr* or "Guest") at a chieftain's court and his entertaining the court with sung/chanted *fornyðislag* tales, accompanied by harp. This court setting is also the performance context for Skaldic poetry,[233] and is the same as the image of the bard or "scop" in *Beowulf*.[234] In a nearly iden-

228. Thorvaldsen, "The Double Scene in Performance." Online: http://www.dur .ac.uk/medieval.www/sagaconf/thorvaldsen.htm/.

229. Although independently of the earlier Myth-and-Ritualists, Norbert Lohfink argues that the literary style of Deuteronomy indicates that the book was composed to be read as Scripture in a worship service: Lohfink, *Das Hauptgebot*).

230. Gunnell, "Eddic Poetry," 87, 91–92; Suzuki, "On the Emergent," 531–54. There might be interesting parallels of biblical material with *ljóðaháttr* poetry, too: compare *Hávamál* 1, 29 with Proverbs and *Solarið* 37 with Psalm 18.

231. Gunnell, "Eddic Poetry," 96.

232. Gunnell, "The Performance of the Poetic," 301–2. It is worth noting that *fornyðislag* is certainly performable in such ways, as attested by its modern performances by the group Sequentia and the opera *The Seeress's Prophecy*; (Nielsen, "The Elder Edda Revisited," 41–42).

233. Gísli Sigurðsson, "On the Classification," 247; Würth, "Skaldic Poetry," 289; Gunnell, *The Origins of Drama*, 330.

234. Jones, "Where Now the Harp?" 486; Cipolla, *Il Racconto di Nornagestr*, 82–83. As "skald" is related to English "scold," so "scop" relates to "scoff." Perhaps the "scoffers" of Proverbs 1 and Psalm 1 [לבים, לבון, אנשי] carry the same connotation (Gandz, "Oral

tical setting, the Roman historian Priscus of Panium (*Historia,* Fragment 8) describes a bard's storytelling in the court of Attila the Hun as "singing" (Gk. ἄδματα πεποιημένα ἔλεγον).[235] The presence or absence of music with Skaldic and Eddic poetry is an ongoing debate.[236] But "music . . . is an indispensable element in the performance of oral literature, particularly oral epics."[237]

The verb used for the performance of Skaldic poetry is usually translated "chant," but its precise meaning is unclear.[238] The modern scholar and performer Benjamin Bagby finds for Eddic poetry that "all aspects of the singer's art are called into use, including the wide and flexible spectrum of vocal utterance: plain speech, heightened speech, sung speech, spoken song, simple syllabic song, melismatic song, as well as the more radical elements of human vocal sound."[239]

Norna-Gestr illustrates serial performance, portions of a longer story given in discrete settings or units, a phenomenon indicated by other tales for performance of sagas, Skaldic poems,[240] and also of the *Sīrat Banī Hilāl* and Homer.[241]

Ancient Near Eastern Performance

Evidence from the ancient Near East supports a very similar portrait of performance contexts for oral literature, including audience-speaker interaction, variety of delivery modes ("genres"), court setting, serial performance, and even the harp.

Tradition," 264). The scoffers in Proverbs are masters of the *mašal,* just as the narrators of the Arabic *sālfah* are masters of the *matal* (Ingham, "Sālfah," 12). In Numbers 21, I translated the term as "ballad singers" (Schmitt, "Hesbonlied," 32).

235. English text in Carey, *Eyewitness to History,* 23–25. On the parity of this example with the Anglo-Saxon and Norse cases, see Opland, *Anglo-Saxon Oral Poetry,* 51, 63.

236. Harris, "Performance," 228–30.

237. Sakata, "The Musical Curtain," 159.

238. Turville-Petre, *Scaldic Poetry,* lxxvi.

239. Bagby, "*Beowulf,* the *Edda,* and the Performance of Medieval Epic," 186. Bagby's performance of *Beowulf* in this style can be found online: http://www.nyu.edu/projects/mcdnar/file.php?id=1019/.

240. Lindow, "Þættir," 180–83.

241. On Homer, see West, "The Singing of Homer," 113–15 and passim; Scodel, *Listening to Homer,* 58, 78–79, 176–77; Reichl, "Introduction," 2. The performance contexts are likely identical (Nagy, "Epic as Music," 55, 61).

In Egypt, performative texts use the verbs "recite" (*šdi*) or "pronounce" (*dm*).[242] Singing is sometimes depicted graphically in such settings,[243] with the singers engaged in stylized "rapt" poses[244] and holding vertical harps akin to Assyrian harps.[245] Contents of *sdd* or oral literature include personal memoires, humorous morality tales, and "Skaldic" encomia on the king.[246] One example of the latter from the court of Merneptah involves singing accompanied by harp.[247] A court setting is commonly depicted, and bard-audience interaction is important for composition.[248] As with the speakers of *siyar* and Skaldic poems, accomplished storytellers (*mdw.ty*) could attain fame for their skill.[249]

The fullest presentation of a performance context is in the text *King Cheops and the Magicians* of Papyrus Westcar (pBerlin 3033).[250] The text is from the Hyksos period (ca. 1600 BCE) but is commonly said to be a Middle Kingdom (XXII Dynasty) composition,[251] although Hans Goedick has challenged a date so early.[252] The story relates how in the court of King Khufu (Cheops), "the king's son Khafra arose [to speak, and he said: I should like to relate to your majesty] another marvel, one which happened in the time of [your] father, Nebka" (1.16–20). He then tells a sort of "marvel tale." This is followed by, "Bauefre arose to speak, and he said: Let me have [your] majesty hear a marvel which took place in the time of your father King Snefru" (4.18–20). There are two more such tales.[253] Each is accompanied by a favorable response from Khufu,

242. Redford, "Scribe and Speaker," 160–61.

243. Ibid., 197.

244. Schlott, "Eine Beobachtungen zu Mimik," 55, 57, 59–63, 69, figs. 3 (V Dynasty grave of En-cheft-ka), 6 (grave of Amanamhet [Thutmosis III]), 15 (XII Dynasty grave of Uchotep).

245. Lawergren and Gurney, "Sound Holes," 37.

246. Redford, "Scribe and Speaker," 169, 183. For example, lines 2–14 of the Song to Merneptah from Hermopolis presented by Roeder, "Zwei Hieroglyphische," 328–40.

247. Redford, "Scribe and Speaker," 188.

248. Ibid., 187, citing the role of Sehtepibre-onkh in the court of Amenemhet II.

249. Ibid., 190.

250. English translation in Simpson, "King Cheops," 15–30.

251. Sánchez Rodriguez, *El Papiro Westcar*, 1; Jenny Berggren, "The 'Ipwt in Papyrus Westcar (7, 5–8; 9,1–5)," 2.

252. Goedick, "Thoughts about the Papyrus Westcar," 23–24, 35.

253. Originally, there were at least five tales; only the last words of the first are preserved, the second and fifth have lacunae, and the third and fourth are complete;

which encourages the performance of the next one. Although, it may be repeated, we cannot assume this is an accurate depiction of real court practices,[254] here we see the court setting, the status of the accomplished bard, and the interplay of audience and poet in the composition-in-performance. Demotic narratives do not, however, lend themselves to division into separate installments or sessions.[255]

Within various Mesopotamian texts, there are numerous prologues that begin, "I will sing . . ." and epilogues that begin with something like this: "This is a song in praise of . . ." or "Whoever recites this text . . ."[256] *Atraḫasis* is written "for singing" (*ana zamāri*), and Anne Kilmer has extensively explored how this would have been done.[257] Harps (*sammû*) are abundantly attested in iconography, especially from the Assyrian period.[258] Some texts (e.g., *Dumuzi and Enkidu*) are designated *balbale*, composed with lyrics.[259]

Some Hittite texts are labeled "songs" (*išḫamai*).[260] One of these songs, the Song of Illuyanka (*COS*, 1:150–51 [#1.56]; *CTH*, 321), is explicitly said to be performed in the Hittite Purulli festival.[261] The *Song of the Ullikummi* is in Hurrian "sung" (*šir-ad-ilu*) before an audience (lines

---

Berggren, "The 'Ipwt," 2).

254. Hays, "The Historicity of Papyrus Westcar," 20–30; Parkinson, "Individual and Society," 141.

255. Tait, "Demotic Literature," 183.

256. Vogelzang, "Some Aspects of Oral and Written Tradition," 266.

257. Kilmer, "Fugal Features of Atrahasis," 133 and passim.

258. Dumbrill, *The Archaeomusicology*, 182, 218; Lawergren and Gurney, "Sound Holes," 40. A lyre, unlike a harp, is characterized by a yoke. They lyre is probably the ALGAR (Dumbrill, *The Archaeomusicology*, 241). The lute is *inu* (ibid., 316). An authentic reproduction of the Sumerian "Lyre of Ur" has been constructed and tuned according to Anne Kilmer's guidelines; Andy Lowings, "The Lyre of Ur Project," lecture presented at the Library of Congress, March 17, 2009. This lyre can be heard online, played as per Kilmer, but unfortunately only either accompanied by replica Sumerian pipes, at http://www.youtube.com/watch?v=LvgtAHV4mzw, or accompanied by English recitation of Gilgamesh, at http://www.youtube.com/watch?v=TSWEeBGhz4M. The sound of the lyre resembles how postbiblical literature described the *nēbel*, a low rumble (Kolyada, *A Compendium of Musical Instruments*, 44).

259. Dumbrill, *The Archaeomusicology*, 399; the connection of *bal* to Akk. *palu*, "dynasty," might indicate the subject matter.

260. Beckman, "Hittite and Hurrian Epic," 256.

261. Beckman, "The Anatolian Myth," 18; Beckman, "The Religion of the Hittites," 104. On the oral-tradition stream from this myth to the Hebrew Bible, see Miller, "The Origin of the Zion Hymns."

1–7), probably accompanied by music.[262] Twenty-nine Hurrian hymns were found at Ugarit with both lyrics and musical notation.[263]

For the Levant, we have much less information. From Ugarit, only *Shahar and Shalem* (*CTA* 23) gives indication that it was performed dramatically.[264] But a number of texts refer to harp playing and singing within the narrative (e.g., *KTU* 1.3.i 18–22).[265] The narrator of the Egyptian story of *Wen-Amun* thought it plausible to depict an Egyptian female skald able to sing in the court at Byblos (2.68–69). A sort of performance scene is found in the Ugaritic Baal cycle. In *Anat* 1 = 4AB (*KTU*/CAT 1.3.i = *CTA* 3.1), at a feast in Baal's court:

> He stood, chanted [*yabuddu*] and sang [*yašîru*],
> Cymbals [*maṣillatâmi*] in the virtuoso's hands
> Sweet of voice the hero sang,
> About Baal on the summit of Zaphon (lines 18–22)[266]

This is remarkably similar to the Papyrus Westcar example, the court of Attila, and *Norna-Gestr* and the skalds, as well as Achilles in *Iliad* 9.

Rock drawings from the central Negeb in the second millennium BCE show lyre players.[267] Lyre players are depicted among the Judean captives being deported from Lachish by Sennacherib, who records receiving singers in tribute from Hezekiah.[268] Other images of lyres were found at Megiddo (one nine-stringed from the thirteenth century and another on a Philistine vase from the late tenth century), Kuntillet Ajrud (ninth century), Ashdod, and Jerusalem (twelve-stringed, on a seventh-century seal).[269] The Megiddo and Kuntillet Ajrud lyres are similar in design.[270] Tambourines or frame drums, like the *ṭār* used for the *Sīrat Banī Hilāl* and perhaps for Homer,[271] are known from figurines from Beth

---

262. Archi, "Transmission," 198–99.

263. Dumbrill, *The Archeaomusicology*, 23–24.

264. Sasson, "Literary Criticism," 94.

265. Wyatt, *Word of Tree*, 136.

266. English translation by Smith, "Warrior Culture." He notes the absence of women in such a public feast, in contrast to those in the private feast of *ANEP*, #157.

267. Keel, *The Symbolism*, fig. 466.

268. Ibid., fig. 470.

269. Burgh, *Listening to the Artifacts*, 10–11.

270. Ibid., 14.

271. Greenwood, "Sounding Out Homer," 504.

Shean nineth-century Tell Taanach, ninth-century Tell el-Farah North, and eighth-century Tel Shiqmona.[272] There are images of small portable lyres in early postexilic seals.[273]

The biblical *kinnôr* and *nēbel* are likely both lyres, not harps or lutes, although *kinnôr* seems in some places to have been used as a generic term for all stringed instruments.[274] The *'asor'* is probably a zither, although in light of comparative philology (Akk. *eširtu*) and some early Christian texts, Kolyada allows that it might have been the Assyrian-style harp, borrowed into Syro-Palestine.[275] The tambourine or frame-drum is the Heb. *Tōp.*[276]

With caution we can examine the Bible's own picture of oral performance. As Foley writes of *Beowulf* and Homer, "We have not lost *all* of the keys to performance. If as audience or readers we are prepared to decode the signals that survive the intersemiotic translation to the medium of texts, and whose recognition will require some knowledge of the enabling referent of tradition, then performance can still be keyed by these features."[277] "We may be able to revivify the . . . extruded texts to some extent by interviewing the poet about his specialized language, by enrolling in a brief tutorial on the traditional poetic idiom."[278]

There are numerous references in the biblical narratives to *musical* performance, although we may question how relevant this is for our purposes. Burgh's thoroughgoing analysis of such passages outlines two categories.[279] His "Style A," more common in the Pentateuch and Deuteronomistic History, involves varied performers and performance spaces. His "Style B," which is the style of Chronicles, involves specific musical personnel and performance spaces and times. Both styles use a variety of instruments, although Style A is more prone to tambourines.[280] Burgh's analysis may be supplemented by Othmar Keel's note that the

272. Catalogued in Burgh, *Listening to the Artifacts*, 31–37.

273. Dumbrill, *The Archaeomusicology*, figs. 103–4.

274. Keel, *The Symbolism*, 346–47; Kolyada, *A Compendium of Musical Instruments*, 32.

275. Ibid., 29–31.

276. Ibid., 106.

277. Foley, *The Singer of Tales in Performance*, 64 (italics original).

278. Foley, "Fieldwork on Homer," 18.

279. Burgh, *Listening to the Artifacts*, 108.

280. Ibid., 108–11, 117. Causse (*Plus vieux*, 23 n. 1) undertook similar analyses.

only instance in which a *nēbel* does not stand with *kinnôr* as a temple instrument is in royal Psalm 144: the *kinnôr* was more common and used by ordinary worshipers (Ps 43:3).[281] The *nēbel* is described primarily in association with the first temple.[282]

Still, the risk in applying this information is that we are looking at mere musical performance. The singing of hymns, love songs, war rally ing cries, and the like is a completely different phenomenon from the oral performance of narrative prose and court poetry.[283]

Of the latter sorts, there are a few places where the *kinnôr* in particular was used for recitation accompaniment. That the lyre was played at feasts is confirmed by Isa 5:12, and the scene might resemble that in *Norna-Gestr* or P. Westcar.[284] There is also evidence that at least the biblical authors understood Israel to have had an oral tradition, an oral literature.[285] That this was actually the case was established in chapter 4, above.

Nevertheless, some argue that Judg 8:14, where a *na'ar* "lad" caught by Gideon, "listed for him the chieftains and elders of Succoth," regardless of its historicity, shows that the biblical authors assumed everyone was literate.[286] Not only is it possible that a *na'ar* actually refers to a kind of soldier (1 Sam 17:11),[287] but the ability to write even seventy-seven names does not satisfy the definition of literacy given herein. This argument also ignores the blatant affirmation of oral tradition at the start of the Gideon cycle, in 6:13: "all his wonderful deeds that our fathers recounted to us."[288]

What is more interesting is the seeming presumption of literacy in Isa 29:11–12: "11 And the vision of all this has become to you like the words of a book that is sealed. When men give it to one who can read, saying, 'Read this,' he says, 'I cannot, for it is sealed.' 12 And when they

---

281. Keel, *The Symbolism*, 349.

282. Kolyada, *A Compendium of Musical Instruments*, 42.

283. Although both seem to be designated, *šîr*; Causse, *Plus Vieux*, 35. Drums, not harps, seem more connected with such songs (Meyers, "Women with Hand-Drums, Dancing: Bible"; online: http://jwa.org/encyclopedia. In which category do we place the descendants of Jubal, all who play the lyre and pipe? Cf. Causse, *Plus Vieux*, 32.

284. Kolyada, *A Compendium of Musical Instruments*, 39.

285. Widengren denied this explicitly ("Oral Tradition," 229).

286. Rabinowitz, *A Witness Forever*, 27.

287. John MacDonald, "The Status and Role of the Na'ar in Israelite Society," 147–70; Leeb, *Away from the Father's House*, 68–90.

288. Gispen, *Mondelinge Overlevering*, 8.

give the book to one who cannot read, saying, 'Read this,' he says, 'I cannot read.'"

There is, certainly, abundant evidence the biblical authors assumed Israelites could read and write (Deut 6:9; 24:1; 17:18; Jer 36:1–4).[289] Yet Deuteronomy also envisions oral transmission of historical memory in 31:19–21:

> Now therefore write this song and teach it to the people of Israel. Put it in their mouths, that this song may be a witness for me against the people of Israel. For when I have brought them into the land flowing with milk and honey, which I swore to give to their fathers, and they have eaten and are full and grown fat, they will turn to other gods and serve them, and despise me and break my covenant. And when many evils and troubles have come upon them, this song shall confront them as a witness (for it will live unforgotten in the mouths of their offspring). For I know what they are inclined to do even today, before I have brought them into the land that I swore to give.

Written texts are uniformly assumed to be proclaimed aloud (Josh 1:8; 2 Kgs 19:14; Isa 29:18; etc.), as the verb for reading *qārā*, "crying out" or "calling," indicates.[290] But the biblical authors seem to consider literacy a developing phenomenon. In spite of numerous descriptions of oral instruction by prophets and priests, the authors do not depict a book as a source of instruction prior to the cult reform of Josiah.[291] Deuteronomy is actually conspicuous in its numerous references to writing, and arguably *the biblical authors themselves* want to connect Deuteronomy with Josiah's reform in 2 Kings 22–23.[292] And even the book of Deuteronomy, as we have just seen, speaks of oral transmission ubiquitously (Deut 4:9; 6:6–7; 6:20–25; 11:18–21; 32:7; and for the Deuteronomistic History, Josh 4:4–9; 4:20–24; 22:24–28; 22:34; Judg 5:10–11; 6:13; etc.).[293] The content of these oral transmissions is the basic great deeds of God in history.[294]

In the biblical depiction, before this was an oral world. Abraham's treaty with Abimelech was unwritten, recorded by planting a tree (Gen

289. Rabinowitz, *A Witness Forever*, 28.

290. Ibid., 29–32; Béré, "*Auditor in fabula*," 1089.

291. Van der Toorn, *Scribal Culture*, 221.

292. Ibid., 224.

293. Gispen, *Mondelinge Overlevering*, 29.

294. Rüger, "Oral Tradition in the Old Testament," 109.

21:30–33).[295] Abraham's purchase of the cave of Machpelah was an oral agreement "in the hearing of the ears" (Gen 23:1–20). Jacob sends only oral missives to Esau (Gen 32:14–22). The wedding of Jacob to Laban's daughters is blatantly missing any written contract (Gen 29:16–30).[296] The biblical authors depict writing in Exodus as only done by God himself (Exod 24:12; 33:15 16) or by Moses on God's orders (Exod 17:14, although there is oral transmission here too; 34:27).[297]

Likewise, even in late texts the oral and written were envisioned side by side. Psalm 78 envisions recounting God's acts from one generation to the next (vv. 2–8), with no mention of writing.[298] Psalm 119 recognizes written and oral sources of Torah (compare vv. 24–29 with 97–100).[299] Isaiah swears by both Torah and תעודה ["repetition"] in Isa 8:20 (cf. 8:16).[300] The city Kiriath-Sefer, "City of Books or Scribes," is also called Kiriath-Sannah (Josh 15:49), "City of Oral Tradition" or "City of Reciters and Bards."[301]

Some texts that envision performance settings for oral narrative that recounts events, in other words, performance contexts that may apply to the material presented in chapter 5, above. Of course, as with *Norna Gestr* and *Cheops and the Magicians*, we are dealing with the author's own perceptions of performance, yet commonly "the narrative is often closely and deliberately connected to the immediate performance space in which the story is told."[302] Such a performance scene, like the Anglo-Saxon "myth of the oral poet, is bound to have a foundation in reality."[303] Still, these are at least scenes imagined by the Israelite authors. We do far better with these than with the oral performance scenes imagined by biblical scholars of the past century, such as covenant renewal festivals held at Shiloh when a

295. Gandz, "Oral Tradition," 249.

296. Silver, *The Story of Scripture*, 47.

297. Gandz, "Oral Tradition," 253.

298. Kofoed, "Remember the Days," 11–12.

299. Smith, *The Pilgrimage Pattern*, 274.

300. Gandz, "Oral Tradition," 261.

301. Ibid., 255 n. 20.

302. Gunnell, "Narratives, Space and Drama," 13.

303. Niles, "Myth," 38.

designated covenant-speaker spoke on behalf of Yahweh,[304] or at Shechem with public recitation of the "Short Historical Credo."[305]

Postbattle celebrations typically include commemoration in song, as with Baal's feast in the Ugaritic material. Exemplars are Exodus 15 (the "Song of the Sea") and Judges 5 (the "Song of Deborah"). Mark Smith notes the use of יְתַנּוּ from תָּנָה in Judg 5:11 with the meaning "commemoration" for this root, as in Judg 11:40.[306] Postbattle laments are also attested (2 Sam 2:19–25a; Psalm 44; Zeph 2:14–18; Baal in *KTU* 1.2.iv 6–7 and *KTU* 1.5.v).[307]

The lament of David over Saul and Jonathan, discussed above, is said to "be taught [ללמד]" to the people of Judah" *and* "behold, it is written in the Book of Jashar" (2 Sam 1:18). Once again we see the familiar oral-and-written duality.[308] Here I am following the Septuagint reading (and Driver, McCarter, ESV, etc.); the Hebrew has, "The bow should be taught . . ." If the Hebrew is preferred, then "The Bow" should be taken as perhaps the tune/mode/meter of the song (as NRSV, NET Bible, etc.), rather than as "use of the bow" (KJV). No iconographic or archaeological evidence exists of an ancient Near East *rabāba*, but Groneberg speculates that the gold-plated *tilpānu*-bow of *EA* 22.42–43, an inventory of gifts from Tušratta, might be not a composite bow (or throwing stick) but a musical instrument's bow.[309] Amzallag and Avriel have proposed a performance mode of complex antiphony for this song.[310]

The reference to the "Book of Jashar," whether it ever existed or not, "foreground[s] the lyric nature of the poem," since other references to the book also involve lyric poetry (Josh 10:12–13).[311]

David's lament is also one of several examples of narrative-heroic poems that occur in the Hebrew Bible paired with prose accounts of the same events. Judges 4 and 5 is another example.[312] We might compare

304. Newman, "The Prophetic Call of Samuel," 87.

305. For Von Rad's Credos, see Miller, *Covenant and Grace*.

306. Smith, "Warrior Culture"; he also notes the parallels of *Iliad* 9.

307. Ibid.

308. Ibid.; Rüger, "Oral Tradition," 119.

309. Groneberg, "*Tilpanu* −Bogen," 117n21. Bowed string instruments are normally considered to have entered the Near East from Central Asia in the tenth century AD.

310. Amzallag and Avriel, "Complex Antiphony in David's Lament," 2, 4, 13.

311. Linafelt, "Private Poetry," 509.

312. Smith, "Warrior Culture."

Icelandic sagas that state a single poem was both memorized by bystand-ers and inscribed on rune staves.[313]

The Septuagint text of 1 Kgs 8:53 refers to a "Sefer Ha-Shir," "Book of the Song," "perhaps suggesting that at least some Israelites thought of tales of the ancient heroes as belonging to an epic-as-song tradition."[314]

It is probable that oral-and-literate ancient Israel had performance settings that were standard for its quasi-secular oral narrative literature. These performance contexts, on the basis of biblical and ancient Near Eastern evidence, probably conform to the *Norna-Gestr* portrait that ap-plies also for Skaldic poetry, the *Sīrat Banī Hilāl*, and Homer. This "pos-sible past" is a court setting with semiprofessional bards performing with musical accompaniment.

---

313. Ross, "Poetry and *fornaldarsögur*."
314. Niditch, "The Challenge of Israelite Epic," 281.

Epilogue

Orality and Historicism

> History [*tārīkh*] is something like a trust; it enters into one's covenant [*dhimmih*]. A man who relates history must fear God and not tip the balance one way or the other. He must give his account free of bias, as it really happened.
>
> —Shammari sālfih[1]

Some early proponents of the idea of "oral tradition" in the Old Testament used the notion to "rescue" the text from higher criticism. When Wellhausen and other pre-Eissfeldt critics had denigrated the historical veracity of the Hebrew Bible, an appeal to oral tradition both salvaged the antiquity of the traditions in "late texts" and provided a basis for historicity in the supposed unfailing power of oral tradition to preserve accurate memories over many generations.[2]

Nevertheless, this is not an entirely accurate picture of the early traditions-history movement. Adophe Lods knew that "La mémoire humaine est chose bien faillible, en Orient comme ailleurs."[3] Although Widengren asserted that Ivan "Engnell contends that oral tradition is absolutely reliable,"[4] Engnell was quite aware that "one must keep in mind the possibility that errors of hearing were made in transmission."[5]

---

1. Sowayan, *Arabian Oral Historical Narrative*, 86–87.

2. Finnegan, "Note on Oral," 195; Finnegan, "How Oral Is Oral Literature?" 55–56.

3. Lods, "Le Rôle de la tradition," 52.

4. Widengren, "Oral Tradition and Written Literature," 227.

5. Engnell, *Rigid Scrutiny*, 9.

Ahlström too sought to "emphasize immediately that the oral transmission is not always of the same reliability."[6]

Claims of the "Longevity of Oral Tradition"[7] are generally properly cautious: "The stability or changeability of a given tradition depends entirely on the stability or changeability of the social, political and ideological circumstances attending it"[8] The medium of transmission, oral vs. written, is not itself as important in the stability of the tradition; it "does not greatly change the degree of continuity or discontinuity that is inherent in all forms of traditions," as Van Seters notes.[9]

But it is equally problematic to jump to conclusions that "oral tradition is untrustworthy."[10] Folklore scholarship in general underwent an "anti-historical reaction" in the 1950s and 60s, following on the work of Moses Finley.[11] Oral tradition came to be seen as essentially unhistorical.[12]

This study has consciously avoided issues of historical veracity up to this point. Nevertheless, a book on oral tradition in the Bible ought to address this concern, and the discussion in this book does bear on the topic.[13]

The historical value of an oral source depends somewhat on genre. The extent of propagandistic elements in, say, praise poetry, can mask genuine illuminating historical data.[14] Formalized historical accounts can be useful when treated with caution.[15] Their chronologies should be particularly suspect.[16] Yet "many oral societies devised strong internal controls over misrepresentation, incorrect and unshared historical

---

6. Ahlström, "Oral and Written Transmission," 69.

7. Wyatt, "'Water, Water Everywhere . . . ,'" 230.

8. Ibid., 232; Davies, "The Reliability," 90.

9. Van Seters, "The Origins of the Hebrew Bible," 92.

10. Paul S. Ash, *David, Solomon and Egypt*. On the problems of such views, see Treitler, "Sinners and Singers," 158.

11. Sherratt, "Archaeological Contexts," 130–31.

12. Perrois, "Tradition orale et histoire," 144.

13. In the ancient world—in Egypt, for instance—oral tradition was considered rather suspect. Hatshepsut's *Pwenet* text contrasts oral tradition with accurate reporting (Redford, "Scribe and Speaker," 171).

14. Finnegan, "A Note on Oral Tradition," 196 ; Pasayat, *Oral Tradition, Society, and History*, 11.

15. Finnegan, "A Note on Oral Tradition," 197.

16. Davies, "The Reliability," 91.

narration."[17] We cannot deny that "certain forms of stories, ballads, or nursery rhymes have come down through the generations in relatively unchanged form."[18]

In addition, it is important to consider what kind of historical information we are seeking. If we embrace the clue-seeking, forensic model of historiography I have defended elsewhere,[19] oral literature can tell us quite a lot.[20] Oral epic, it may be argued, presents truth on different terms than modern textual histories.[21] Historians in Nordic countries are only just rediscovering an interest in patently legendary materials after a long period of avoiding them because they were not historical.[22] Oral literature offers "invaluable doorways into the day-to-day world-view of the people of the past who told and received" it.[23]

But even events can be preserved authentically, if we look for "stable point[s] present in every account" that do not "appear to be an addition from elsewhere."[24] When we cannot explain why or how a given element should have entered into a tradition at a point late in its transmission, we may be looking at history.[25]

The situation of Homer is perhaps most similar here. Evidence now exists that there was a real, historical war in which Troy was destroyed by Mycenaean Greeks.[26] Over time, however, events were combined arbitrarily and reinterpreted to produce a story that bears very little resemblance to "what actually happened."[27]

17. Jawaharlal Handoo, "'People are Still Hungry for Kings,'" 72; Davies, "Reliability," 90.

18. Finnegan, *Oral Traditions and the Verbal Arts*, 113. Petroglyph iconography in the American southwest of dead adult male bighorns and the religious system itself within which the art was made remains unchanged for 11,000 years (Whitley, "Archaeological Evidence," 18–19).

19. Miller, "Yahweh and His Clio," 158–59.

20. Finnegan, "A Note on Oral Tradition," 198.

21. Foley, "Traditional History in South Slavic Oral Epic," 357.

22. Gunnell, "Legends and Landscape," 306.

23. Ibid., 311.

24. Vaughan, "Fact and Fiction," 223.

25. Ibid., 227.

26. Raaflaub, "Epic and History," 59.

27. Ibid.

Elsewhere, I have suggested that an orally derived "historical" text may be imagined, if you will, as something like a painting.[28] Textualized oral lore paints a picture of the world it describes. To define this metaphor better, consider a Renaissance painting of the assassination of Julius Caesar. The dress, the architecture may be Renaissance. There may be elements in the painting that are Romanesque or from other periods between the Roman and Renaissance, which the artist included, knowing that they were "past." This does not mean that Caesar was not assassinated. And so, classicists have tried to locate this element or that "in the Bronze Age, the Dark Ages, and in Homer's own time."[29] Since the poet made a conscious effort to avoid recent innovations if he knew them to be such, the latter category is small.[30] "The society depicted in the *Iliad* to a large extent matches up with that deduced from archaeological and other data for Greek society around 800 BCE," considerably later than the war described.[31] Yet many elements—most notably Ajax's shield, but other objects and verbal motifs—belong to the mid-second millennium or earlier.[32] Given the infrequent, inconsistent, and contradictory appearances of these elements, it is improbable that they were consciously introduced in the eighth century as "archaisms."[33] J. K. Davies provides nine useful criteria for evaluating individual logoi from the Homeric epics for their historical accuracy: accurate material culture, sociocultural accuracy, lack of anachronisms, lack of fantastic details, a story kernel of a kind suited to survival in collective memory, historical probability, external confirmation, a means for oral transmission, and lack of other (e.g., etiological) explanation for the logos.[34] He readily admits that all nine will rarely be satisfied.[35]

If we turn to the Arabic material, the *Sīrat Banī Hilāl* has been woven from a skein of actual events,[36] but with the focus shifted to he-

---

28. Miller, "A Taphonomic Approach." Calvet's "sedimentary" analogy is similar (Calvet, *Tradition Orale*, 95–96).

29. Raaflaub, "Epic and History," 61.

30. Ibid.

31. Edwards, "Homer's *Iliad*," 312.

32. Sherratt, "Archaeological Contexts," 135, 139.

33. Ibid., 136.

34. Davies, "The Reliability," 98–100.

35. Ibid., 101.

36. Reynolds, "*Sīrat Banī Hilāl*," 80.

roic individuals.[37] *Sīrat ʾAntar ibn Shaddād* incorporates historical fact and fabricated embellishment, historical personages and their fictitious actions.[38] "The frame of the *sīra* is essentially correct, though the main characters appear to be fictitious."[39] At the same time, historical events, historical political systems, and historical customs are included.[40] Actual historical figures appear in actual historical battles that have nothing to do with that figure, or that may have occurred long after the figure was dead.[41] Historical figures with similar names are merged, chronologies are altered, but the story line may still remains basically accurate.[42] When historically accurate material is used, it is used according to the furtherance of the author's literary ends.[43] The *suwālif*, likewise, are of mixed and sometimes negligible historical value.[44] The situation resembles the Homeric epics, then. We do not have an accurate historical narrative. We have an authentic plot line filled with authentic details but fictitious in some of the narrative's most important particulars and often with no way to tell the fictitious from the real.[45] We should not be tempted to say of the *siyar*, as Peter Heath does of the *Sīrat ʾAntar ibn Shaddād*, "that these works are woefully bad history."[46] We might see them as "heavily curated artifacts" that nevertheless have much to tell about their time of origin.[47]

Historicity is also a question for those dealing with the Icelandic material. On the one hand, "the depth of historical memory, i.e., the interval between the earliest memorized events and the time of their recording in writing, constituted several centuries."[48] The sagamen thought the oral

---

37. Reynolds, "Epic and History," 407.

38. Cherkaoui, *Le roman de ʾAntar* 172 ; Heath, *The Thirsty Sword*, 24.

39. Reynolds, "*Sīrat Banī Hilāl*," 83.

40. Cherkaoui, "Historical Elements," 408.

41. Ibid., 411, 415, 421.

42. Ibid., 412–13, 416, 421.

43. Ibid. 407–8, 420.

44. Sowayan, *Arabian Oral Historical Narrative*, 17.

45. Garcin, "*Sīra/s* et histoire," 33–34 ; Cherkaoui, "Historical Elements," 416. This seems to be the case in oral balladry as a whole (Nicolaisen, "Names and Narratives, " 262–64, 266–67).

46. Heath, "A Critical Review," 40.

47. Sowayan, *Arabian Oral Historical Narrative*, 45.

48. Melnikova, "The Incorporation of Oral Historical Tradition," 2.

lore they were using was historically accurate.[49] On the other hand, "The remembrances about the past underwent continual changes . . . ceaseless revision."[50] Much in the stories of the poetic Edda "is a late invention."[51] And it mattered little to the sagamen "whether a verse was composed to commemorate a real event or whether it was composed as part of a story, so long as there is reason to believe that it is old."[52]

The Icelandic material shows that the painting model outlined above is not sufficient. The painting of the past is not merely an accumulation of elements from the "target time" ("narrative time") and all other moments up to and including the author's own time ("time of narration").[53] Many of the elements that work their way into oral historical narratives are mythological in origin, and this must be accounted for in the biblical material.[54]

And yet, as in the Arabic oral literature, many elements have their origin over two centuries before the writing of the text.[55] "Skeptical assessment of skaldic verse as a possible source for . . . history seems generally correct. But on occasion skaldic testimony has the value of corroborating details found in other minor sources. On occasion, too, information in the skaldic verses, though not fully confirmed elsewhere, has a general plausibility that encourages acceptance."[56] Some of the overall stories, minus many details, are known independently from Iceland, England, and Germany. Anglo-Saxon poetry attests to the story of Weland (or Völund; see above) circulating in England four hundred years before the

49. Beard, "Berserkir," 99; Andersson, "From Tradition," 9; Quinn, "From Orality to Literacy in Medieval Iceland," 50. The late twelfth-century Norwegian Theodoricus Monachus was less trusting (*Historia de antiquitate*, cited in Hermann, "Concepts of Memory," 289–91). Tacitus was very skeptical of the restored value of Germanic lays (Green, *Medieval Listening and Reading*, 239.

50. Melnikova, "The Incorporation of Oral Historical Tradition," 2.

51. Taylor, "*Völundarkviða, Þrymskviða*, and the Function of Myth," 264; Vésteinn Ólason, "Icelandic Saga," 46.

52. Gordon, "Oral Tradition," 75. Würth, "Historiography," 156, is less certain of this.

53. Although it is all of that (Ross, "From Iceland to Norway," 58).

54. Melnikova, "The Incorporation of Oral Historical Tradition," 8; Gordon, "Oral Tradition," 69.

55. Gunnell, "From *Grímnismál* to Graffiti," (online: www.hanko.uio.no/planses/TerryGunnel.html). Gísli Sigurðsson does not think we have the ability to separate out the historical from the fictional; "Orality Harnessed," 26.

56. Poole, "Skaldic Verse," 298.

written Icelandic *Völundarkviða* appeared.[57] The sagas "are based on the oral memory of people in Iceland. They are not spun out of thin air."[58] We have more cases of authentic plot lines filled with authentic details but fictitious in some of the narratives' most important particulars. But if we reject somewhat the hard distinction between "history" and "fiction," as Lars Lönnroth and Heather O'Donoghue have suggested,[59] then the poems and sagas are still "historical."

We should, therefore, be chary when approaching the orally derived narratives of the Old Testament. They probably preserve authentic historical plot lines and are filled with authentic details. But we should also expect that some of the key ingredients of the narratives are not historically genuine. This should certainly not deter us from using these texts for the great deal they reveal about local geography, society, attitudes, and ideas.[60]

Still, excavating the orally derived texts in the Bible for kernels of historical truth, like similarly excavating literary texts, seems much less interesting than "shift[ing] the emphasis away from what is remembered to a consideration of how and why it is remembered."[61]

---

57. Taylor, "*Völundarkviða*," 266.

58. Gísli Sigurðsson, "Orality and Literacy," 296.

59. Lönnroth, "The Transformation of Literary Genres," 341; O'Donoghue, *Skaldic Verse*, 12.

60. Gunnell, "Legends and Landscape," 313–14. The *local* nature of this material deserves much more study, as ethnographic research shows the deeply imbedded nature of folk material in the landscape of its tradents (ibid., 317–18).

61. Townsend, "Whatever Happened to York Viking Poetry?" 51.

Conclusion

We have seen that any continued reliance on the oral-formulaic school of Parry and Lord, and Goody and Ong by biblical scholars would be highly misguided. There is no formulaic test for orality in a written text, oral poets do not always compose on the spot, societies are seldom entirely oral or entirely literate, and there is no philosophical difference between those that are.

Literary authors in antiquity composed from both oral and written sources, interweaving them with their own contributions, always composing for oral/aural performance. In ancient Israel, this was part of a stream of tradition embedded in an oral-and-written educational system throughout the Iron II period. Oral and written literatures were simultaneously part of ancient Israel for the entire time of the Hebrew Bible's composition. We must abandon a model of oral literature becoming a written Bible, to be re-oralized in the Jewish community. There was an interplay of oral and written composition and performance throughout Israel's history.

The oral literature of ancient Israel resembled the Eddic and Skaldic poetry of Iceland and the oral narrative poetry of Arabia. These were performed in court settings, with audience-speaker interaction, a variety of delivery genres, serial performance, and musical accompaniment. When this material became textualized in the Bible, it was similar to the Icelandic family sagas and Arabic *siyar*. Several specific examples from the Bible were outlined in this volume, but it must be remembered that all of the Old Testament narrative books were part of an oral-written stream of tradition.

This does not mean that such examples of orally derived literature are historically reliable. They preserve authentic plots and are filled with authentic details, but they are fictitious in many respects, even down to the main characters.

The biblical text cannot be fully understood without understanding its oral nature, especially as biblical scholarship moves into postmodern and nonpositivistic directions. William Graham writes, "Implicit in the loss of the fundamental orality of the written word is also the loss of an important perspective on the functional aspect of scripture . . . The oral dimension is, however, the one most intimately bound up with the major personal and communal roles of scripture in religious life, especially those that move not only in the intellectual or ideational realm."[1]

Oral tradition cannot be the research interest of traditions historians alone. We have seen how, among other things, redaction- and text-criticism are extensions of orality; in the future we may explore how so, too, are actualization and contextualization.[2]

---

1. Graham, *Beyond the Written Word*, 155.

2. Draper, "'Less Literate Are Safer,'" 314. On the theological importance of orality, see Johannes Beumer, *Die mündliche Überlieferung als Glaubensquelle* (Handbuch der Dogmengeschichte 1.4; Freiburg: Herder, 1962), 1–14; and, from an outsider's perspective, see Schleicher, "General Reflections," 136.

Bibliography[1]

Aarne, Antti, and Stith Thompson. *The Types of the Folktale*. 2nd ed. Folklore Fellows Communications 184. Helsinki: Academia Scientiarum Fennica, 1964.

Abrahams, Roger D. "Creativity, Individuality, and the Traditional Singer." *Studies in the Literary Imagination* 3 (1970) 5–34.

Acker, Paul. *Revising Oral Theory: Formulaic Composition in Old English and Old Icelandic Verse*. Garland Studies in Medieval Literature 16. New York: Garland, 1998.

Ahlström, Gosta W. "Oral and Written Transmission." *HTR* 59 (1966) 69–81.

Albertz, Rainer, and Bob Becking, editors. *Yahwism after the Exile: Perspectives on Israelite Religion in the Persian Era*. Studies in Theology and Religion 5. Assen: Van Gorcum, 2003.

Albright, W. F. "The Oracles of Balaam." *JBL* 63 (1944) 207–33.

———. "Some Oriental Glosses on the Homeric Problem." *AJA* 54 (1950) 162–76.

Alt, Albrecht. "The Origins of Israelite Law." In *Essays on Old Testament History and Religion*, 101–72. Garden City, NY: Doubleday, 1966.

Alster, Bendt. *Dumuzi's Dream: Aspects of Oral Poetry in a Sumerian Myth*. Mesopotamia 1. Copenhagen: Akademisk, 1972.

———. "Interaction of Oral and Written Poetry in Early Mesopotamian Literature." In *Mesopotamian Epic Literature: Aural or Oral?* edited by Marianna E. Vogelzang and Herman L. J. Vanstiphout, 23–70. Lewiston, NY: Mellen, 1992.

Amit, D., G. D. Stiebel, and O. Peleg Barkat, editors. *New Studies in the Archaeology of Jerusalem and Its Region*. Jerusalem: Hebrew University of Jerusalem Press, 2009.

Amit, Yairah. *History and Ideology: An Introduction to the Historiography of the Hebrew Bible.*. Biblical Seminar 60. Sheffield, UK: Sheffield Academic, 1999.

Amodio, Mark C. "Contemporary Critical Approaches and Studies in Oral Tradition." In *Teaching Oral Traditions*, edited by John Miles Foley, 95–105. Modern Language Association Options for Teaching. New York: Modern Language Association, 1998.

———. *Writing the Oral Tradition*. Poetics of Orality and Literacy. Notre Dame, IN: University of Notre Dame Press, 2004.

Amzallag, Nissim, and Mikhal Avriel. "Complex Antiphony in David's Lament and Its Literary Significance." *VT* 60 (2010) 1–14.

Andersson, Theodore M. "From Tradition to Literature in the Sagas." In *Oral Art Forms and Their Passage into Writing*, edited by Else Mundal and Jonas Wellendorf, 7–18. Copenhagen: Museum Tusculanum Press, 2008.

"Antar." *Journal of Sacred Literature* 9 (1850) 1–35.

---

1. N.B. Because most modern Icelanders have no surnames, it is conventional to list them in bibliographies alphabetically by first name rather than patronymic.

Bibliography

Apo, Satu, "The Relationship between Oral and Literary Tradition as a Challenge in Fairy-Tale Research." *Marvels & Tales: Journal of Fairy-Tale Studies* 21 (2007) 19–33.

Archi, Alfonso. "Orality, Direct Speech and the Kumarbi Cycle." *AoF* 36 (2009) 209–29.

———. "Transmission of Recitative Literature by the Hittites." *AoF* 34 (2007) 185–203.

Armistead, Samuel G. "Epic and Ballad." *Olifant* 8 (1981) 376–88.

Ásdís Egilsdóttir. "From Orality to Literacy." In *Reykholt som Makt- og Lærdomssenter*, edited by Else Mundal, 215–28. Snorrastofa 3. Reykholt: Snorrastofa, Menningar- og Miðaldasetur, 2006.

Ash, Paul S. *David, Solomon and Egypt: A Reassessment*. JSOTSup 297. Sheffield, UK: Sheffield Academic, 1999.

Ashcraft, Mark H. *Human Memory and Cognition*. New York: HarperCollins, 1994.

Assmann, Jan. *Religion and Cultural Memory: Ten Studies*. Cultural Memory in the Present. Stanford: Stanford University Press, 2006.

Attwood, Katrina. "The Saga of Gunnlaug Serpent-tongue." In *The Sagas of Icelanders: A Selection*, edited by Jane Smiley, 558–94. New York: Viking, 2000.

Avishur, Y. "Additional Parallels of an Akkadian Proverb Found in the Iraqi Vernacular Arabic." *Die Welt des Orient* 12 (1981) 37–38.

Bagby, Benjamin. "*Beowulf*, the *Edda*, and the Performance of Medieval Epic." In *Performing Medieval Narrative*, edited by Evelyn B. Vitz et al., 181–92. Woodbridge, Suffolk, UK: Brewer, 2005.

Baines, John. "Myth and Literature." In *Ancient Egyptian Literature: History and Forms*, edited by Antonio Loprieno, 361–78. PÄ 10. Leiden: Brill, 1996.

———. *Visual and Written Culture in Ancient Egypt*. New York: Oxford University Press, 2007.

Bakker, Egbert J. "Epic Remembering." In *Orality, Literacy, Memory in the Ancient Greek and Roman World*, edited by E. Anne Mackay, 65–77. Orality and Literacy in Ancient Greece 7. Mnemosyne Supplement 298. Leiden: Brill, 2008.

———. "Homer, Hypertext, and the Web of Myth." In *Varieties and Consequences of Literacy and Orality*, edited by Ursula Schaefer and Edda Spielmann, 149–60. Tübingen: Narr, 2001.

Bandhu, C. M. "Common Languages and Common Narratives." *Folklore and Folkloristics* 1 (2008) 20–27.

Barber, Elizabeth W., and Paul T. Barber. *When They Severed Earth from Sky: How the Human Mind Shapes Myth*. Princeton: Princeton University Press, 2005.

Bartok, Bela, and Albert B. Lord. *Serbo-Croatian Folksongs*. Columbia University Studies in Musicology 7. New York: Columbia University Press, 1951.

Bauman, Richard. "Verbal Art as Performance." In *Performance*, edited by Philip Auslander, 3:32–60. New York: Routledge, 2003.

Beard, D. J. "The Berserkir in Icelandic Literature." In *Approaches to Oral Tradition*, edited by Robin Thelwall, 99–114. Occasional Papers in Linguistics and Language Learning 4. Belfast: New University of Ulster, 1978.

Beckman, Gary. "The Anatolian Myth of Illuyanka." *JANES* 14 (1982) 11–25.

———. "Hittite and Hurrian Epic." In *A Companion to Ancient Epic*, edited by John Miles Foley, 255–63. Blackwell Companions to the Ancient World. Literature and Culture. Malden, MA: Blackwell, 2005.

———. "The Religion of the Hittites." *BA* 52 (1989) 98–108.

Béré, Paul. "*Auditor in fabula*—la Bible dans son contexte oral." *OTE* 19 (2006) 1089–105.

Bibliography

Berggren, Jenny. "The 'Ipwt in Papyrus Westcar (7, 5–8; 9,1–5)." PhD diss., Uppsala University, 2006.

Berlejung, Angelika. "Assyrians in the West." Paper presented at the Twentieth International Organization for the Study of the Old Testament, Helsinki, August 1–6, 2010.

Beumer, Johannes. *Die mündliche Überlieferung als Glaubensquelle.* Handbuch der Dogmengeschichte 1.4. Freiburg: Herder & Herder, 1962.

Biale, David. "The God with Breasts: El Shaddai in the Bible." *HR* 21 (1981) 240–56.

Birgisson, Bergveinn. "What Have We Lost by Writing?" In *Oral Art Forms and Their Passage into Writing*, edited by Else Mundal and Jonas Wellendorf, 163–84. Copenhagen: Museum Tusculanum Press, 2008.

Birkeland, Harris. *Zum Hebräischen Traditionswesen.* ANVAO Historisk-Filosofisk Klasse 1938,1. Oslo: Dybwad, 1939.

Blanton, Richard E., "Beyond Centralization: Steps toward a Theory of Egalitarian Behavior in Archaic States." In *Archaic States*, edited by Gary M. Feinman and Joyce Marcus, 135–72. Santa Fe: School of American Research Press, 1998.

Blenkinsopp, Joseph, *Treasures Old and New: Essays in the Theology of the Pentateuch.* Grand Rapids: Eerdmans, 2004.

Block, Daniel I. "Will the Real Gideon Please Stand Up? Narrative Style and Intentions in Judges 6–9" *JETS* 40 (1997) 353–66.

Bogatyrev, Peter. "Folklore as a Special Form of Creativity." In *The Prague School: Selected Writings, 1929–1946*, edited by Peter Steiner, 32–46. University of Texas Press Slavic Series 6. Austin: University of Texas Press, 1982.

Boley, Jacqueline. "The Storyteller's Art in Old Hittite: The Use of Sentence Connectives and Discourse Particles." *Res Antiquae* 1 (2004) 67–110.

Bowman, Richard G. "Narrative Criticism." In *Judges and Method: New Approaches in Biblical Studies*, edited by Gale A. Yee, 17–33. 2nd ed. Minneapolis: Fortress, 2007.

Brink, Stefan. "*Verba Volant, Scripta Manent?* Aspects of Early Scandinavian Oral Society." In *Literacy in Medieval and Early Modern Scandinavian Culture*, edited by Pernille Hermann, 77–120. The Viking Collection 16. Odense: University Press of Southern Denmark, 2005.

Brockington, John. "The Textualization of the Sanskrit Epics." In *Textualization of Oral Epics*, edited by Lauri Honko, 193–215. Trends in Linguistics. Studies and Monographs 128. Berlin: de Gruyter, 2000.

Bruno, Arvid. *Das Hebräische Epos: Eine Rhythmische und Textkritische.* Uppsala: Almqvist & Wiksell, 1935.

Burgess, Jonathan S. "The Epic Cycle and Fragments." In *A Companion to Ancient Epic*, edited by John Miles Foley, 344–52. Blackwell Companions to the Ancient World. Literature and Culture. Malden, MA: Blackwell, 2005.

Burgh, Theodore W. *Listening to the Artifacts: Music Culture in Ancient Palestine.* New York: T. & T. Clark, 2006.

Burkhart, Dagmar. "Märchen nach dem Märchen." *Fabula* 49 (2008) 47–69.

Butler, Christopher S. "Formulaic Language." In *The Dynamics of Language Use: Functional and Contrastive Perspectives*, edited by Christopher S. Butler et al., 221–42. Pragmatics & Beyond, new ser., 140. Amsterdam: Benjamins, 2005.

———. "Functional Approaches to Language Use." In *The Dynamics of Language Use: Functional and Contrastive Perspectives*, edited by Christopher S. Butler, et al., 3–17. Pragmatics & Beyond, new ser., 140. Amsterdam: Benjamins, 2005.

Bibliography

Byock, Jesse L. "Saga Form, Oral Prehistory, and the Icelandic Social Context." *New Literary History* 16 (1984) 153–73.

Byrne, Ryan. "The Refuge of Scribalism in Iron I Palestine." *BASOR* 345 (2007) 1–31.

Caie, Graham D. "*Ealdgesegena worn:* What the Old English *Beowulf* Tells Us about Oral Forms." In *Oral Art Forms and Their Passage into Writing*, edited by Else Mundal and Jonas Wellendorf, 109–20. Copenhagen: Museum Tusculanum Press, 2008.

Calvet, Louis-Jean. *La Tradition orale.* Que sais-je? 2181. Paris: Presses Universitaires de France, 1984

Campbell, Antony F. *Joshua to Chronicles: An Introduction.* Louisville: Westminster John Knox, 2004.

———. "The Reported Story." *Semeia* 46 (1989) 77–85.

Campbell, Antony F., and Mark O'Brien. *Rethinking the Pentateuch: Prolegomena to the Theology of Ancient Israel.* Louisville: Westminster John Knox, 2005.

———. *Unfolding the Deuteronomistic History: Origins, Upgrades, Present Text.* Minneapolis: Fortress, 2000.

Canova, Giovanni. "Il Poeta Epico nella Tradizione Araba: Nota e Testimonianze." *Quaderni di Studi Arabi* 1 (1983) 87–104.

Carey, John, editor. *Eyewitness to History.* Cambridge: Harvard University Press, 1987

Carr, David M. "The Rise of Torah." In *The Pentateuch as Torah: New Models for Understanding Its Promulgation and Acceptance*, edited by Gary N. Knoppers and Bernard Malcolm Levinson, 39–46. Winona Lake, IN: Eisenbrauns, 2007.

———. "The Tel Zayit Abecedary in (Social) Context." In *Literate Culture and Tenth-Century Canaan: The Tel Zayit Abecedary in Context*, edited by Ron E. Tappy and P. Kyle McCarter, 113–30. Winona Lake, IN: Eisenbrauns, 2008.

———. "Torah on the Heart: Literary Jewish Textuality within Its Ancient Near Eastern Context." *Oral Tradition* 25 (2010) 17–39.

———. *Writing on the Tablet of the Heart: Origins of Scripture and Literature.* Oxford: University Press, 2005.

Casanowicz, Immanuel M. "Paronomasia in the Old Testament." *JBL* 12 (1893) 105–67.

Causse, Antonin. *Les plus vieux chants de la Bible.* Études d'Histoire et de Philosophie Religieuses Publiées par la Faculté de Théologie Protestante de l'Université de Strasbourg 14. Paris: Alcan, 1926.

Cherkaoui, Driss. "Historical Elements in the *Sīrat 'Antar.*" *Oriente Moderno* 83 (2003) 407–25.

———. *Le Roman de 'Antar.* Paris: Présence Africaine, 2000.

Chesnutt, Michael. "Orality in a Norse-Icelandic Perspective." *Oral Tradition* 18 (2003) 197–99.

———. "Popular and Learned Elements in the Icelandic Saga-Tradition." In *Proceedings of the First International Saga Conference*, edited by Peter Foote et al., 28–65. London: Viking Society for Northern Research, 1973.

Christensen, D. L. "Numbers 21:14–15 and the Book of the Wars of the Lord." *CBQ* 36 (1974) 359–60.

Cipolla, Adele. *Il Racconto di Nornagestr: Edizione Critica, Traduzione e Comento.* Medioevi Testi 1. Verona: Fiorini, 1996.

Clark, Francelia M. *Theme in Oral Epic and in Beowulf.* Milman Parry Studies in Oral Tradition. New York: Garland, 1995.

Cogan, Mordechai, and Hayim Tadmor. *II Kings: A New Translation.* AB 11. Garden City, NY: Doubleday, 1988.

Bibliography

Connelly, Bridget. *Arab Folk Epic and Identity*. Berkeley: University of California Press, 1986.

Constantine, Mary-Ann. "Thoughts on Oral Tradition." *Oral Tradition* 18 (2003) 187–88.

Cooper, Jerrold S. "Babbling On: Recovering Mesopotamian Orality." In *Mesopotamian Epic Literature: Oral or Aural?* edited by Marianna E. Vogelzang and Herman L. J. Vanstiphout, 103–22. Lewiston, NY: Mellen, 1992.

Coote, Robert. "Reflections." In *Text and Tradition: The Hebrew Bible and Folklore*, edited by Susan B. Niditch, 229–30. SemeiaSt. Atlanta: Scholars, 1990.

Cross, Frank Moore. *From Epic to Canon: History and Literature in Ancient Israel*. Baltimore: Johns Hopkins University Press, 1998.

———. "Telltale Remnants of Oral Epic in the Older Sources of the Tetrateuch." In *Exploring the Longue Durée: Essays in Honor of Lawrence E. Stager*, edited by J. David Schloen, 83–88. Winona Lake, IN: Eisenbrauns, 2009.

Culley, Robert C. "Exploring New Directions." In *The Hebrew Bible and Its Modern Interpreters*, edited by Douglas A. Knight and Gene M. Tucker, 181–83. The Bible and Its Modern Interpreters 1. Chico, CA: Scholars, 1985.

———. "Five Tales of Punishment in the Book of Numbers." In *Text and Tradition: The Hebrew Bible and Folklore*, edited by Susan B. Niditch, 25–34. SemeiaSt. Atlanta: Scholars, 1990.

———. *Oral Formulaic Language in the Biblical Psalms*. Near and Middle Eastern Series 4. Toronto: University of Toronto Press, 1967.

———. "Oral Traditions and the OT: Some Recent Discussion." *Semeia* 5 (1976) 1–33.

———. *Studies in the Structure of Hebrew Narrative*. Semeia Supplements. Philadelphia: Fortress, 1976.

Davidson, E. T. A. *Intricacy, Design & Cunning in the Book of Judges*. Philadelphia: Xlibris, 2008.

Davies, J. K. "The Reliability of the Oral Tradition." In *The Trojan War: Its Historicity and Context*, edited by Lin Foxhall and John K. Davies, 87–110. Bristol: Bristol Classical, 1984.

Davis, Donald. *Jack Always Seeks His Fortune: Authentic Appalachian Jack Tales*. American Storytelling. Little Rock, AR: August House, 1992.

Day, John. *God's Conflict with the Dragon and the Sea: Echoes of Canaanite Myth in the Old Testament*. Cambridge Oriental Publications 35. Cambridge: Cambridge University Press, 1985.

———. *Yahweh and the Gods and Goddesses of Canaan*. JSOTSup 265. New York: Continuum, 2002.

Deignan, Alice. *Metaphor and Corpus Linguistics*. Converging Evolution in Language and Communication Research, 6. Amsterdam: Benjamins, 2005.

Doniger, Wendy. "Minimyths and Maximyths and Political Points of View." In *Myth and Method*, edited by Laurie L. Patton and Wendy Doniger, 109–27. Studies in Religion and Culture. Charlottesville: University Press of Virginia, 1996.

Donner, H., and W. Röllig *Kanaanäische und aramäische Inschriften*. 3 vols. Wiesbaden: Harrassowitz, 1962.

Dowden, Ken. *The Uses of Greek Mythology*. Approaching the Ancient World 1. London: Routledge, 1992.

Draper, Jonathan A. "'Less Literate Are Safer': The Politics of Orality and Literacy in Biblical Interpretation." *ATR* 84 (2002) 303–18.

Bibliography

Dumbrill, Richard J. *The Archaeomusicology of the Ancient Near East*. Victoria, BC: Trafford, 2005.

Dundes, Alan. *Holy Writ as Oral Lit*. Lanham, MD: Rowman & Littlefield, 1999.

Durand, Jean-Marie. "Écrit et parole au Proche-Orient ancien." In *L'Appropriation de l'Oral*, edited by Danielle Hébrard and Annie Prassoloff, 51–56. Paris: Université Paris Diderot, 1990.

Dietrich, M. et al. editors. *Die keilaphabetischen Texte aus Ugarit*. AOAT 24/1. Neukirchen-Vluyn: Neukirchener, 1976.

Dijkstra, Manfred. "Jacob." In *DDD*, 459–61.

Dronke, Ursula. *The Poetic Edda*. 2 vols. Oxford: Clarendon, 1969.

Echols, Charles L. *"Tell Me, O Muse": The Song of Deborah (Judges 5) in Light of Heroic Poetry*. Library of Hebrew Bible/Old Testament Studies 487. New York: T. & T. Clark, 2008.

Edmunds, Lowell. "Epic and Myth." In *A Companion to Ancient Epic*, edited by John Miles Foley, 31–44. Blackwell Companions to the Ancient World. Literature and Culture. Malden, MA: Blackwell, 2005.

Edwards, I. E. S. et al., editors. *The History of the Middle East and the Aegean Region, 1800–1380 BC*. Cambridge Ancient History 2.2. Cambridge: Cambridge University Press, 1973.

Edwards, Mark W. "Homer's *Iliad*." In *A Companion to Ancient Epic*, edited by John Miles Foley, 302–14. Blackwell Companions to the Ancient World. Literature and Culture. Malden, MA: Blackwell, 2005.

Edzard, D. O. "Sumerian Epic." *Bulletin of the Canadian Society for Mesopotamian Studies* 27 (1994) 7–14.

Ego, Beatte, "In der Schriftrolle ist für mich geschrieben." In *Die Textualisierung der Religion*, edited by Joachim Schaper, 82–104. FAT 62. Tübingen: Mohr/Siebeck, 2009.

Elman, Yaakov. "Authoritative Oral Tradition in Neo-Assyrian Scribal Circles." *Journal of Ancient Near Eastern Studies* 7 (1975) 19–32.

Engnell, Ivan. *A Rigid Scrutiny: Critical Essays on the Old Testament*. Translated and edited by John T. Willis. Nashville: Vanderbilt University Press, 1969.

Esler, Philip F. "Ezra-Nehemiah as a Narrative of (Reinvented) Israelite Identity." *BibInt* 11 (2003) 413–26.

Fairclough, Norman. "Semiosis, Ideology, and Mediation." In *Mediating Ideology in Text and Image: Ten Critical Studies*, edited by Inger Lassen et al., 19–35. Discourse Approaches to Politics, Society, and Culture 18. Amsterdam: Benjamins, 2006.

Faulkes, Anthony. *Poetical Inspiration in Old Norse and Old English Poetry*. Dorothea Coke Memorial Lecture in Northern Studies. London: Viking Society for Northern Research, 1997.

Fausbøll, V., editor. *Buddhist Birth-Stories*. New and rev. ed. Broadway Translations. London: Routledge, 1925.

Fine, Elizabeth C. *The Folklore Text: From Performance to Print*. Bloomington: Indiana University Press, 1984.

Finkelstein, Israel. *'Izbet Sartah: An Early Iron Age Site Near Rosh Ha'ayin*. British Archaeological Reports International 299. Oxford: British Archaeological Reports, 1985.

Finlay, Alison. "Skalds, Troubadours, and Sagas." *Saga book of the Viking Society for Northern Research* 24 (1995) 105–53.

Bibliography

Finnegan, Ruth H. "How Oral Is Oral Literature?" *BSOAS* 37 (1974) 52–64.

————. *Literacy and Orality: Studies in the Technology of Communication.* Oxford: Blackwell, 1988.

————. "Literacy versus Non-literacy: The Great Divide? Some Comments on the Significance of Literature in Non-Literate Cultures." In *Modes of Thought: Essays on Thinking in Western and Non-Western Societies,* edited by Robin Horton and Ruth Finnegan, 112–44. London: Faber & Faber, 1973.

————. "A Note on Oral Tradition and Historical Evidence." *History and Theory* 9 (1970) 195–201.

————. *The Oral and Beyond: Doing Things with Words in Africa.* Chicago: University of Chicago Press, 2007.

————. "'Oral Tradition': Weasel Words or Transdisciplinary Door to Multiplexity?" *Oral Tradition* 18 (2003) 84–86.

————. *Oral Traditions and the Verbal Arts: A Guide to Research.* Association of Social Anthropologists Research Methods 4. ASA Research Methods in Social Anthropology. London: Routledge, 1992.

————. "Problems in the Processing of 'Oral Texts.'" In *Oral Tradition and Innovation: New Wine in Old Bottles?,* edited by E. R. Sienaert et al., 1–23. Durban: University of Natal Oral Documentation and Research Centre, 1991.

————. "What Is Oral Literature Anyway?" In *Oral Literature and the Formula,* edited by Benjamin A. Stolz and Richard S. Shannon III, 175–76. Ann Arbor: Center for the Coordination of Ancient and Modern Studies, University of Michigan, 1976.

Foley, John Miles. "Analogues: Modern Oral Epics." In *A Companion to Ancient Epic,* edited by John Miles Foley, 196–212. Blackwell Companions to the Ancient World. Literature and Culture. Malden, MA: Blackwell, 2005.

————. "The Challenge of Translating Traditional Oral Epic." In *Dynamics of Tradition,* edited by Lotte Tarkka, 248–65. Studia Fennica folkloristica. Helsinki: Finnish Literature Society, 2003.

————. "Editing and Translating the Traditional Oral Epic." In *Epea and Grammata: Oral and Written Communication in Ancient Greece,* edited by Ian Worthington and John Miles Foley, 3–28. Mnemosyne Bibliotheca Classica Batava Supplement 230. Leiden: Brill, 2002.

————. "Fieldwork on Homer." In *New Directions in Oral Theory,* edited by Mark C. Amodio, 15–42. Medieval & Renaissance Texts & Studies, 287. Tempe: Arizona Center for Medieval and Renaissance Studies, 2005.

————. "Folklore and Oral Tradition." Paper presented at the 1994 annual meeting of the Society of Biblical Literature, Chicago.

————. *Immanent Art: From Structure to Meaning in Traditional Oral Epic.* Bloomington: Indiana University Press, 1991.

————. "The Implications of Oral Tradition." In *Oral Tradition in the Middle Ages,* edited by W. F. H. Nicolaisen, 31–58. Medieval & Renaissance Texts & Studies 112. Binghamton, NY: Medieval & Renaissance Texts & Studies, 1995.

————. "Plenitude and Diversity: Interactions between Orality and Writing." In *The Interface of Orality and Writing: Speaking, Seeing, Writing in the Shaping of New Genres,* edited by Annette Weissenrieder and Robert B. Coote, 103–18. WUNT 260. Tubingen: Mohr/Siebeck, 2010.

————. "Reading Homer through Oral Tradition." *College Literature* 34.2 (2007) 1–28.

————. *The Singer of Tales in Performance.* Voices in Performance and Text. Bloomington: Indiana University Press, 1995.

————. "Traditional History in South Slavic Oral Epic." In *Epic and History*, edited by David Konstan and Kurt A. Raaflaub, 347–61. The Ancient World: Comparative Histories 4. Chichester, UK: Wiley-Blackwell, 2010.

————. *Traditional Oral Epic: The Odyssey, Beowulf, and the Serbo-Croatian Return Song.* Berkeley: University of California Press, 1990.

————. Review of *The Singer of Tales*, by Albert B. Lord. *Cultural Analysis* 1 (2000) 85–96.

Frank, Roberta. "Skaldic Poetry." In *Old Norse–Icelandic Literature*, edited by Carol J. Clover and John Lindow, 157–96. Medieval Academy Reprints for Teaching, 42. Toronto: University of Toronto Press, 2005.

Friedman, Albert B. "The Oral-Formulaic Theory of Balladry—A Re-rebuttal." In *The Ballad Image: Essays Presented to Bertrand Harris Bronson*, edited by James Porter, 215–40. Los Angeles: University of California Press, 1983.

Gade, Kari Ellen, editor. *Poetry from the Kings' Sagas.* 2 vols. Skaldic Poetry of the Scandinavian Middle Ages 2. Turnhout: Brepols, 2009.

Gandz, Solomon. "Oral Tradition and the Bible." In *Jewish Studies in Memory of George A. Kohut*, edited by Salo W. Baron and Alexander Marx, 248–69. New York: The Alexander Kohut Memorial Foundation, 1935.

Garcin, Jean-Claude, "*Sīra*/s et histoire." *Arabica* 51 (2004) 33–54.

Garfinkel, Yosef, and Saar Ganor. "Khirbet Qeiyafa." *Journal of Hebrew Scriptures* 8 (2007–2008) article 22. Online: www.arts.ualberta.ca/JHS/Articles/article_99.pdf.

Garfinkel, Yosef, and Saar Ganor, editors. *Khirbet Qeiyafa.* Vol. 1, *Excavation Report 2007–2008.* Jerusalem: Israel Exploration Society, 2009.

Garsiel, Moshe. "Word Play and Puns as Rhetorical Device in the Book of Samuel." In *Puns and Pundits: Word Play in the Hebrew Bible and Ancient Near Eastern Literature*, edited by Scott B. Noegel, 181–204. Bethesda, MD: CDL, 2000.

Gass, Erasmus. "Modes of Divine Communication in the Balaam Narrative." *BN*, new ser., 139 (2008) 19–38.

Gaster, Theodor H. *Myth, Legend, and Custom in the Old Testament.* New York: Harper & Row, 1969.

Gelb, Ignace J. "Comparative Method in the Study of the Society and Economy of the Ancient Near East." *Rocznik Orientalistyczny* 41 (1980) 29–36.

Gerhardsson, Birger. Review of *Mündliche und schrifliche Tradition*, by A. H. J. Gunneweg. *SEÅ* 25 (1960) 175–81.

Gilan, Amir. "Epic and History in Hittite Anatolia." In *Epic and History*, edited by David Konstan and Kurt A. Raaflaub, 51–65. The Ancient World: Comparative Histories 4. Chichester, UK: Wiley-Blackwell, 2010.

Giles, Terry, and William Doan. "Performance Criticism of the Hebrew Bible." *Religion Compass* 2 (2008) 273–86.

Gísli Sigurðsson. *The Medieval Icelandic Saga and Oral Tradition.* Publications of the Milman Parry Collection of Oral Literature 2. Cambridge: Harvard University Press, 2004.

————. "On the Classification of Eddic Heroic Poetry in View of the Oral Theory." In *Poetry in the Scandinavian Middle Ages*, 245–55. Spoleto: Presso la sede del Centro Studi, 1990.

Bibliography

————. "Orality and Literacy in the Sagas of Icelanders." In *A Companion to Old Norse-Icelandic Literature and Culture*, edited by Rory McTurk, 285–301. Blackwell Companions to Literature and Culture 31. Malden, MA: Blackwell, 2005.

————. "Orality Harnessed: How to Read Written Sagas from an Oral Culture?" In *Oral Art Forms and Their Passage into Writing*, edited by Else Mundal and Jonas Wellendorf, 19–28. Copenhagen: Museum Tusculanum Press, 2008.

Gispen, W. H. *Mondelinge Overlevering in het Oude Testament*. Meppel: B. ten Brink en M. Stenvert & Zoom, 1932.

Gliick, J. J. "Paronomasia in Biblical Literature." *Semitics* 1 (1970) 50–78.

Glucksberg, Sam. *Understanding Figurative Language: From Metaphors to Idioms*. Oxford Psychological Series 36. Oxford: University Press, 2001.

Goatly, Andrew. *The Language of Metaphors*. London: Routledge, 1997.

Goedick, Hans. "Thoughts about the Papyrus Westcar." *ZÄS* 120 (1993) 23–26.

Gómez Aranda, Mariano. "Transmisión Oral y Transmisión Escrita: La Biblia Hebrea." In *Entre la Palabra y el Texto: Problemas en la Interpetación de Fuentes Orales y Escritas*, edited by Luis Díaz G. Viana and Matilde Fernández Montes, 247–67. Oiartzun, Spain: Sendoa, 1997.

Goody, Jack. *The Domestication of the Savage Mind*. Themes in the Social Sciences. Cambridge: Cambridge University Press, 1977.

————. *The Interface between the Written and the Oral*. Studies in Literacy, Family, Culture, and the State. Cambridge: Cambridge University Press, 1987.

————. *The Logic of Writing and the Organization of Society*. Studies in Literacy, Family, Culture, and the State. Cambridge: Cambridge University Press, 1986.

Goody, Jack, and Ian Watt. "The Consequences of Literacy." *Comparative Studies in Society and History* 5 (1963) 304–45.

Gordon, Cyrus H. *Ugaritic Textbook: Grammar, Texts in Transliteration, Cuneiform Selections, Glossary, Indices*. AnOr 38. Rome: Pontifical Biblical Institute, 1965.

Gordon, Edmund I. *Sumerian Proverbs: Glimpses into Everyday Life in Ancient Mesopotamia*. Museum Monographs 19. Philadelphia: University Museum, University of Pennyslvania, 1959.

Gordon, Ida. "Oral Tradition and the Sagas of Poets." In *Studia Centenalia*, edited by B. S. Benedikz, 69–75. Reykjavik, Iceland: Typis Isafoldianis, 1961.

Goyet, Florence, "Narrative Structure and Political Construction." *Oral Tradition* 23 (2008) 15–27.

Graham, William A. *Beyond the Written Word: Oral Aspects of Scripture in the History of Religion*. Cambridge: Cambridge University Press, 1987.

Green, D. H. *Medieval Listening and Reading: The Primary Reception of German Literature, 800–1300*. Cambridge: Cambridge University Press, 1994.

Greenwood, Emily. "Sounding Out Homer." *Oral Tradition* 24 (2009) 503–18.

Griffiths, Paul J. *Religious Reading: The Place of Reading in the Practice of Religion*. New York: Oxford University Press, 1999.

Groneberg, B. R. M. "*Tilpanu* =Bogen." In *Reallexikon der Assyriologie* 81 (1987) 115–23.

Guillaume, A. "Paronomasia in the Old Testament." *JSS* 9 (1964) 282–90.

Gunkel, Herman. *Genesis*. 2nd ed. HKAT. Göttingen: Vandenhoeck & Ruprecht, 1902.

————. *Genesis*. 3rd ed. HKAT. Göttingen: Vandenhoeck & Ruprecht, 1910.

Gunn, David M. "The 'Battle Report': Oral or Scribal Convention?" *JBL* 93 (1974) 513–18.

————. "Narrative Patterns and Oral Tradition in Judges and Samuel." *VT* 24 (1974) 286–317.

Bibliography

————. *The Story of King David: Genre and Interpretation.* JSOTSup 6. Sheffield, UK: JSOT Press, 1978.

————. "'Threading the Labyrinth': A Response to Albert B. Lord." In *Text and Tradition: The Hebrew Bible and Folklore,* edited by Susan B. Niditch, 19–24. SemeiaSt. Atlanta: Scholars, 1990.

Gunnell, Terry. "Eddic Poetry." In *A Companion to Old Norse-Icelandic Literature and Culture,* edited by Rory McTurk, 82–100. Blackwell Companions to Literature and Culture 31. Malden, MA: Blackwell, 2005.

————. "From *Grímnismál* to Graffiti." Online: www.hanko.uio.no/planses/TerryGunnel .html.

————. "*Grýla, Grýlur, Grøleks* and *Skeklers*: Folk Drama in the North Atlantic in the Early Middle Ages?" Online http://jol.ismennt.is/english/gryla-terry-gunnell.htm.

————. "Legends and Landscape in the Nordic Countries." *Cultural and Social History* 6 (2009) 305–22.

————. "Narratives, Space and Drama." *Folklore* 33 (2006) 7–26.

————. *The Origins of Drama in Scandinavia.* Woodbridge, UK: Brewer, 1995.

————. "The Performance of the Poetic Edda." In *The Viking World,* edited by Stefan Brink, 299–303. London: Routledge, 2008.

————. "The Play of Skírnir." *Nordic Theatre Studies* 7 (1995) 21–35.

————. "The Saga of Hrafnkel Frey's Godi." In *The Sagas of Icelanders,* edited by Jane Smiley, 436–62. New York: Viking, 2000.

————. "'Til holts ek gekk . . .' The Performance Demands of *Skírnismál, Fáfnismál,* and *Sigrdrífumál* in Liminal Time and Sacred Space." In *Old Norse Religion in Long-Term Perspectives,* edited by Anders Andrén, et al., 238–42. Vägar till Mildgård 8. Lund: Nordic Academic Press, 2006.

Gurney, O. R. "The Tale of the Poor Man of Nippur and Its Folklore Parallels." *Anatolian Studies* 22 (1972) 149–58.

Guy, Jeff. "Literacy and Literature." In *Oral Tradition and Innovation: New Wine in Old Bottles?* edited by E. R. Sienaert et al., 395–413. Durban, South Africa: University of Natal Oral Documentation and Research Centre, 1991.

Hahn, Ferdinand. "Zur Verschriftlichung mündlicher Tradition in der Bibel." *ZRGG* 39 (1987) 307–317.

Hainsworth, J. B. "The Fallibility of an Oral Heroic Tradition." In *The Trojan War: Its Historicity and Context,* edited by Lin Foxhall and John K. Davies, 111–36. Bristol, UK: Bristol Classical Press, 1981.

————. *The Idea of Epic.* Eidos Studies in Classical Kinds 3. Berkeley: University of California Press, 1991.

Haldar, Alfred. "Tradition and History." *BiOr* 31 (1974) 26–37.

Hallo, William W. "Context of Scripture." In *Proceedings of the 11th World Congress of Jewish Studies,* vol. A, 9–15. Jerusalem: World Union of Jewish Studies, 1994.

————, editor. *The Context of Scripture.* 3 vols. Leiden: Brill, 2003.

Handoo, Jawaharlal. "'People Are Still Hungry for Kings' – Folklore and Oral History." In *Dynamics of Tradition,* edited by Lotte Tarkka, 67–74. Studia Fennica folkloristica Helsinki: Finnish Literature Society, 2003.

Harper, R. F., editor. *Assyrian and Babylonian Letters.* 14 vols. Chicago: University of Chicago Press, 1892–1914.

Bibliography

Harris, Joseph. "The Performance of Old Norse Eddic Poetry." In *The Oral Epic: Performance and Music*, edited by Karl Reichl, 225–32. Intercultural Music Studies 12. Berlin: Verlag für Wissenschaft und Bildung, 2000.

Harris, Joseph, and Thomas D. Hill. "Gestr's 'Prime Sign,'" *Arkiv for nordisk filologi* 104 (1989) 103–22.

Harris, Richard L. "Proverbs in Saxon and in the Sagas." Paper presented at the annual meeting of the Medieval Academy, Vancouver, BC. April 4, 2008.

Harvilahti, Lauri. "Folklore and Oral Tradition." *Oral Tradition* 18 (2003) 200–202.

———. "Textualising an Oral Epic." *Folklore Fellows Network* 26 (2004) 3–5.

Hayes, Katherine M. *The Earth Mourns: Prophetic Metaphor and Oral Aesthetic.* SBLABib 8. Leiden: Brill, 2002.

Hays, H. M. "The Historicity of Papyrus Westcar." *ZÄS* 129 (2002) 20–30.

Heath, Peter. "A Critical Review of Modern Scholarship on *Sīrat 'Antar ibn Shaddād* and the Popular *Sīra.*" *Journal of Arabic Literature* 15 (1984) 19–44.

———. *The Thirsty Sword: Sīrat 'Atar and the Arabic Popular Epic.* Salt Lake City: University of Utah Press, 1996.

Held, Moshe. "Philological Notes on the Mari Covenant Rituals." *BASOR* 200 (1970) 32–40.

Hendel, Ronald S. *The Epic of the Patriarch: The Jacob Cycle and the Narrative Traditions of Canaan and Israel.* HSM 42. Atlanta: Scholars, 1987.

Hendel, Russell J. "Biblical Puns." *Jewish Bible Quarterly* 34 (2006) 190–97.

Henderson, W. J. "Tradition and Originality in Early Greek Lyric." In *Oral Tradition and Innovation: New Wine in Old Bottles?* edited by E. R. Sienaert et al., 249–56. Durban: University of Natal Oral Documentation and Research Centre, 1991.

Henkelman, Wouter F. M. "The Birth of Gilgameš (Ael. *NA* XII.21). A Case-Study in Literary Receptivity." In *Altertum und Mittelmeerraum: Altertum und Mittelmeeraum die anitke Welt diesseits und jenseitzs der Levante*, edited by Robert Rollinger and Briggite Truschnegg, 807–56. Oriens et Occidens 12. Stuttgart: Steiner, 2006.

Herdner, A., editor. *Corpus des tablettes en cunéiformes alphabétiques découvertes à Ras Shamra-Ugarit.* Paris: Imprimerie Nationale, 1963.

Hermann, Pernille "Concepts of Memory and Approaches to the Past in Medieval Icelandic Literature." *Scandinavian Studies* 81 (2009) 287–308.

Hermann Pálsson. *Oral Tradition and Saga Writing.* Studia Medievalia Septentrionalia 3. Vienna: Fassbender, 1999.

Hertzberg, Hans W. *Josua, Richter, Ruth.* ATD. Gottingen: Vandenhoeck & Ruprecht, 1985.

Hess, Richard S. "Writing about Writing." *VT* 66 (2006) 342–46.

Heusler, Andreas. *Die Anfänge der isländischen Saga.* Abhandlungen der Königlichen Preussischen Akademie der Wissenschaften, philosophish-historische Klasse 1913, 9. Berlin: Königlichen Preussischen Akademie der Wissenschaften, 1913.

Hollander, Lee Milton. *The Skalds: A Selection of Their Poems.* Ann Arbor Paperbacks. Ann Arbor: University of Michigan Press, 1945.

Hom, Mary K. Y. H. "'A Mighty Hunter before YHWH.'" *VT* 60 (2010) 63–68.

Honeck, Richard P. *Proverb in Mind: The Cognitive Science of Proverbial Wit and Wisdom.* Mahwah, NJ: Erlbaum, 1997.

Honko, Lauri. "Comparing the Textualization of Oral Epics." *Folklore Fellows Newsletter* 13 (1996) 2–3, 7–8.

———. "Oral and Semiliterary Epics." *Folklore Fellows Newsletter* 10 (1995) 1–6.

Bibliography

----------. "The Quest for the Long Epic." In *Dynamics of Tradition*, edited by Lotte Tarkka, 191–212. Studia Fennica folkloristica. Helsinki: Finnish Literature Society, 2003.

----------. "The Quest for Oral Text." *Folklore Fellows Newsletter* 12 (1996) 1, 6.

----------. "Text as Process and Practice." In *Textualization of Oral Epics*, edited by Lauri Honko, 3–55. Trends in Linguistics. Studies and Monographs 128. Berlin: de Gruyter, 2000.

Hoop, Raymond de. *Genesis 49 in Its Literary and Historical Context*. OtSt 29. Leiden: Brill, 1999.

Hylander, Ivar. *Der Literarische Samuel-Saul-Komplex*. Uppsala: Almqvist & Wiksell, 1932.

Ilmari Soisalon-Soinen, "Der Charakter der ältesten alttestamentlichen Erzähltraditionen." *Temenos* 4 (1969) 128–39.

Ingham, Bruce. "The *Sālfah* as a Narrative Genre." *Asian Folklore Studies* 52 (1993) 5–32.

Irvin, Dorothy. *Mytharion*. AOAT 32. Kevelaer: Butzon & Berker, 1978.

Izre 'el, Shlomo. "The Study of Oral Poetry." In *Mesopotamian Epic Literature: Oral or Aural?* edited by Marianna E. Vogelzang and Herman L. J. Vanstiphout, 155–226. Lewiston, NY: Mellen, 1992.

Jaffee, Martin S. "The Hebrew Scriptures." In *Teaching Oral Traditions*, edited by John Miles Foley, 321–29. Modern Language Association Options for Teaching. New York: Modern Language Association, 1998.

----------. *Torah in the Mouth: Writing and Oral Tradition in Palestinian Judaism 200 BCE– 400 CE*. Oxford: Oxford University Press, 2001.

Janowksi, Bernd, and Gernot Wilhelm, editors. *Staatsverträge, Herrscherinschriften und andere Dokumente zur politischen Geschichte*. Texte aus der Umwelt des Alten Testaments n.s. 2. Gütersloh: Güthersloher, 2005.

Jason, Heda. "Deborah and Barak." *Shnaton* 5–6 (1981–82) 79–87.

----------. "Folk Literature in Its Cultural Context." In *Oral and Written/Literate in Literature and Culture*, edited by Svetozar Petrović, 69–98. Vojvodina Academy of Science and Arts Symposium 4. Novi Sad: Vojvodina Academy of Science and Arts, 1988.

----------. "The Poor Man of Nippur: An Ethnopoetic Analysis." *JCS* 31 (1979) 189–215.

----------. "The Story of David and Goliath: A Folk Epic?" *Bib* 60 (1979) 36–70.

----------. "The Study of Israelite and Jewish Oral and Folk Literature: Problems and Issues." *Asian Folklore Studies* 49 (1990) 69–108.

Jason, Heda, and Aharon Kempinski, "How Old Are Folktales?" *Fabula* 22 (1981) 1–27.

Jeffrey, Peter. Letter from Peter Jeffrey. "Communications." *Journal of the American Musicological Society* 47 (1994) 175–79.

Jensen, Minna Skafte. "In What Sense Can the *Iliad* and the *Odyssey* Be Considered Oral Texts?" In *Homer's "Odyssey,"* edited by Lillian E. Doherty, 18–28. Oxford Readings in Classical Studies 13. Oxford: Oxford University Press, 2009.

----------. "The Oral-Formulaic Theory Revisited." In *Oral Art Forms and Their Passage into Writing*, edited by Else Mundal and Jonas Wellendorf, 43–52. Copenhagen: Museum Tusculanum Press, 2008.

----------. "Performance." In *A Companion to Ancient Epic*, edited by John Miles Foley, 45–54. Blackwell Companions to the Ancient World. Literature and Culture. Malden, MA: Blackwell, 2005.

----------. "The Writing of the *Iliad* and the *Odyssey*." In *Textualization of Oral Epics*, edited by Lauri Honko, 57–67. Trends in Linguistics. Studies and Monographs 128. Berlin: de Gruyter, 2000.

Bibliography

Jesch, Judith. "Sagas and Scaldic Poetry." In *Artikler udgivet I anledning af Preben Meulengracht Sørensens 60 års fødselsdag*, edited by Jan Maack, 7–18. Aarhus: Norrønt Forum, 2000.

———. "Skaldic Verse, a Case of Literacy *Avant la Lettre*." In *Literacy in Medieval and Early Modern Scandinavian Culture*, edited by Pernille Hermann, 187–209. The Viking Collection 16. Odense: University Press of Southern Denmark, 2005.

Jolles, Frank. "Interfaces between Oral and Literate Societies." In *Oral Tradition and Innovation: New Wine In Old Bottles?* edited by E. R. Sienaert et al., 257–71. Durban: University of Natal Oral Documentation and Research Centre, 1991.

Jón Aðalsteinsson. *A Piece of Horse Liver*. Reykjavik, Iceland: Haskolautgafan Felagsvisindastofnun, 1998.

Jónas Kristjánsson. "Íslendingadrápa and Oral Tradition." *Gripla* 1 (1975) 76–91.

Jones, Chris. "Where Now the Harp? Listening for the Sounds of Old English Verse, from *Beowulf* to the Twentieth Century." *Oral Tradition* 24 (2009) 485–502.

Joubert, Annekie. *The Power of Performance: Linking Past and Present in Hananwa and Lobedu Oral Literature*. Trends in Linguistics. Studies and Monographs 160. Berlin: de Gruyter, 2004.

Joüon, Paul. *Grammaire de l'Hébreu Biblique*. 2 vols. in 1. Rome: Pontifical Biblical Institute, 1923.

Katz, Joshua T. "Oral Tradition in Linguistics." *Oral Tradition* 18 (2003) 261–62.

Kawashima, Robert S. *Biblical Narrative and the Death of the Rhapsode*. Indiana Studies in Biblical Literature. Bloomington: Indiana University Press, 2004.

———. "Comparative Literature and Biblical Studies: The Case of Allusion." *Proof* 27 (2007) 324–44.

———. "From Song to Story: The Genesis of Narrative in Judges 4 and 5." *Proof* 21 (2001) 151–78.

Keel, Othmar. *The Symbolism of the Biblical World: Ancient Near Eastern Iconography and the Book of Psalms*. 1978. Winona Lake: Eisenbrauns, 1997.

Keesing, Felix M., and Marie M. Keesing. *Elite Communication in Samoa: A Study of Leadership*. Stanford Anthropological Series 3. Stanford: Stanford University Press, 1956.

Kellogg, Robert. "The Prehistory of Eddic Poetry." In *Poetry in the Scandinavian Middle Ages*, 187–99. Spoleto: Presso la sede del Centro Studi, 1990.

Kurpershoek, P. Marcel, editor. *Oral Poetry and Narratives from Central Arabia*. 4 vols. Studies in Arabic Literature 17. Leiden: Brill, 1994.

Khamis, Said A. M. "From Written through Oral to Mediated Oral." In *Interfaces between the Oral and the Written: Versions and Subversions in African Literatures 2*, edited by Alain Ricard and Flora Veit-Wild, 203–18. Matatu 31–32. Amsterdam: Rodopi, 2005.

Kilmer, Anne D. "Fugal Features of Atrahasis." In *Mesopotamian Poetic Language: Sumerian and Akkadian*, edited by M. E. Vogelzang and H. L. J. Vanstiphout, 127–39. Cuneiform Monographs 6. Proceedings of the Groningen Group for the Study of Mesopotamian Literature 2. Groningen: Styx, 1996.

Kirkpatrick, Patricia G. "The Jacob-Esau Narratives." In *The Function of Ancient Historiography in Biblical and Cognate Studies*, edited by Patricia G. Kirkpatrick and Timothy Golz, 1–17. Library of Hebrew Bible/Old Testament Studies 489. New York: T. & T. Clark, 2008.

Bibliography

————. *The Old Testament and Folklore Study*. JSOTSup 62. Sheffield, UK: JSOT Press, 1988.

Knierim, Rolf P. "Old Testament Form Criticism Reconsidered." *Int* 27 (1973) 435–68.

Knight, Douglas A. *Rediscovering the Traditions of Israel*. Rev. ed. SBLDS 9. Missoula: SBL, distributed by Scholars Press, 1975.

Koch, Klaus. *Growth of the Biblical Tradition*. London: Adam & Charles Black, 1969.

Kofoed, Jens B. "Remember the Days of Old (Deut 32, 7)—Oral and Written Transmission in the Hebrew Bible." *SEE-J Hiphil* 1 (2004). Online: http://www.see-j.net/index.php/hiphil/article/viewPDFInterstitial/2/2.

Kolyada, Yelena. *A Compendium of Musical Instruments and Instrumental Terminology in the Bible*. BibleWorld. London: Equinox, 2009.

Komlósi, Lászlo, and Elizabeth Knipf. "Contrastive Analysis of Entrenchment and Collocational Force in Variable-sized Lexical Units." In *The Dynamics of Language Use: Functional and Contrastive Perspectives*, edited by Christopher S. Butler et al., 243–63. Pragmatics and Beyond, new ser., 140. Amsterdam: Benjamins, 2005.

Korpel, Marjo C. A. *A Rift in the Clouds: Ugaritic and Hebrew Descriptions of the Divine*. Ugaritische-Biblisch Literatur 8. Munster: Ugarit, 1990.

Kratz, Corrine A. "Persuasive Suggestions and Reassuring Promises: Emergent Parallelism and Dialogic Encouragement in Song." *Journal of American Folklore* 103 (1990) 42–67.

Kugel, James L. *The Idea of Biblical Poetry: Parallelism and Its History*. Baltimore: Johns Hopkins University Press, 1981.

Kuiken, Don et al. "Forms of Self-Implication in Literary Reading." *Poetics Today* 25 (2004) 171–203.

LaBarbera, Robert. "The Man of War and the Man of God: Social Satire in 2 Kings 6:8—7:20." *CBQ* 46 (1984) 637–51.

Laessö, Jørgen. "Literacy and Oral Tradition in Ancient Mesopotamia." In *Studia Orientalia Ioanni Pedersen*, edited by F. Hvidberg, 205–18. Hauniae, Denmark: Munksgaard, 1953.

Lakoff, George. "The Death of Dead Metaphor." *Metaphor and Symbolic Activity* 2 (1987) 143–47.

Lambert, W. G., editor. *Babylonian Wisdom Literature*. Oxford: Clarendon, 1960.

Laroche, Emmanuel, editor. *Catalogue des textes hittites*. 1956. Paris: Klincksieck, 1971.

Larsen, Mogens T. "The Mesopotamian Lukewarm Mind: Reflections on Science, Divination, and Literacy." In *Language, Literature, and History*, edited by Francisca Rochberg-Halton, 203–25. AOS 67. New Haven: American Oriental Society, 1987.

Lasine, Stuart. "Jehoram and the Cannibal Mothers (2 Kings 6.24–44): Solomon's Judgment as an Inverted World." *JSOT* 50 (1991) 27–53.

Lawergren, Bo, and O. R. Gurney. "Sound Holes and Geometrical Figures: Clues to the Terminology of Ancient Mesopotamian Harps." *Iraq* 49 (1987) 37–52.

Lederman, Zvi. "An Early Iron Age Village at Khirbet Raddana." PhD diss., Harvard University, 1999.

Leeb, Carolyn S. *Away from the Father's House: The Social Location of* Na'ar *and* Na'arah *in Ancient Israel*. JSOTSup 301. Sheffield, UK: Sheffield Academic, 2000.

Lemaire, A. "Notes d'épigraphie nord-ouest sémitique." *Sem* 35 (1985) 251–56.

Leson, Mark. "The Function of Etiological Legends in the Hebrew Bible." Paper presented at the Catholic Biblical Association Chesapeake Bay Regional Meeting, Washington, DC, January 2009.

Bibliography

Levin, Yigal. "Nimrod the Mighty, King of Kish, King of Sumer and Akkad." *VT* 52 (2002) 350–66.

Linafelt, Tod. "Private Poetry and Public Eloquence in 2 Samuel 1:17–27: Hearing and Overhearing David's Lament for Jonathan and Saul." *Journal of Religion* 88 (2008) 497–526.

Lindow, John. "*Þættir* and Oral Performance." In *Oral Tradition in the Middle Ages*, edited by W. F. H. Nicolaisen, 179–86. Medieval and Renaissance Texts & Studies 112. Binghamton, NY: Medieval & Renaissance Texts & Studies, 1995.

Lindquist, Maria. "King Og's Iron Bed." Paper presented at the Society of Biblical Literature Annual Meeting, Atlanta, 2010.

Lods, Adolphe. *Histoire de la littérature hébraïque et juive*. Bibliothèque historique Paris: Payot, 1950.

———. "Le role de la tradition orale dans la formation des récits de l'Ancien Testament." *RHR* 88 (1923) 51–64.

Lohfink, Norbert. *Das Hauptgebot: Eine Untersuchung literarischer Einleitungsfragen zu Dtn 5–11*. AnBib 20. Rome: Pontifical Biblical Institute, 1963.

Long, Burke O. "Framing Repetitions in Biblical Historiography." *JBL* 106 (1987) 385–99.

Lönnroth, Lars. "New Dimensions and Old Directions in Saga Research." *Scandinavica* 19 (1980) 57–61.

———. *Njáls Saga: A Critical Introduction*. Berkeley: University of California Press, 1976.

———. "The Transformation of Literary Genres in Iceland from Orality to Literacy." In *Scandinavia and Christian Europe in the Middle Ages*, edited by Rudolf Simek and Judith Meurer, 341–44. Bonn: Universität Bonn, 2003.

Loprieno, Antonio. "Puns and Word Play in Ancient Egyptian." In *Puns and Pundits: Word Play in the Hebrew Bible and Ancient Near Eastern Literature*, edited by Scott B. Noegel, 3–22. Bethesda, MD: CDL, 2000.

Lord, Albert B. "Characteristics of Orality." *Oral Tradition* 2 (1987) 54–72.

———. "Composition by Theme in Homer and Southslavic Epos." *TAPA* 82 (1951) 71–80.

———. *Epic Singers and Oral Tradition*. Myth and Poetics. Ithaca: Cornell University Press, 1991.

———. "Formula and Non-Narrative Theme in South Slavic Oral Epic and the OT." *Semeia* 5 (1976) 93–105.

———. "Homer as Oral Poet." *HSCP* 72 (1967) 1–46.

———. "Homer, Parry, and Huso." *AJA* 52 (1948) 34–44.

———. "The Merging of Two Worlds: Oral and Written Poetics and Poetry as Carriers of Ancient Values." In *Oral Tradition in Literature: Interpretation in Context*, edited by John Miles Foley, 19–64. Columbia: University of Missouri Press, 1986.

———. "Oral Poetry." In *The Princeton Encyclopedia of Poetry and Poetics*, edited by Alex Preminger, 591–93. Enlarged ed. Princeton: Princeton University Press, 1974.

———. "Perspectives on Recent Work on the Oral Traditional Formula." *Oral Tradition* 1 (1986) 467–503.

———. *The Singer of Tales*. Harvard Studies in Comparative Literature 24. Cambridge: Harvard University Press, 1960.

———. *The Singer of Tales*. Edited by Stephen Mitchell and Gregory Nagy. 2nd ed. Cambridge: Harvard University Press, 2000.

———. *The Singer Resumes the Tale*. Edited by Mary Louise Lord. Myth and Poetics. Ithaca: Cornell University Press, 1995.

————. "The Traditional Song." In *Oral Literature and the Formula,* edited by Benjamin A. Stolz and Richard S. Shannon III, 1–15. Ann Arbor: Center for the Coordination of Ancient and Modern Studies, University of Michigan, 1976.

Lunn, Nick. "Paronomastic Constructions in Biblical Hebrew." *Notes on Translation* 10.4 (1996) 31–52.

Lutzky, Harriet. "Shadday as a Goddess Epithet." *VT* 48 (1998) 15–36.

MacDonald, John. "The Status and Role of the Na'ar in Israelite Society." *JNES* 35 (1976) 147–70.

Macdonald, M. C. A. "Literacy in an Oral Environment." In *Writing and Ancient Near Eastern Society: Papers in Honour of Alan R. Millard,* edited by Piotr Bienkowski et al., 49–118. Library of Hebrew Bible/Old Testament Studies 426. New York: T. & T. Clark, 2005.

Martin, Richard P. "Epic as Genre." In *A Companion to Ancient Epic,* edited by John Miles Foley, 9–19. Blackwell Companions to the Ancient world. Literature and Culture. Malden, MA: Blackwell, 2005.

————. "Homer's *Iliad* and *Odyssey.*" In *Teaching Oral Traditions,* edited by John Miles Foley, 339–58. Modern Language Association Options for Teaching. New York: Modern Language Association, 1998.

McCarthy, William Bertrand. "Recent Scholarship in Oral Theory and Ethnopoetics." *Journal of American Folklore* 120 (2007) 360–76.

Melnikova, Elena A. "The Incorporation of Oral Historical Tradition in the Early Historical Texts." *Sagas and Societies* 12 (2002) 1–16.

Meyers, Carol. "Women with Hand-Drums, Dancing: Bible." In *Jewish Women,* edited by P. Hyman and D. Ofer. Online: http://jwa.org/encyclopedia.

Michałowski, Piotr. "Orality and Literacy and Early Mesopotamian Literature." In *Mesopotamian Epic Literature: Oral or Aural?* edited by Marianna E. Vogelzang and Herman L. J. Vanstiphout, 227–46. Lewiston, NY: Mellen, 1992.

Miller, Geoffrey P. "Foreword: The Development of Ancient Near Eastern Law." *Chicago-Kent Law Review* 70 (1995) 1623–30.

Miller, Robert D., II. "The 'Biography' of Moses in the Pentateuch." In *Moses: A History of Reception, 2nd–15th Century,* edited by Jane Beal, n.p. Commentaria Series. Leiden: Brill, forthcoming.

————. *Chieftains of the Highland Clans: A History of Israel in the Twelfth and Eleventh Centuries BC.* The Bible in Its World. Grand Rapids: Eerdmans, 2004.

————. *Covenant and Grace in the Old Testament.* Forthcoming.

————. "How Post-Modernism (and W. F. Albright) Can Save Us from Malarkey." *Bible and Interpretation.* November 2003. Online: http://www.bibleinterp.com/articles/Miller_Malarkey.shtml/.

————. "The Origin of the Zion Hymns." In *The Composition of the Book of Psalms,* edited by Erich Zenger, 667–75. BETL 238. Leuven: Peeters, 2010.

————. "A Taphonomic Approach to Understanding Historiography." Paper presented at the XLVe Rencontre Assyriologique Internationale, Cambridge, Massachusetts, 1998.

————. "When Pharaohs Ruled: On the Translation of Judges 5:2." *JTS* 59 (2008) 650–54.

————. "Yahweh and His Clio: Critical Theory and the Historical Criticism of the Hebrew Bible." *Currents in Biblical Research* 4 (2005) 145–65.

Bibliography

Mills, Margaret A. "Domains of Folklore Concern." In *Text and Tradition: The Hebrew Bible and Folklore*, edited by Susan B. Niditch, 231–42. SemeiaSt. Atlanta: Scholars, 1990.

Minchin, Elizabeth. "Spatial Memory and the Composition of the *Iliad*." In *Orality, Literacy, Memory in the Ancient Greek and Roman World*, edited by E. Anne Mackay, 9–34. Orality and Literacy in Ancient Greece 7. Mnemosyne Supplement 298. Leiden: Brill, 2008.

Mitchell, Gordon. "War, Folklore, and the Mystery of a Disappearing Book." *JSOT* 68 (1995) 113–19.

Mitchell, Stephen A. "Reconstructing Old Norse Oral Tradition." *Oral Tradition* 18 (2003) 203–6.

———. "The Sagaman and Oral Literature." In *Comparative Research on Oral Traditions: A Memorial for Milman Parry*, edited by John Miles Foley, 407–15. Columbus, OH: Slavica, 1987.

Mobley, Gregory. *The Empty Men: The Heroic Tradition of Ancient Israel*. ABRL. New York: Doubleday, 2006.

Moor, Johannes Cornelis de. *An Anthology of Religious Texts from Ugarit*. Nisaba 16. Leiden: Brill, 1987.

———. *Mondelinge Overlevering in Mesopotamië, Ugarit, en Israël*. Leiden: Brill, 1965.

Moore, A. W. *The Folk-Lore of the Isle of Man*. 1891. Charleston, SC: Forgotten Books, 2007.

Moore, George F. *Judges*. Sacred Books of the Old and New Testaments. Edinburgh: T. & T. Clark, 1898.

Morris, William, and Eirikr Magnusson. *The Story of the Volsungs*. London: Walter Scott Press, 1888.

Mundal, Else. "Introduction." In *Oral Art Forms and Their Passage into Writing*, edited by Else Mundal and Jonas Wellendorf, 1–6. Copenhagen: Museum Tusculanum Press, 2008.

———. "Oral or Scribal Variation in *Vǫluspá*." In *Oral Art Forms and Their Passage into Writing*, edited by Else Mundal and Jonas Wellendorf, 209–27. Copenhagen: Museum Tusculanum Press, 2008.

Muraoka, T. *Emphatic Words and Structures in Biblical Hebrew*. Jerusalem: Magnes, 1985.

Na'aman, Nadav. *The Past That Shapes the Present: The Creation of Biblical Historiography in the Late First Temple Period and after the Downfall*. N.p.: Bailik Institute, 2000.

Nagy, Gregory. "Epic as Music." In *The Oral Epic: Performance and Music*, edited by Karl Reichl, 41–68. Intercultural Music Studies 12. Berlin: Verlag für Wissenschaft und Bildung, 2000.

Naveh, Joseph. "Some Considerations on the Ostracon from Izbet Sartah." *IEJ* 28 (1978) 31–35.

Neef, Heinz-Dieter. *Deboraerzählung und Deboralied*. Biblisch-Theologische Studien 49. Neukirchen-Vluyn: Neukirchener, 2002.

Nelson, Douglas L. et al. "Spreading Activation or Spooky Action at a Distance?" *Journal of Experimental Psychology* 29 (2003) 42–52.

Newman, Murray H. "The Prophetic Call of Samuel." In *Israel's Prophetic Heritage*, edited by Bernhard W. Anderson and Walter Harrelson, 86–97. New York: Harper & Row, 1962.

Nicolaisen, W. F. H. "Names and Narratives." *Journal of American Folklore* 97 (1984) 259–72.

Bibliography

Niditch, Susan. "The Challenge of Israelite Epic." In *A Companion to Ancient Epic*, edited by John Miles Foley, 227–88. Blackwell Companions to the Ancient World. Literature and Culture. Malden, MA: Blackwell, 2005.

———. "Epic and History in the Hebrew Bible." In *Epic and History*, edited by David Konstan and Kurt A. Raaflaub, 86–102. The Ancient World: Comparative Histories 4. Chichester, UK: Wiley-Blackwell, 2010.

———. "The Hebrew Bible and Oral Literature." In *The Interface of Orality and Writing: Speaking, Seeing, Writing in the Shaping of New Genres*, edited by Annette Weissenrieder and Robert B. Coote, 3–18. WUNT 260. Tübingen: Mohr/Siebeck, 2010.

———. *Judges: A Commentary*. OTL. Louisville: Westminster John Knox, 2008.

———. "Oral Tradition and Biblical Scholarship." *Oral Tradition* 18 (2003) 43–44.

———. *Oral World and Written Word: Ancient Israelite Literature*. Library of Ancient Israel. London: SPCK, 1997.

Nielsen, Eduard. "Historical Perspectives and Geographical Horizons: On the Question of North-Israelite Elements in Deuteronomy." *ASTI* 11 (1978) 77–89.

———. *Oral Tradition: A Modern Problem in Old Testament Introduction*. SBT 11. London: SCM, 1954.

Nielsen, Eva. "The Elder Edda Revisited: Past and Present Performances of the Icelandic Eddic Poems." PhD diss., Florida State University, 2005.

Niesiołowski-Spanò, Łukasz. "Two Aetiological Narratives in Genesis and their Dates." *Studia Judaica* 9 (2006) 367–81.

Niles, John D. "The Myth of the Anglo-Saxon Oral Poet." *Western Folklore* 62 (2003) 7–61.

Noegel, Scott B. "Mesopotamian Epic." In *A Companion to Ancient Epic*, edited by John Miles Foley, 233–45. Blackwell Companions to the Ancient World. Literature and Culture. Malden, MA: Blackwell, 2005.

Nordal, Guðrún. "The Art of Poetry and the Sagas of Icelanders." In *Learning and Understanding in the Old Norse World*, edited by Judy Quinn, et al., 219–38. Medieval Texts and Cultures of Northern Europe 18. Turnhout: Brepols, 2007.

———. "The Dialogue between Audience and Text." In *Oral Art Forms and Their Passage into Writing*, edited by Else Mundal and Jonas Wellendorf, 185–202. Copenhagen: Museum Tusculanum Press, 2008.

———. *Tools of Literacy: The Role of Skaldic Verse in Icelandic Textual Culture of the Twelfth and Thirteenth Centuries*. Toronto: University of Toronto Press, 2001.

———. "Why Skaldic Verse? Fashion and Cultural Politics in Thirteenth-Century Iceland." In *Sagas and Societies*, edited by T. Jonuks et al., 1–10. Tübingen: Universitat Tübingen, 2002.

Notarius, Tania. "Poetic Discourse and the Problem of Verbal Tenses in the Oracles of Balaam." *Hebrew Studies* 49 (2008) 55–86.

Nyberg, H. S. *Muntlig Tradition*. Edited by Bo Utas. Acta Societatis Litteteratum Humaniorum Regiae Upsaliensis 51. Uppsala: Swedish Science Press, 1954.

———. *Studien zum Hoseabuche: zugleich ein Beitrag zur Klärung des Problems der alttestamentlichen Textkritik*. UUÅ 6. Uppsala: Almqvist & Wiksells, 1935.

O'Connor, Michael P. *Hebrew Verse Structure*. Winona Lake: Eisenbrauns, 1980.

O'Donoghue, Heather. *Skaldic Verse and the Poetics of Saga Narrative*. Oxford: Oxford University Press, 2005.

Bibliography

Oesterreicher, Wulf. "Types of Orality in Text." In *Written Voices, Spoken Signs: Tradition, Performance, and the Epic Text*, edited by Egbert Bakker and Ahuvia Kahane, 190–214. Cambridge: Harvard University Press, 1997.

O'Keeffe, Katherine O'Brien. "The Performing Body on the Oral-Literate Continuum." In *Teaching Oral Traditions*, edited by John Miles Foley, 46–58. Modern Language Association Options for Teaching. New York: Modern Language Association, 1998.

Olrik, Axel. *Principles for Oral Narrative Research.* Folklore Studies in Translation. Bloomington: Indiana University Press, 1992.

Ong, Walter J. "A Comment on 'Arguing about Literacy.'" *College English* 50 (1988) 700–701.

———. "Literacy and Orality in our Times." *Association of Departments of English Bulletin* 58 (1978) 1–7.

———. *Orality and Literacy: The Technologizing of the Word.* New Accents. London: Methuen, 1982.

———. "The Psychodynamics of Oral Memory and Narration. In *The Pedagogy of God's Image: Essays on Symbol and the Religious Imagination*, edited by Robert Masson, 55–73. The Annual Publication of the College Theological Society 1981. Chico, CA: Scholars, 1982.

———. "Writing Is a Technology that Restructures Thought." In *The Written Word: Literacy in Transition*, edited by Gerd Baumann, 23–50. Wolfson College Lectures 1985. Oxford: Clarendon, 1986.

O'Nolan, Kevin. "Formula in Oral Tradition." In *Approaches to Oral Tradition*, edited by Robin Thelwall, 24–35. Occasional Papers in Linguistics and Language Learning 4. Belfast: New University of Ulster, 1978.

Opland, Jeff. *Anglo-Saxon Oral Poetry: A Study of the Traditions.* New Haven: Yale University Press, 1980.

Palsson, Herman, and Paul Edwards, translators. *Egil's Saga*, by Snorri Sturluson. Harmondsworth, UK: Penguin, 1976.

Parpola, Simo, comp. *Letters from Assyrian Scholars.* 2 vols. Winona Lake: Eisenbrauns, 2007.

Parkinson, R. B. "Individual and Society in Middle Kingdom Literature." In *Ancient Egyptian Literature: History and Forms*, edited by Antonio Loprieno, 137–56. PÄ 10. Leiden: Brill, 1996.

———. *Poetry and Culture in Middle Kingdom Egypt: A Dark Side to the Perfection.* Athlone Publications in Egyptology and Ancient Near Eastern Studies. New York: Continuum, 2002.

Parry, Adam. "Have We Homer's *Iliad*?" *Yale Classical Studies* 20 (1966) 175–216.

Parry, Milman. *The Making of Homeric Verse: The Collected Papers of Milman Parry*, edited by A. Parry. Oxford: Clarendon, 1971.

———. "Studies in the Epic Technique of Oral Verse-Making." *HSCP* 41 (1930) 73–147; 43 (1932) 1–50.

———. "Whole Formulaic Verses in Greek and Southslavic Heroic Song." *TAPA* 64 (1933) 179–97.

Parry, Milman, and Albert B. Lord, editors. *Serbo-Croatian Heroic Songs.* 3 vols. Cambridge: Harvard University Press, 1954–1974.

Pasayat, Chitrasen. *Oral Tradition, Society, and History.* New Delhi: Mohit, 2008.

Pelias, Ronald J., and James Vanoosting. "A Paradigm for Performance Studies." In *Performance*, 1:215–31, edited by Philip Auslander. New York: Routledge, 2003.

Bibliography

Perkins, Richard. "Objects and Oral Tradition in Medieval Iceland." In *Úr Dölum til Dala*, edited by Rory McTurk and Andrew Wawn, 239–66. Leeds Texts and Monographs, new ser., 11. Leeds: School of English, University of Leeds, 1989.

Perrois, Louis. "Tradition orale et histoire : intérêt et limites d'une enquête de terrain sur les migrations Kota (Gabon)" *Cahiers O.R.S.T.O.M. séries Sciences humaines* 13 (1976) 143–46.

Person, Raymond R., Jr. *The Deuteronomic History and the Book of Chronicles: Scribal Works in an Oral World*. Society of Biblical Literature: Ancient Israel and Its Literature 6. Atlanta: Society of Biblical Literature, 2010.

———. *The Deuteronomic School: History, Social Setting, and Literature*. SBLStBl 2. Atlanta: Society of Biblical Literature, 2002.

———. "A Rolling Corpus and Oral Tradition." In *Troubling Jeremiah*, edited by A. R. Pete Diamond et al., 263–71. JSOTSup 260. Sheffield, UK: Sheffield Academic, 1999.

Petrović, Sonja. "Oral and Written Art Forms in Serbian Medieval Literature." In *Oral Art Forms and Their Passage into Writing*, edited by Else Mundal and Jonas Wellendorf, 85–108. Copenhagen: Museum Tusculanum Press, 2008.

Phelan, Peggy. "Narrative and Performance." *Narrative* 8:2 (2000) n.p.

Phillpotts, Bertha S. *Edda and Saga*. The Home University Library of Modern Knowledge. London: Thornton Butterworth, 1931.

———. *The Elder Edda and Ancient Scandinavian Drama*. Cambridge: Cambridge University Press, 1920.

Polak, Frank H. "The Oral and the Written: Syntax, Stylistics and the Development of Biblical Prose Narrative." *Journal of Ancient Near Eastern Studies* 26 (1988) 59–105.

———. "Style Is More Than Person." In *Biblical Hebrew: Studies in Chronology and Typology*, edited by Ian Young. JSOTSup 369. London: T. & T. Clark, 2003.

Poole, Russell. "Composition Transmission Performance: The First Ten lausavísur." *Kormáks saga alvíssmál* 7 (1997) 37–60.

———. "Skaldic Verse and Anglo-Saxon History: Some Aspects of the Period 1009–1016." *Speculum* 62 (1987) 265–98.

Porter, J. R. "Samson's Riddle in Judges XIV. 14, 18." *JTS* 13 (1962) 106–9.

Powell, Marvin A. "Weights and Measures." In *ABD* 6:879–908.

Pretzler, Maria. "Pausanias and Oral Tradition." *Classical Quarterly* 55 (2005) 235–49.

Quinn, Judy. "From Orality to Literacy in Medieval Iceland." In *Old Icelandic Literature and Society*, edited by Margaret Clunies Ross, 30–60. Cambridge Studies in Medieval Literature 42. Cambridge: Cambridge University Press, 2000.

Raaflaub, Kurt A. "Epic and History." In *A Companion to Ancient Epic*, edited by John Miles Foley, 55–70. Blackwell Companions to the Ancient World. Literature and Culture. Malden, MA: Blackwell, 2005.

Rabinowitz, Isaac. *A Witness Forever*. Occasional Publications of the Department of Near Eastern Studies and the Program of Jewish Studies, Cornell University 1. Bethesda, MD: CDL, 1993.

Ranković, Slavica. "Who Is Speaking in Traditional Texts? On the Distributed Author of the Sagas of Icelanders and Serbian Epic Poetry." *New Literary History* 38 (2007) 293–307.

Reckendorf, Hermann. *Über Paronomasie in den semitischen Sprachen*. Giessen: Töpelmann, 1909.

Bibliography

Redford, Donald B. "Scribe and Speaker." In *Writings and Speech in Israelite and Ancient Near Eastern Prophecies*, edited by Ehud Ben Zvi and Michael H. Floyd, 145–218. SBLSymS 10. Atlanta: Society of Biblical Literature, 2000.

Reichl, Karl. "Introduction: The Music and Performance of Oral Epics." In *The Oral Epic: Performance and Music*, edited by Karl Reichl, 1–40. Intercultural Music Studies 12. Berlin: Verlag für Wissenschaft und Bildung, 2000.

Rendsburg, Gary A. "Word Play in Biblical Hebrew." In *Puns and Pundits: Word Play in the Hebrew Bible and Ancient Near Eastern Literature*, edited by Scott B. Noegel, 137–62. Bethesda, MD: CDL, 2000.

Rendtorff, Rolf. *The Problem of the Process of Transmission in the Pentateuch*. JSOTSup 89. Sheffield, UK: JSOT Press, 1990.

Renz, Johannes. "Die vor- und ausserliterarische Texttradition." In *Die Textualisierung der Religion*, edited by Joachim Schaper, 53–81. FAT 62. Tübingen: Mohr/Siebeck, 2009.

Reynolds, Dwight F. "Epic and History in the Arabic Tradition." In *Epic and History*, edited by David Konstan and Kurt A. Raaflaub, 392–410. The Ancient World: Comparative Histories 4. Chichester, UK: Wiley-Blackwell, 2010.

———. *Heroic Poets, Poetic Heroes: The Ethnography of Performance in an Arabic Oral Epic Tradition*. Myth and Poetics 18. Ithaca: Cornell University Press, 1995.

———. "Sīrat Banī Hilāl." *Oral Tradition* 4 (1989) 80–100.

Ringgren, Helmer. "Oral and Written Transmission in the Old Testament: Some Observations." *ST* 3 (1949) 34–59.

Roeder, Günthe. "Zwei Hieroglyphische Inschriften aus Hermopolis." *Annales du Service des Antiquités d'Egypt* 52 (1954) 315–442.

Rofé, Alexander, *Deuteronomy: Issues and Interpretation*. London: T. & T. Clark, 2002.

———. "The Family-Saga as a Source for the History of the Settlement." *ErIsr* 24 (1982) 187–91.

———. *Introduction to the Composition of the Pentateuch*. The Biblical Seminar 58. Sheffield, UK: Sheffield Academic, 1999.

Röllig, Wolfgang. "Aspekte der Archivierung und Kanonisierung von Keilschriftliteratur im 8./7. Jh. V. Chr." In *Die Textualisierung der Religion*, edited by Joachim Schaper, 35–52. FAT 62. Tübingen: Mohr/Siebeck, 2009.

Rollston, Christopher. "The Phoenician Script of the Tel Zayit Abecedary and Putative Evidence for Israelite Literacy." In *Literate Culture and Tenth-Century Canaan: The Tel Zayit Abecedary in Context*, edited by Ron E. Tappy and P. Kyle McCarter, 61–96. Winona Lake: Eisenbrauns, 2008.

———. "Scribal Education in Ancient Israel." *BASOR* 344 (2006) 47–74.

———. *Writing and Literacy in the World of Ancient Israel*. SBLABS 11. Atlanta: Society of Biblical Literature, 2010.

Rose, Martin "Names of God in the Old Testament." In *ABD* 4:1004–11.

Rosenblatt, Louise M. *The Reader, the Text, the Poem: The Transactional Theory of the Literary Work*. Carbondale: Southern Illinois University Press, 1978.

Ross, Margaret Clunies. "From Iceland to Norway: Essential Rites of Passage for an Early Icelandic Skald." *Alvíssmál* 9 (1999) 55–72.

———. *A History of Old Norse Poetry and Poetics*. Woodbridge, Suffolk: D. S. Brewer, 2005.

———. "Poetry and *fornaldarsögur*." Online: http://www.dur.ac.uk/medieval.www/saga conf/clunies.htm.

Bibliography

Rothenberg, Jerome. "2 July 1975." In *Alcheringa: Ethnopoetics (Selections)*, edited by Jerome Rothenberg and Dennis Tedlock, n.p. San Francisco: Duration, n.d.

Rüger, Hans-Peter. "Oral Tradition in the Old Testament." In *Jesus and the Oral Gospel Tradition*, edited by Henry Wansbrough, 107–20. JSNTSup 64. Sheffield, UK: JSOT Press, 1991.

Russo, Joseph. "Oral Theory: Its Development in Homeric Studies and Applicability to Other Literatures." In *Mesopotamian Epic Literature: Oral or Aural?* edited by Marianna E. Vogelzang and Herman L. J. Vanstiphout, 7–22. Lewiston, NY: Mellen, 1992.

Ryholt, Kim. *The Political Situation in Egypt during the Second Intermediate Period c.1800–1550 B.C.* Copenhagen: Museum Tuscalanum Press, 1997.

Sakata, Hiromi L. "The Musical Curtain: Music as Structural Marker in Epic Performance." In *The Oral Epic: Performance and Music*, edited by Karl Reichl, 159–69. Intercultural Music Studies 12. Berlin: Verlag für Wissenschaft und Bildung, 2000.

Sale, Mary. "The Oral-Formulaic Theory Today." In *Speaking Volumes: Orality and Literacy in the Greek and Roman World*, edited by Janet Watson, 53–80. Mnemosyne, bibliotheca classica Batava Supplement 218. Leiden: Brill, 2001.

Sánchez Rodriguez, Ángel. *El Papiro Westcar*. Colección Estudios de Egiptología. Seville: ASADE, 2003.

Sanders, Seth L. "What Was the Alphabet For? The Rise of Written Vernaculars and the Making of Israelite National Literature." *Ma'arav* 11 (2004) 25–56.

———. "Writing and Early Iron Age Israel: Before National Scripts, Beyond Nations and States." In *Literate Culture and Tenth-Century Canaan*, edited by Ron E. Tappy and P. Kyle McCarter, 97–112. Winona Lake: Eisenbrauns, 2008.

Sasson, Jack M. "Comparative Observations on the Near Eastern Epic Traditions." In *A Companion to Ancient Epic*, edited by John Miles Foley, 215–32. Blackwell Companions to the Ancient World. Literature and Culture. Malden, MA: Blackwell, 2005.

———. "Literary Criticism, Folklore Scholarship, and Ugaritic Literature." In *Ugarit in Retrospect*, edited by Gordon D. Young, 81–98. Winona Lake: Eisenbrauns, 1981.

Satterthwaite, Philip E. "The Elisha Narratives." *TynBul* 49 (1998) 1–28.

Schaper, Joachim. "Exilic and Post-Exilic Prophecy and the Orality/Literacy Problem." *VT* 55 (2005) 324–42.

———. "The Living Word Engraved in Stone." In *Memory in the Bible and Antiquity*, edited by Stephen C. Barton et al., 9–24. WUNT 212. Tübingen: Mohr/Siebeck, 2007.

———. "A Theology of Writing: The Oral and the Written, God as Scribe, and the Book of Deuteronomy." In *Anthropology and Biblical Studies: Avenues of Approach*, edited by Louise J. Lawrence and Mario I. Aguilar, 97–119. Leiden: Deo, 2004.

Schieffelin, Edward L. "Problematizing Performance." In *Ritual, Performance, Media*, edited by Felicia Hughes-Freeland, 194–207. ASA Monographs 35. Lodon: Routledge, 1997.

Schier, Kurt. "Einige methodische Überlegungen zum Problem von mündlicher und literarischer Tradition im Norden." In *Oral Tradition, Literary Tradition: A Symposium*, edited by Hans Bekker Nielsen et al., 98–115. Odense: Odense University Press, 1977.

Schippers, Arie. "An Episode in the Life of a Hero in the *Sīrat Banī Hilāl.*" *Oriente Moderno* 22 (2003) 347–59.

Bibliography

Schleicher, Marianne. "General Reflections: Addressed by Scripture." In *Receptions and Transformations of the Bible*, edited by Kirsten Nielsen, 136–40. Religion and Normativity 2. Aarhus: Aarhus University Press, 2009.

Schlott, Adelheid. „Eine Beobachtungen zu Mimik und Gestik von Singenden." *Göttinger Miszellen* 152 (1996) 55–70.

Schmitt, Hans-Christoph. "Das Hesbonlied Num. 21,27aβb–30 und die Geschichte der Stadt Hesbon." *ZDPV* 104 (1988) 26–43.

Schniedewind, William M. *How the Bible Became a Book: The Textualization of Ancient Israel*. Cambridge: Cambridge University Press, 2004.

———. "How the Bible Became a Book." *Bible and Interpretation*. 2005. Online: http://www.bibleinterp.com/articles/Schniedewind-How_the_Bible_Became_a_Book.shtml.

———. "Orality and Literacy in Ancient Israel." *RelSRev* 26 (2000) 327–32.

———. Review of *Holy Writ as Oral Lit*, by Alan Dundes; and *Underdogs and Tricksters: A Prelude to Biblical Folklore*, by Susan Niditch. *Western Folklore* 59 (2000) 334–36.

———. *Society and the Promise to David: The Reception History of 2 Samuel 7:1–17*. New York: Oxford University Press, 1999.

Schniedewind, William M., and Daniel Sivan. "Elijah-Elisha Narratives: A Test Case for the Northern Dialect of Hebrew." *JQR* 87 (1997) 303–37.

Schwiderski, Dirk. *The Old and Imperial Aramaic Inscriptions*. 2 vols. Fontes et Subsidia ad Bibliam Pertinentes 2. Berlin: de Gruyter, 2004.

Scodel, Ruth. *Listening to Homer: Tradition, Narrative, and Audience*. Ann Arbor: University of Michigan Press, 2002.

———. "Social Memory in Aeschylus' *Oresteia*." In *Orality, Literacy, Memory in the Ancient Greek and Roman World*, edited by E. Anne Mackay, 115–41. Mnemosyne Supplement 298. Orality and Literacy in Ancient Greece 7. Leiden: Brill, 2008.

Seybold, Klaus. "Zur mündlichen Überlieferung im alten Israel." In *Vergangenheit in mündlicher Überlieferung*, edited by J. Von Ungern-Sternberg and H. Reinau, 141–48. Colloquium Räuericum 1. Stuttgart: Teubner, 1988.

Shear, Ione Mylonas. *Kingship in the Mycenaean World and Its Reflections in the Oral Tradition*. Prehistory Monographs 13. Philadelphia: INSTAP Academic, 2004.

Sherratt, Susan. "Archaeological Contexts." In *A Companion to Ancient Epic*, edited by John Miles Foley, 119–41. Blackwell Companions to the Ancient World. Literature and Culture. Malden, MA: Blackwell, 2005.

Sherzer, Joel. *Verbal Art in San Blas*. Cambridge Studies in Oral and Literate Culture 21. Cambridge: Cambridge University Press, 1990.

Silver, Daniel Jeremy. *The Story of Scripture: From Oral Tradition to the Written Word*. New York: Basic Books, 1990.

Simpson, William Kelly, translator. "King Cheops and the Magicians." In *The Literature of Ancient Egypt*, 15–30. New Haven: Yale University Press, 1973.

Ska, Jean-Louis, "From History Writing to Library Building." In *The Pentateuch as Torah: New Models for Understanding Its Promulgation and Acceptance*, edited by Gary N. Knoppers and Bernard M. Levinson, 145–67. Winona Lake: Eisenbrauns, 2007.

———. "Le Pentateuque à l'heure de ses usagers." *Bib* 87 (2006) 98–110.

———. "A Plea on Behalf of the Biblical Redactors." *ST* 59 (2005) 4–18.

———. Review of *The Life of Moses*, by John Van Seters. *Bib* 76 (1995) 419–22.

Slyomovics, Susan. "The Death-Song of 'Āmir Khafājī." *Journal of Arabic Literature* 18 (1987) 62–78.

Bibliography

————. *The Merchant of Art: An Egyptian Hilali Oral Epic Poet in Performance.* University of California Publications in Modern Philology 120. Berkeley: University of California Press, 1987.

Smith, Mark S. *The Pilgrimage Pattern in Exodus.* JSOTSup 239. Sheffield, UK: Sheffield Academic Press, 1997.

————. "Warrior Culture in Early Israel and the 'Voice' of David in 1 Samuel 2." Paper presented at the Seventy-second International Meeting of the Catholic Biblical Association of America, Creighton University, August 1, 2009.

Snodgrass, A. M. *The Dark Age of Greece: An Archaeological Survey of the Eleventh to the Eighth Centuries B.C.* Edinburgh: Edinburgh University Press, 1971.

Solberg, Olav. "The Scandinavian Medieval Ballad." In *Oral Art Forms and Their Passage into Writing,* edited by Else Mundal and Jonas Wellendorf, 121–34. Copenhagen: Museum Tusculanum Press, 2008.

Sowayan, Saad A. *The Arabian Oral Historical Narrative: An Ethnographic and Linguistic Analysis.* Semitica Viva 6. Wiesbaden: Harrassowitz, 1992.

————. "The Bedouin: Oral Narrative as a Literary Product and Historical Source." In *Text and Tales: Studies in Oral Tradition,* edited by Jarich Oosten, 66–78. CNWS Publications 22. Leiden: Research School CNWS, 1994.

Spalinger, Anthony J. *The Transformation of an Ancient Egyptian Narrative.* Göttinger Orientforschungen, 4/40. Wiesbaden: Harrassowitz, 2002.

Sparks, Kenton L. *Ancient Texts for the Study of the Hebrew Bible: A Guide to the Background Literature.* Peabody, MA: Hendrickson, 2005.

Stager, Lawrence E. "Inscribed Potsherd from the Eleventh Century B.C." *BASOR* 194 (1969) 45–52.

Stahl, Janet. "Accuracy, Fidelity, and Stability?" *Orality Newsletter* 8 (2008) n.p.

Stephenson, R. Rex. *The Jack Tales: Folk Stories from the Blue Ridge Mountains.* Schulenburg, TX: Clark, 1991.

Stern, Elsie R. "'One of These Things Is Not Like the others': Uses of Interdisciplinary Research in the Studies of Second Temple Orality and Textuality." Paper presented at the Society of Biblical Literature annual Meeting. Atlanta 2010.

Suzuki, Seiichi. "On the Emergent Trochaic Cadence / x in Old Norse *Fornyrðslag* Meter." *Journal of Germanic Linguistics* 20 (2008) 53–79.

Syren, Roger, "Before the Text and After." In *Text & Experience: Towards a Cultural Exegesis of the Bible,* edited by Daniel Smith-Christopher, 225–37. The Biblical Seminar 35. Sheffield, UK: Sheffield Academic, 1995.

Tait, W. John. "Demotic Literature." In *Ancient Egyptian Literature: History and Forms,* edited by Antonio Loprieno, 175–90. PÄ 10. Leiden: Brill, 1996.

Taylor, Paul B. "*Völundarkviða, Þrymskviða,* and the Function of Myth." *Neophilogus* 78 (1994) 263–81.

Taylor, Paul B., and W. H. Auden, translators. *The Elder Edda: A Selection.* London: Faber, 1969.

Thiel, Winfried. "Erwägungen zur Aramäisch-Israelitischen Geschichte im 9. Jh. v. Chr." In *Nachdenken über Israel, Bibel und Theologie.* BEATAJ 37. Frankfurt: Lang, 1994.

Thomas, Rosalind. *Literacy and Orality in Ancient Greece.* Key Themes in Ancient History. Cambridge: Cambridge University, 1992.

————. *Oral Tradition and Written Record in Classical Athens.* Cambridge Studies in Oral and Literate Culture 18. Cambridge: Cambridge University Press, 1986.

Bibliography

————. "Performance Literature and the Written Word: Lost in Transcription?" *Oral Tradition* 20 (2005) 1–6.

Thompson, Thomas L. "Why Talk about the Past? The Bible, Epic and Historiography." In *In Search of Philip R. Davies: Whose Festschrift Is It Anyway?* edited by Duncan Burns and John W. Rogerson, 1–19. Library of Hebrew Bible/Old Testament Studies 484. New York: Continuum, 2009.

Thorvaldsen, Bernt Ø. "The Double Scene in Performance." In *Imagining Paradise*. Online: http://www.dur.ac.uk/medieval.www/sagaconf/thorvaldsen.htm.

————. "The Eddic Form and Its Contexts: An Oral Art Form Performed in Writing." In *Oral Art Forms and Their Passage into Writing*, edited by Else Mundal and Jonas Wellendorf, 151–62. Copenhagen: Museum Tusculanum Press, 2008.

Todorov, Tzvetan. *The Poetics of Prose*. Translated by Richard Howard. Ithaca: Cornell University Press, 1977.

Toorn, Karel van der. *Scribal Culture and the Making of the Hebrew Bible*. Cambridge: Harvard University Press, 2007.

Toorn, Karel van der, and P. W. van der Horst. "Nimrod before and after the Bible." *HTR* 83 (1990) 1–29.

Townsend, Matthew. "Norse Poets and English Kings: Skaldic Performance in Anglo-Saxon England." *Offa* 58 (2001) 269–75.

————. "Whatever Happened to York Viking Poetry? Memory, Tradition and the Transmission of Skaldic Verse', *Saga-Book of the Viking Society* 27 (2003) 48–90.

Treitler, Leo. "Letter from Leo Treitler." Communications. *Journal of the American Musicological Society* 47 (1994) 179.

————. "Sinners and Singers: A Morality Tale." *Journal of the American Musicological Society* 47 (1994) 137–71.

Tulinius, Torfi H. "Sagas of Icelandic Prehistory." In *A Companion to Old Norse–Icelandic Literature and Culture*, edited by Rory McTurk 447–61. Blackwell Companions to Literature and Culture 31. Malden, MA: Blackwell, 2005.

Turville-Petre, E. O. G. *Scaldic Poetry*. Oxford: Clarendon, 1976.

Ünal, Ahmet. "The Power of Narrative in Hittite Literature." *BA* 52 (1989) 130–43.

Van Seters, John. *Abraham in History and Tradition*. New Haven: Yale University Press, 1975.

————. *The Edited Bible: The Curious History of the "Editor" in Biblical Criticism*. Winona Lake, Eisenbrauns, 2006.

————. *The Life of Moses: The Yahwist as Historian in Exodus-Numbers*. Contributions to Exegesis and Theology 10. Kampen: Kok Pharos, 1994.

————. "Myth, Legend, and History." *Excursus* 1 (1988) 2–9.

————. "Oral Patterns or Literary Conventions in Biblical Narrative." *Semeia* 5 (1976) 139–54.

————. "The Origins of the Hebrew Bible." *Journal of Ancient Near Eastern Religions* 7 (2007) 87–108.

————. *The Pentateuch: A Social-Science Commentary*. London: T. & T. Clark, 2004.

————. "The Role of the Scribe in the Making of the Hebrew Bible." *Journal of Ancient Near Eastern Religions* 8 (2008) 99–129.

————. "The Terms 'Amorite' and 'Hittite' in the Old Testament." *VT* 22 (1972) 64–81.

————. Review of *Oral World and Written Word*, by Susan Niditch *JAOS* 118 (1998) 436–37.

Vansina, Jan. *Oral Tradition as History*. Madison: University of Wisconsin Press, 1985.

Bibliography

Vaughn, Trefor D. "Fact and Fiction in a Legend." *Folklore* 119 (2008) 218–32.

Vermeylen, Jacques. "Comment sont tombé les héros?" In *Analyse Narrative et Bible*, edited by Camille Focant and André Wénin, 97–116. BETL 191. Leuven: Peeters, 2005.

Vésteinn Ólason. "Family Sagas." In *A Companion to Old Norse-Icelandic Literature and Culture*, edited by Rory McTurk, 101–18. Blackwell Companions to Literature and Culture 31. Malden, MA: Blackwell, 2005.

———. "The Icelandic Saga as a Kind of Literature." In *Learning and Understanding in the Old Norse World*, edited by Judy Quinn et al., 27–48. Medieval Texts and Cultures of Northern Europe 18. Amsterdam: Brepols, 2007.

Vet, Thérèse de. "Context and the Emerging Story." *Oral Tradition* 23 (2008) 159–79.

———. "The Joint Role of Orality and Literacy in the Composition, Transmission, and Performance of the Homeric Texts." *TAPA* 126 (1996) 43–76.

Vidal, Jordi. "King Lists and Oral Transmission." *Ugarit-Forschungen* 32 (2000) 555–66.

Virolleaud, C. *L'Astrologie chaldéenne Supplément*. Paris: Geuthner, 1905.

Vogelzang, Marianna E. "Some Aspects of Oral and Written Tradition in Akkadian." In *Mesopotamian Epic Literature: Oral or Aural?* edited by Marianna E. Vogelzang and Herman L. J. Vanstiphout, 265–80. Lewiston, NY: Mellen, 1992.

Voigt, Vilmos. "Skaldic Poetry Everywhere?" Conference paper online: http://www.dur .ac.uk/medieval.www.sagaconf.vogt.htm.

Waltke, Bruce K., and Michael P. O'Connor. *An Introduction to Biblical Hebrew Syntax*. Winona Lake: Eisenbrauns, 1990.

Watson, Wilfred G. E. "Puns Ugaritic Newly Surveyed." In *Puns and Pundits: Word Play in the Hebrew Bible and Ancient Near Eastern Tradition*, edited by Scott B. Noegel, 117–36. Bethesda, MD: CDL, 2000.

Wendland, Ernst. "Performance Criticism." *T.I.C. Talk* 65 (2008) 1–11.

West, M. L. "The Singing of Homer and the Modes of Early Greek Music." *Journal of Hellenic Studies* 101 (1981) 113–29.

Westenholz, Joan G. "Historical Events and the Process of their Transformation in Akkadian Heroic Traditions." In *Epic and History*, edited by David Konstan and Kurt A. Raaflaub, 26–50. The Ancient World: Comparative Histories 4. Chichester, UK: Wiley-Blackwell, 2010.

———. "Oral Traditions and Written Texts in the Cycle of Akkade." Pages 123–54 in *Mesopotamian Epic Literature: Oral or Aural?* edited by Marianna E. Vogelzang and Herman L. J. Vanstiphout. Lewiston, NY: Mellen, 1992.

Westermann, Claus. *Das mündliche Wort*. ArbT 82. Stuttgart: Calwer, 1996.

Whitley, David S. "Archaeological Evidence for Conceptual Metaphors as Enduring Knowledge Structures." *Time and Mind* 1 (2008) 7–29.

Widengren, George. "Oral Tradition and Written Literature among the Hebrews in the Light of Arabic Evidence." *AcOr* 23 (1958) 201–62.

Wilcke, Claus. *Wer Las und Schrieb in Babylonien und Assyrien?* Sitzungberichte der Bayerischen Akademie der Wissenschaften, Philosophische-historische Klasse 6. Munich: Bayerische Akademie der Wissenschaft, 2000.

Wilson, Robert R. "Deuteronomy, Ethnicity, and Reform: Reflections on the Social Setting of the Book of Deuteronomy." In *Constituting the Community: Studies on the Polity of Ancient Israel in Honor of S. Dean McBride Jr.*, edited by John T. Strong and Steven S. Tuell, 107–24. Winona Lake: Eisenbrauns, 2005.

Bibliography

Winter, Irene J. "Royal Rhetoric and the Development of Historical Narrative in Neo-Assyrian Reliefs." *Studies in Visual Communication* 7 (1981) 2–38.

Wolf, Alois. "Zur Rolle des Epischen im mittelalterlichen Norden." Pages 251–70 in *New Methods in the Research of Epic*, edited by Hildegard L. C. Tristram. ScriptOralia 107. Tübingen: Narr, 1998.

Worthen, W. B. "Drama, Performativity, and Performance." *Publications of the Modern Language Association* 113 (1998) 1093–1107.

Wundt, Wilhelm. *Logikk*. Vol. 3, *Logik der Geisteswissenschaften*. Stuttgart: Enke, 1921.

———. *Völkerpsychologie*. Leipzig: Engelmann, 1909.

Würth, Stefanie. "Historiography and Pseudo-History." In *A Companion to Old Norse-Icelandic Literature and Culture*, edited by Rory McTurk, 155–72. Blackwell Companions to Literature and Culture 31. Malden: Blackwell, 2005.

———. "The Rhetoric of *Vǫlsunga saga*." In *Fornaldarsagornas Struktur och Ideologi*, edited by Ármann Jakobsson et al., 101–112. Nordiska Texter och Undersökningar 28. Uppsala: Swedish Science Press, 2003.

———. "Skaldic Poetry and Performance." In *Learning and Understanding in the Old Norse World*, edited by Judy Quinn et al., 263–84. Medieval Texts and Cultures of Northern Europe 18. Amsterdam: Brepols, 2007.

Wyatt, Nick. "Epic in Ugaritic Literature." In *A Companion to Ancient Epic*, edited by John Miles Foley, 246–95. Blackwell Companions to the Ancient World. Literature and Culture. Malden, MA Blackwell, 2005.

———. *The Mythic Mind: Essays on Cosmology and Religion in Ugaritic and Old Testament Literature*. BibleWorld. London: Equinox, 2005.

———. "The Mythic Mind Revisited." *SJOT* 22 (2008) 161–75.

———. *Space and Time in the Religious Life of the Near East*. Biblical Seminar 85. Sheffield, UK: Sheffield Academic, 2001.

———. "'Water, Water Everywhere . . .': Musings on the Aqueous Myths of the Near East." In *De la Tablilla a la Inteligencia Artificial*, edited by A. González et al., 211–59. Madrid: CSIC, 2003

———. *Word of Tree and Whisper of Stone: And Other Papers on Ugaritarian Thought*. Gorgias Ugaritic Studies 1. Piscataway, NJ: Gorgias, 2007.

Yassif, Eli. *The Hebrew Folktale: History, Genre, Meaning*. Translated by Jacqueline S. TeitelbaumFolklore Studies in Translation 11. Bloomington: Indiana University Press, 1999.

Young, Ian M. "Israelite Literacy: Interpreting the Evidence Part I." *VT* 48 (1998) 239–53.

———. "Israelite Literacy: Interpreting the Evidence Part II." *VT* 48 (1998) 408–22.

Zakovitch, Yair. "Humor and Theology or the Successful Failure of Israelite Intelligence." In *Text and Tradition: The Hebrew Bible and Folklore*, edited by Susan B. Niditch, 75–98. SemeiaSt. Atlanta: Scholars, 1990.

———. "Yes, There Was an Israelite Epic in the Biblical Period." *International Folklore Review* 8 (1991) 18–25.

Zerubavel, Eviatar. *Time Maps: Collective Memory and the Social Shape of the Past*. Chicago: University of Chicago Press, 2003.

Zlotnick, Dov. "Memory and the Integrity of the Oral Tradition." *Journal of Ancient Near Eastern Studies* 16–17 (1984–1985) 229–41.

Zumthor, Paul. *Oral Poetry: An Introduction*. Translated by Kathryn Murphy-Judy. Theory and History of Literature 70. Minneapolis: University of Minnesota Press, 1990.

Zwettler, Michael. *The Oral Tradition of Classical Arabic Poetry*. Columbus: Ohio State University Press, 1978.

Index

Index

Made in United States
North Haven, CT
26 July 2023

39553877R00104